Dittmer

DIALOGIC EDUCATION

EDUCATION

Conversation About Ideas and Between Persons

Ronald C. Arnett

Southern Illinois University Press
Carbondale and Edwardsville

Library of Congress Cataloging-in-Publication Data
Arnett, Ronald C., 1952–
  Dialogic education : conversation about ideas and between persons
/ Ronald C. Arnett.
     p. cm.
  Includes bibliographical references and index.
  1. Communication in education. 2. Teacher-student relationships.
3. College teaching. I. Title.
LB1033.5.A76 1992
378.1'25—dc20   91-45964
ISBN 0-8093-1804-0   CIP

The paper used in this publication meets the
minimum requirements of American National
Standard for Information Sciences—Permanence
of Paper for Printed Library Materials,
ANSI Z39.48–1984. ∞

CONTENTS

PREFACE

STUDENT: Professor, why did you choose this vocation? How did you decide to be a teacher? Did a vocational aptitude test point you in this direction? Did you want summers off to study and travel? Were your parents teachers?

TEACHER: I chose teaching out of a love of learning, study, and a desire to pass on information and values to the next generation. Aristotle considered politics the most noble profession, one motivated by a concern for the "common good." I entered teaching with that kind of commitment. I wanted my life to count, as I helped others make a difference in service to the human community. I chose teaching because it is a profession concerned about the "common good."

The young student questioning his favorite professor was impressed by the dignity of the response. He, too, followed a similar path and became a teacher. This book is written under the assumption that college teaching is still a noble and significant way to spend a life in service and learning. At this juncture in my own career, I still affirm the hope about the teaching vocation that I heard from my professor. My career has witnessed the tail end of the "good" years of plentiful resources and abundant job opportunities for faculty and students and has entered the "career concerned" years of higher education, when the struggle for resources and employment has been difficult. Throughout my career, however, I have been convinced that college teaching offers a significant opportunity to contribute to the "common good."

My confidence in the teaching profession comes not only from my own response to teaching, but from inspiration I continue to receive from colleagues and students. This book reflects deep appreciation for colleagues who meet the demands of their vocations, motivated by the desire to serve their discipline and the next generation of scholars and leaders.

This book is geared to understanding the professorate from the perspective of dialogic education at the undergraduate level of instruction. It is written from the vantage point of someone in love with the teaching process who has learned as a student, professor, chair, and dean that good teaching and scholarship are the only fundamental reasons for colleges and universities to exist. My experiences at a state university, a large comprehensive Catholic university, and a small liberal arts college have permitted me to associate with many excellent teachers, scholars, and administrators committed to the type of education that I hold to be significant in the pursuit of education and the development of human character. This book reflects many of the learnings from those places and people, summarized in the notion of dialogic education.

This book is not offered as *the* truth or *the* perspective on education. Instead, this work assumes a more modest hope of inviting conversation about education and teaching, using examples and stories from a variety of locations and colleagues. This book is my attempt, as a philosopher of communication, to understand the dynamics of education as I have witnessed it in the lives of many colleagues and friends. In short, I invite the reader into conversation with me in my attempt to understand education from the perspective of dialogic communication. This book is not meant to tell "how to teach," but rather to suggest what might take place between teacher and student in the midst of dialogue. Throughout the book, I remain guided by a hope that together in conversation they can probe the richness of subject content and support the humanness of one another as partners in learning.

Finally, I wish to thank Deb Hammond for her typing, retyping, and thoughtful comments on the manuscript. Dr. Richard Johannesen and Dr. Rob Anderson offered significant suggestions on this work, both in general and specific form. I value their wisdom and friendship. And most importantly, I dedicate this book to my closest learning partner and friend—my wife, Millie. Her comments on this manuscript were insightful and clarifying. It is my wish that our children, Adam and Aimee, might learn from dedicated and concerned teachers and perhaps consider lending their lives in service through education.

This book is grounded in an assumption that learning is a lifelong task about ideas and people. I feel most fortunate to be part of a vocation that is charged to make learning the center of our lives. I offer this book as part of an ongoing conversation about assisting the "common good" as an educator concerned about content and the human spirit. To my colleagues and former teachers who have inspired and continue to inspire not only competence but dedication and commitment in their students, I offer this book with thanks.

PART 1

Conversation,
Relationships,
and Values

1

Introduction: Dialogue and Education

Hope in education—

The neglect of teaching in the university is an ominous symptom. I believe it signals a weakening of our will to live. For if we do not nurture our young and identify with them, we forfeit any hope in the regeneration and continuation of the species; we are walled up defensively within the confines of our egos and our momentary gratifications. But this means that we are not fully alive ourselves.

> Bruce Wilshire,
> *The Moral Collapse of the University:*
> *Professionalism, Purity, and Alienation*

Commitment to the future—

In the crusade against ignorance, there have been no easy victories, but no lasting defeats. . . . To believe in education is to believe in the future, to believe in what may be accomplished through the disciplined use of intelligence, allied with cooperation and good will. If it seems naively American to put so much stock in schools, colleges, universities, and the endless prospect of self-improvement and social improvement, it is an admirable, and perhaps even a noble, flaw.

> Diane Ravitch,
> *The Troubled Crusade:*
> *American Education, 1945–1980*

This book-length essay examines a noble vocation: college teaching centered on undergraduate instruction. Dialogic education is concerned with the life of information, relationships, and values that shape the character of students, faculty, and institutions; it is an educational life offering fair examination of ideas and an invitation to join conversation about ideas grounded in relationships concerned about the personhood of students.

One of my former students, who is working on his doctorate in education, asked me what advice to give a teacher unable to make dialogue happen with some students. I responded that dialogue between persons is not always possible, nor should it be expected at all times. Dialogue is an invitation, not a demand, nourished not so much by the guarantee that it will happen as by patience. Dialogic education does not require or expect each moment to be a deep dialogue. Our task as dialogic educators is less grandiose. We simply need to offer information and evaluation in a civil fashion, looking for opportunities for "conversation about ideas" relationships, and values, both inside and outside the normal classroom setting.

In fact, the civil person willing to live without dialogue often lays the foundation for its occurrence—offering openness without demand. The moment we begin to pride ourselves on our ability to "be in dialogue" we move from what Buber called "being" and unveil the door of "seeming."[1] I do not envision this book about special moments of great depth of conversation with students, but rather as a reminder of the importance of a foundation of ideas, relationships, and values as core elements for inviting dialogue in education.

The notion of character is a major underlying theme in *Dialogic Education: Conversation About Ideas and Between Persons*.[2] Dialogic education is a form of character education shaped by scholarship, relationships, and the ethos of an institution.[3] Character is shaped by virtues, practice, relationships, and conversation about ideas in the search for excellence. I envision dialogic educators in conversation, reluctant to offer prescriptive solutions to educational questions. This book outlines a way of viewing the shaping of character within a dialogic context, sensitive to ideas, relationships, and values, and wary of propaganda and ideological blinders placed on our discourse.

Another tacit assumption guiding this book is gratitude—gratefulness for the opportunity to be a teacher and learner. This book is a form of thanks to teachers, colleagues, and students. I am, indeed, grateful for my chance to be part of this profession and to be part of so many lives.

If today our common life in society is, as many observers seem to think, a life lacking shared purpose and commitment—a life, that is, with little in common—perhaps at least a part of the problem is this: We have understood that common life largely in terms of rights and entitlement, in terms of the language of obligation, and not in terms of a virtue like gratitude. What a terrible misunderstanding this could be if it should be true that "there are obligations and debts which of their very nature cannot be adequately fulfilled and discharged."[4]

Dialogic Education: Conversation About Ideas and Between Persons offers a positive and constructive look at a vocation that has experienced significant criticism. During the past few years, we have been inundated with studies, reports, and books stressing problems on college and university campuses caused by a real and, at times, a perceived decline in standards.

This work does not question the importance of critical examinations of higher education. Every vocation requires careful scrutiny. A warning from the Committee on Academic Freedom in the United States (1915), charged by the first president of the American Association of University Professors, John Dewey, reveals the need for critical examination.

> The responsibility [for judging quality] cannot, in this committee's opinion, be rightfully evaded. If this profession should prove itself unwilling to purge its ranks of the incompetent and the unworthy, or to prevent the freedom which it claims in the name of science from being used as a shelter for inefficiency, for superficiality, or for uncritical and intemperate partisanship, it is certain that the task will be performed by others—by others who lack certain essential qualifications for performing it, and whose action is sure to breed suspicions and recurrent controversies deeply injurious to the internal order and the public standing of universities.[5]

Because we are open to criticism of various aspects of higher education, for example, the declining quality of students and the "careerism" of students and faculty, some counterbalancing is necessary. This work is offered as a reminder of the positive and constructive news about higher education: conversation about ideas and between persons on a campus is a worthy way to spend a life.

Teaching as More Than Dispensing Information

The following quotation from John Gardner describes the potential danger associated with some contemporary professionals. His warning suggests that higher education needs to invite values embodying a long-term concern for others, encouraging us to take questions about content and values seriously.

> I have to tell you candidly that an education at any of the great universities, followed by a graduate degree, followed by a plunge into the world of young professionals moves you steadily further from the bedrock of everyday American experience. If you're lucky you will escape the root ailments of the young urban professional— an overvaluing of intellect as against character, of getting there first as against growing in mind and spirit, of food for the ego as against food for the hunger of the heart.[6]

Gardner is suggesting that a great university provides knowledge but may fail to offer an education beyond questions of self-advancement. I believe dialogue between persons permits education to extend beyond information acquisition, while simultaneously emphasizing up-to-date information necessary for knowledge application.

Dialogic education, as described in this book, assumes that the development of human character and commitment to lifelong learning needs to be part of a quality education. Great teaching in a liberal education tradition not only permits the acquisition of information but reveals why such information should be used for the betterment of the human community. As Nietzsche stated, if one can find a *why* in life, one can bear any *how*.[7] It is most often in conversation that students and teachers discover the *whys*, which can undergird the technical *hows*. My bias as a teacher attempting to offer dialogic education is that the mix of information acquisition, relationships, and value discussion is necessary in the educational process of conversation between persons.

Invitation to Conversation

This book is an invitation to conversation about higher education centered on undergraduate instruction. My goal is not to suggest *the* answer or *the* perspective or to outline *the* view of dialogic education. I suggest no new teaching techniques, no detailing of the use of media, syllabi, lectures, or homework assignments. Other sources provide how-to pointers on teaching. This book is a reminder about why I became a college professor—to work with ideas and people. I welcome you, as a reader, into a conversation about education from a dialogic perspective.

A friend of mine likened his return to teaching from a job in industry to one of the experiences of the central character in Herman Hesse's novel, *Siddhartha*, whose main pursuit was a sense of meaning in life. In Siddhartha's first encounter with the ferryman, he took little notice of him. In his eagerness to find meaning, Siddhartha decided to travel throughout the world, engaging in activities ranging from hedonism to asceticism. After this life of diversity, he again met the ferryman, still taking people across the river in the same location many times each day.

Siddhartha was surprised to see how content the ferryman had remained in the same location and how frustrated his own much traveled life had become.[8] Similarly, my colleague who returned to teaching found faculty members who expressed satisfaction in working with students. We move students across similar hurdles each year, yet there are always unique individuals, challenges, and demands. Like the ferryman in Hesse's novel, educators, too, can rediscover a sense of meaning in the educational task. There is uniqueness and opportunity in what many would call belabored repetition of conversation with students.

The following chapters provide the basis for this conversation, examining what is possible when the ingredients for dialogic education are available. I stress the possibilities available to teachers and students as they work dialogically at their respective educations, possibilities central to such a view of learning. The following quotation on liberal education by William Darkey reveals the tie between education and conversation that is central to my work: "Conversational exchange between student and teacher is an essential condition for learning. This implies that educational institutions are obliged to provide conditions in which such conversations can occur."[9] In essence, *Dialogic Education: Conversation About Ideas and Between Persons* suggests that the quality of conversation between teacher and student shapes the educational environment, as well as providing a narrative or story context from which information can be understood. Dialogic education begins with an assumption that people in conversation about ideas can add information breadth and relational awareness as complements to disciplinary depth.

2

Ideas, Persons, and Value Discussion

The vulnerable teacher—

The freedom to commit oneself, to create, is habitual in a person who has made himself vulnerable, open to his experience and that of others, in whatever form he may encounter it. The word *vulnerable* derives from *vuln*, Latin for *wound*. To become powerfully vulnerable is to expose oneself to possible wounds. One cannot create valuable things without risk. If he brings to the moment the best of his past experience, he comes on strong; and if he suffers then a wound, it will not disable him, because he is at his best, moving out of his full experience, healthy and strong. He is emotional as well as intellectual. He is growing out of himself and others.

Ken Macrorie,
The Vulnerable Teacher

Education of character—

EDUCATION worthy of the name is essentially education of character.... Personality is something which in its growth remains essentially outside the influence of the educator; but to assist in the moulding of character is his greatest task. Personality is a completion, only character is a task. One may cultivate and enhance personality, but in education one can and one must aim at character.

Martin Buber,
Between Man and Man

Introduction

Dialogic education is an attitude *and* a concrete commitment to conversation about ideas, persons, and values. Dialogic educa-

8

tion, as outlined in this book, is not a standard method or an unusual technique of instruction. The term *dialogic education* and the title of this book are reminders for me and hopefully for others about why we became educators—a love of inquiry and a joy at working with people in the learning process.

Over my years in higher education, I have heard an increasing number of colleagues discuss the importance of campus politics, underprepared students, and demands placed on family by an active professional life. While the above voices have seemed to grow louder, conversations about ideas and about students have seemed to grow more quiet. This book could have the following descriptive subtitle: *Why I Became an Educator*. This work is a reminder that ideas and people are the center of education, not politics, gripes about students, or discussions of the inadequacies of colleagues and our place of employment.

This book-length essay on dialogic education is not offered as *the* answer on what education or even dialogic education should resemble. Such an aim could not be accomplished without violating the unique relationship that needs to be built between each teacher and student. What makes a department or a campus special is the teachers' willingness to allow the uniqueness of their own outlook to meet in dialogue with the special needs and hopes of students.

I offer this book as a conversation about dialogic education on the undergraduate campus. This first chapter outlines the basic ingredients in dialogic education: that the teacher is vital in inviting conversation about class content, while recognizing the importance of relationships in education; that education is an act of information and value questioning that permits one to test the viability of one's learning, in hopes of preparing students for complex informational and ethical challenges; and that there is a basic trust that a quality future collectively and individually is intricately tied to our commitment to inquiry and people.

Dialogic education asks the question, What will be the impact on others when information is implemented? The basic premise of dialogic education is that the learning and the use of our knowledge involves us *and* others, recognizing that our interpretation of information is governed as much by our value orientation as by the facts assembled. The following quotation from Martin Buber points to the relational and value dimension of the teaching task.

"The human race begins in every hour," with every newborn child, but the world is nonetheless, already there. How those new living beings, "determined yet still determinable," encounter the already existent creation, and what they make of the world, is decided by the countenance of each historic hour. Each choice of the world which the consciously willing educator, primarily the teacher, offers to the rather malleable child, will have an important part in such a decision. It is the teacher who knows the environment and is a selective sieve through which the majority of creation must pass when it again would encounter a new soul. But even the newborn child is a "fact of creation." Thus understood, education, both conscious and subconscious, occurs in every minute through the encounter between the "old" and recurrently "young" creature. If this encounter is brought about and guided consciously, we speak of an actual educational procedure. Today the teacher is the most important, though not by any means the sole executor of it.[1]

A teacher interested in dialogue attempts to assist students by offering information and value questioning with a relational openness to the student and by encouraging the testing of information with other perspectives that frame our contemporary, complex, and often conflict-ridden world. As I stated to an incoming group of professors, "If you can present multiple perspectives on ideas and take people seriously, attempting to learn from both, you will enjoy one of the finest vocations possible—college teaching." Dialogic education, as outlined in this work, takes ideas and people seriously and regards the vocation of educator as a fine way of life.[2]

Why Dialogic Education?

Defining Dialogue

I ground dialogue in this book-length essay in three basic attitudes: a willingness to enter conversation about ideas, taking a position in openness that can still be altered given additional information; a commitment to keep relationships affirming, even as disagreements over theory occur; and a willingness to ask value questions about information application. In communication literature, the term *dialogue* is defined in a helpful fashion by Rob Anderson, who combines the work of Richard Johannesen, John Stewart, Martin Buber, and Carl Rogers.[3] The following is paraphrased from Anderson's outline of the ingredients needed for human dialogue.

1. *Presence.* Dialogue requires a willingness to follow the conversation as it leads in "unrehearsed" directions.

2. *Unanticipated consequences.* Dialogue cannot be predicted to assure an outcome known a priori to an exchange.

3. *Otherness.* The mystery and uniqueness of the other is accepted.

4. *Vulnerability.* Willingness to engage in some risk when knowing the outcome of an exchange is not apparent at the outset of a conversation.

5. *Mutual implication.* We discover in message interpretation something about our communicative partner and much about ourselves in the unique way we hear the message.

6. *Temporal flow.* Dialogue presumes some historical continuity of communicative partners and a sensitivity to the time of the address—past, present, and future anticipations enter the conversation.

7. *Authenticity.* A presumption of honesty, until proven otherwise, is offered to the other.[4]

The ingredients of dialogue pointed to by Anderson frame this work, viewing dialogue as reaching out to the other in an authentic fashion, willing to try to meet and follow the unpredictable consequences of the exchange. In addition, one other element is referred to repeatedly in this book—the importance of a position or a place to begin a dialogue. On a campus, dialogue is invited by a common commitment to inquiry and a sensitivity to a particular place—a campus, department, or cadre of faculty and students. This work assumes the importance of two "common centers" that can pull people together, both of which will be discussed at length: inquiry, that is, conversation about ideas; and an academic "home" of a department or campus. The common center of inquiry is a philosophical commitment and the common center of an academic home is a concrete place from which to work, study, and teach.

Changing Dialogic Beginnings

Dialogue is not a formula; each relationship offers a different and unique starting place for discourse. An educated person needs to know how to study with careful intent while remaining open to multiple possibilities.[5] Dialogic education requires care and openness to how we might best meet the needs of students, remaining sensitive to unique calls of our historical period. For instance, twenty years ago when I first received my Ph.D., I asked students to call me by my first name. I now ask students to use the title professor or doctor. I am certainly no more enamored with having a Ph.D. than I was when I first received the degree. I do, however, feel that a larger number of my students need to be reminded more of the responsibilities of being a student than was the case when I first began teaching. Martin Buber contended that sociocultural roles remind us that our special obligations to one another are important.[6]

Many of my colleagues find the use of an academic title limiting for them as teachers; my response is that each teacher must do whatever is necessary to keep inquiry and conversation between persons alive in the classroom. My approach is not for all; each teacher needs to find his or her own unique ways to keep the classroom a rich place of learning. But each of us needs to be reminded that a role carries unique responsibilities, calling for particular commitments and obligations.

Dialogic education involves the creative blending of content and relationship between teacher and student. This approach would be violated if teachers were offered a prescription for dialogue with students. Dialogic education shapes character, not through prescription, but through an invitation to conversation about content without forgetting the part people must play in learning and information implementation.

The following Hasidic tale is an analogy, suggesting the multiple and unique ways in which dialogic education might be enacted. There was a great and beloved rabbi, who when he passed away was greatly missed. There were many mourners who appreciated the man and his leadership. In hopes of maintaining the tradition of the great rabbi, the congregation asked the rabbi's son to assume the role of teacher and leader of the congregation. When the son accepted the role of rabbi, there was a sigh of relief. The people were pleased that the vision and action of the former rabbi would continue to inspire and nourish the congregation.

Like most young leaders, the revered rabbi's son implemented changes, not all of which were appreciated by the congregation. One day the young rabbi overheard members of the congregation complaining about him and saying, "If only he were more like his father, then all would be right with his leadership." Upon hearing their complaint, the young rabbi paused for a long while, looking off somewhere beyond the members of the congregation, who stood before him. Finally, the young rabbi turned his attention back to his people and said in a quiet voice that he did not understand. The young rabbi reminded people that he was his father's son. " 'I do just as my father did. He did not imitate and I do not imitate.' "[7]

Being a dialogic educator is not something to be imitated. As Carl Rogers was fond of saying, it is better to have a quality relationship with another than to possess a great counseling theory if one hopes to be of help to another human being.[8] In this case, it is better to want to meet a student, using one's own interpersonal and professional skills than it is to follow a rigid set of guidelines in accordance with a given theory. In fact, the act of imitation would violate the importance of inviting a unique relationship between teacher and student within the confines of a given campus culture.

The Struggles Before Us

I asked an exceptional student in the course "Human Conflict" what she sought from the class. Her answer was a basic version of what I have stated above. "I need to know the information, why it is important, how to apply it and what its impact might be on myself and others when applied." The student went on to suggest that linking the philosophical and the practical is important. Indeed, information that we attempt to apply does have consequences for ourselves and others, and the way we teach one another has an impact on the way we put some of our learning into action.

We are at an interesting point in education, a demanding and critical juncture. The expectations for higher education are great, the criticism intense, and the campuses frequently divided. Articles in *The Chronicle of Higher Education* and even the cover story of *Newsweek* have discussed the issue of "political correctness," an effort to encourage "correct" thinking on social issues.[9] Ted Koppel examined the question of political correctness on his "Nightline" broadcast of 13 May 1991. Also, a controversial work by Dinesh D'Souza, *Illiberal Education: The Politics of Race and Sex on Campus*, is generating considerable conversation.[10] Even those believing in the advancement of "multicultural" education have significant differences in their perspectives.[11] On the other end of the spectrum has been the work of such people as Allan Bloom in *The Closing of the American Mind*,[12] who lament social advocacy in education and ask for a renewal of classic education.

In addition, there are reports tabulating the rise of hate and violence on campuses, such as "Hate in the Ivory Tower" and a Carnegie report discussing the increase of "incivility" on campuses.[13]

These are but a small sampling of the problems and differences present on campuses today. Ernest Boyer puts the situation in perspective with an observation based on his long association with higher education, its goals and limitations: "The start of the new decade now presents, at least from my perspective, perhaps the most challenging moment in higher education in forty years. It affords us an unusual opportunity for American colleges and universities to return to their roots and to consider not more regulations, but the enduring values of a true learning community."[14] Boyer suggests that the time is demanding, but like all difficult moments, it offers an opportunity for creativity and exciting discoveries.

The demanding task before us is to find ways of keeping the conversation going between faculty, from Bloom to "politically correct" colleagues. Answers to the woes of higher education are not necessarily clear cut, but we might do well to be cautious about pushing ideological positions on one another, whether from the right or the left of the political spectrum. Recently, I was thrust into conflict by two opposing ideological camps. First, a professor accused me of keeping his article from being published due to a "politically correct" position that excluded scholarship about "conservative" positions. Later, I was accused of being a neoconservative for being part of a committee that voted to permit a conference on Communication and Christianity to be held on a "conservative" campus. If we push our own agenda on others, we may find ourselves moving more toward propaganda than education. I offer no answers to the increasing political conflicts on campuses due to different ideological perspectives, other than to suggest that a college or university profits from varying viewpoints and that this book attempts to describe the campus as a place for inquiry and conversation.

I am not a politician, nor a holder of *the* truth. My hope rests with learning as much as I can, both from inquiry and students, both in and outside the classroom. My work with dialogic communication, the teachers who have shaped my life, time with students both in and outside the classroom, and my own teaching stance all point to the importance of keeping academic conversation vibrant and alive.

A Modest Proposal

It is possible to point to the general nature of dialogic education without judging the rightness of the approach for all or suggesting that this book outlines the only approach to dialogue in education. The precise concrete application of any approach to education needs to fit the academic and personal inclinations of a given teacher and campus. Thus, my approach to dialogic education is better termed a modest proposal than *the* answer to educational problems.[15] I do, however, believe that any environment conducive to free inquiry will place humility as a necessary virtue.

Education can be viewed as an ongoing conversation focusing on the development of a "humane intellectual,"[16] interested in learning how information can constructively impact the human community aesthetically and practically. As Buber suggested, dialogic education can be viewed as education of character and education of the whole person. Carl Rogers, also well known for his work in dialogue, proposed that education needs to address the intellect and the personhood of the learner.[17] John Dewey discussed the social aspects of education that need to accompany cognitive development.[18] Similar messages have come from educators such as Ernest L. Boyer, Warren Bryan Martin, and Parker J. Palmer.[19]

In light of the above references, let us clarify that my aim is to complement the recent pleas for "upgrading" the content level of higher education. I am in agreement with many pronouncements in recent years calling for more content in education. However, dialogic education calls for two other ingredients as well: acknowledging the long-term impact of how we teach and learn together, suggesting that the quality of relationships does affect learning; and openly claiming a value dimension to education, emphasizing the importance of questioning how information, when applied, will affect human beings.

The way in which we learn has as much impact on us as the information we memorize. The style of learning is itself another form of content given by the teacher through modeling. A child can be told to stay away from strangers in order to avoid the possibility of a tragedy that all parents so deeply fear, but the way in which the child is told to "watch out" for other adults will have an impact. Telling a child that some people are not to be trusted and that in order to be safe the child must listen to only a select few adults can make the child unduly cautious or fearful. What determines if the result is caution or just generalized fear of adults is tied more to the way in which information is offered to the child than to general information about adult misconduct. The way in which a parent cautions a child will determine not just whether the child listens; it will also shape the child's view of the "stranger."

From a dialogic educational standpoint, the hope is to offer caution within a context that life is still good and consists of many fine people. However, most good things in life require time to develop; it is not often helpful to push relationships to premature points of trust. Relationships, like most of life's accomplishments, take time to mature. In essence, one hopes to offer caution qualified by the notion that people are so important that we need to take time to know and understand them.

The way in which we offer the message of caution will determine if our daughter or son will envision an unfriendly world or recognize the importance of inviting relationships to build naturally, taking time for the child and, in some cases, for Mom and Dad to get to know the adult involved. One of the basic assumptions of dialogic education is that the way in which we pass on the *how* of knowledge implementation will have an impact, just as the information acquired makes a difference.

The goal of dialogic education is a humane intellectual, a person able to understand that information and the manner in which the information is taught has an immediate and a long-term impact, requiring learning and teaching to be offered and used with care. In essence, dialogic education is based on the interplay of information, relationship building, value discussion, and the development of a person of character in an ideologically complex world community.

Outlining Dialogic Education

While each chapter of this book begins with quotations from various insightful authors, no one author has been the model for this book. The central organizing theme or pivotal point of the book is evident in its subtitle, *Conversation About Ideas and Between Persons*. My observation in working with students is that dialogue centered on the class content and sensitive to the personal aspirations of students opens up possibilities of growth for the learning participants.

Even though no one author points to *the* way in which this work uses the term *dialogic education*, Paulo Freire does offer a handle on what the term implies. Freire's understanding of dialogic education begins with the assumption that both reflection and action are central to dialogue. His understanding of dialogue is akin to Toulmin's call in "The Recovery of Practical Philosophy" for a practical use of philosophy and communication.[20]

Dialogue requires knowingly inviting the "active" interaction of teacher and student in the learning process. Such "action" is based on the following: love of commitment to others; humility to learn from others; mutual trust between the learning partners; a sense of hope that the world can be made better through learning by partners in education; a concerted effort to lessen the limits of the other, to broaden the other's horizons, permitting him or her to see the world through multiple paradigms; and a willingness to invest time and energy in a form of education that requires close interplay and collaboration of teacher and student.[21]

Freire reveals dialogic education as including the importance of *how*, as well as *what* one learns. Our underlying philosophy of education communicates as does the information that is offered to students. Richard Bernstein, in *Beyond Objectivism and Relativism: Science, Hermeneutics, and Praxis*, reminds us that we live in a time when the philosophical and the pragmatic have crisscrossed.[22] Freire and Bernstein suggest that the orientation from which we approach a problem affects the very nature of what we see and the solutions discovered.

The paradigm from which we choose to study determines what is discovered, making no paradigmatic selection neutral without larger ethical and practical implications. Thus, the dialogic paradigm of information, relationship, and value discussion is not a neutral view of what can be learned on a college or university campus. Such a view of education encourages students to understand the potential long-term impact of the information learned.

To more clearly define the way in which I use the term *dialogic education*, it is helpful to examine the implications of the terms that compose the subtitle of this book, *Conversation About Ideas and Between Persons*. The words in the subtitle point to a definition of dialogic education that propels this work. The interplay of intellect, relationship building, and value discussion offer the foundation for dialogic education.

Conversation

The act of conversation is central to this interpretation of dialogic education. A phrase by Calvin Schrag points to the type of conversation suggested in this work: communicative praxis. Schrag suggests that communicative meaning is the result of the interplay of communication and action. He conceptualizes the interplay of discourse and action, language and perception, and speech and embodiment. He suggests a balance of "metaphors of discourse, such as word, script, and text . . . [with the] metaphors of action, such as work, labor, and play, if the texture of communicative praxis is to be properly displayed."[23]

Schrag ends his book, *Communicative Praxis and the Space of Subjectivity*, by suggesting that a new humanism will not be centered on the person. It will need to be centered on discourse and action. The human being will be decentered but not ignored. The human being in such a vision becomes a participant in an ongoing conversation.[24] Extending Schrag's view, I conceptualize conversation as more central to education than any sole teacher, student, or university; each is necessary, but not singularly sufficient, for conversation to occur. Conversation involves ideas, people, and the organizational culture in which interaction takes place, requiring sensitivity to the importance of speech, human relationships, and the educational "home" in which the learning is invited. Dialogic education is a form of communicative praxis, inviting conversation about ideas and between people, while asking value questions of how and why particular information will be put into action.

Using the term *conversation* in conjunction with education suggests that dialogic education is a collective and an active process, not one conducted in isolation. Conversation is initiated when one reads a piece of literature, beginning a silent conversation with the author. But more significantly for undergraduates, dialogic education is dependent on the willingness of teacher and student to be in conversation both inside and outside the classroom.

As an undergraduate student, I remember sitting in the classroom watching a gifted teacher struggle to get us to take up her invitation to join in conversation about the material. Finally, in exasperation she threw her hands in the air and asked for our help. The material had open-ended possibilities, the teacher was willing, but the class was reluctant. That failed classroom effort reminds me today, as a teacher, that try as I might, conversation about ideas cannot be guaranteed. Even the most gifted of teachers on a given day with a certain student or particular class will not always have an invitation to join the conversation accepted.

Remembering the anguish on this fine teacher's face reminds me that dialogic learning is not dependent solely on the teacher, the student, or the content; each contributes to the enterprise. In essence, the term *conversation* in the subtitle of this work suggests that dialogic education is not a solitary activity; rather, it is a bringing together of ideas, relationships, and values within an organizational culture in symbolic interaction with the goal of transmitting and understanding information.

Conversation about Ideas

Conversation on a campus is centered on ideas emerging from study and inquiry, suggesting that dialogic education is centered around "conversation about ideas," whether the humanities, social science, science, or professional study is our task. The word *idea* will be used in a general manner throughout this book in conjunction with conversation. An idea is a starting place for conversation. Conversation about ideas is equated with a commitment to inquiry, propelled by wanting to find out, to know, that rejects the desire to locate additional support for an ideological position accepted a priori or prior to the commencement of a particular study.

I agree with Richard Weaver that "ideas have consequences."[25] John Lyne offers a blend of "idealism" and "rhetoric" that gets to the heart of how the term *ideas* is used throughout this book. He traces the various ways of understanding idealism and suggests that an idealism for today needs to combine the tools of tradition, the present, and an anticipated future, finding a way to link and lead us to both familiar and new insights. Such an idealism cannot ignore the material world or the reality of human pain and limits, but neither will it be content without exploring what might be possible if we just look and understand differently.

> If the past is recuperable only in memory, and the future is with us only in anticipation, and both processes are symbolic, then we have a double dependency on symbolization. That complex state of dependency involves incipient valuing and actions, as the pragmatists insist. And so, the dependency is also an enablement. For the idealist, a considered placement in the world beyond the moment is also required. In navigating through experience, being "realistic" is not enough: life requires a broader sense of direction. This is found only as the material world is transformed into a significant world, charged with a dual sense of what is given and what is yet to be realized. When we must look to the past or to the future searching for direction, a place in a trajectory, this is when idealism most commends itself as a rhetorical stance.[26]

Ideas are viewed as the glue that pulls together data, facts, tradition, and hopes for the future. But ideas open to challenge can give meaning to action and behavior that otherwise might be viewed as insignificant or simply burdensome. Conversation about ideas, as pointed to in this work, implies that no one set of ideas is valid for all circumstances; application and questioning are part of the life of ideas. Otherwise we walk into ideological rigidity and the dangers detailed by Eric Hoffer in *The True Believer*.

One of the main rhetorical points of the phrase "conversation about ideas" is that it offers a potential key to bringing diversity together through a common search and a common commitment to inquiry. Students and faculty come together on a campus for many diverse reasons, varying from a commitment to a general educa-tion, to a hope that new skills will enhance a professional life, to not knowing what else to do in life. At times a teacher may feel as if no one has entered the classroom for the love of learning. In spite of the diversity of reasons for joining a campus, students can still be invited into conversation about ideas.

I often discuss with students that there are two major rhetori-cal topics that can unite people of diverse interests under a com-mon objective: sports and complaints. Some people can be brought together by discussion of sports because they love to play, others because they love to argue over who is the best or worst, and still others because they can use conversation about sports as a way to make contact with others. In addition, people will often team together if they can find a common complaint. When one is unwill-ing or unable to use sports or complaining as a reason for coming together, it is necessary to look for another topic that might bring diversity together.

For instance, some go to church because of a belief in God, others due to a belief in the denomination, others to help their children, others to assist their businesses, and still others attend because they are used to getting up early on Sunday. What pulls the people together is a common assumption that going to church is a worthy activity, even if the reasons for going are quite diverse.

The fact that people do not talk about sports or go to church for the same reasons does not mean that we cannot learn together and share a common conversation, even as we recognize the di-verse reasons we come together. We only get in trouble when we begin to insist on one particular motivation for coming together, thus missing the opportunity of bringing people of diverse motiva-tions together under a larger common center.

If one insists on a narrowly defined common center, problems will be invited. I have seen some skilled faculty make *excellence* into a negative word. They tie excellence not only to what is learned, but to the motivation for learning. They want a purity of learning for its own sake, rejecting an instrumental view of learning. When a professor makes such a narrow demand, a large number of students become frustrated with the course. The narrow common center more accurately becomes an elite position that excludes more than it invites.

If we wait until classrooms are filled with eager learners with "pure" motivations, wanting to learn for the love of learning alone, we may never have an opportunity to teach. But if we take students as they are, inviting discussion of ideas as our common center, regardless of individual motivation, we may keep some semblance of unity on the campus, while doing what we are required to do—educating our students.

Students and teachers need to be reminded of the common center that brings us together on a university campus—the discussion of ideas. If relationships become primary, we are better called a social agency than a college or university. If value questions become primary, we are better called a church than a college or university. Again, note that in dialogic education relationships and value questions are an integral part of the learning. But once either one overtakes conversation about ideas as our central task, we forfeit the primary reason or purpose for the college or university to exist.

In essence, dialogic education involves three components. Two, relationships and values, are of secondary importance and one, ideas, is primary. Before discussing this further, it is important to note that dialogic education does not abstractly separate these three ingredients. Each term works hand in hand with the other two terms. In fact, dialogic education is an idea based in the value of the importance of civil conversation between persons, presupposing the importance and necessity of relationships in education.

As all three ingredients are assumed to be co-present, of first and foremost importance is conversation about ideas. This content base is then facilitated by taking relationships seriously, and encouraging the asking of value questions, such as: "What will be the impact of this information on the human community?" It is not a matter of choosing one dialogic education element over the other two, but a point of emphasis, with conversation about ideas as primary.

A commitment to conversation about ideas sets the agenda for our time together. We are invited in from a vast sea of multiple and conflicting agendas to a common life together, the discussion of ideas, not to a common view of what the ideas mean or how they should be applied, or even why one should tolerate taking time to talk about them. We share a common realization that the beginning of education must be content and the ability to talk about that information.

Dialogic education is based on the hope that the teacher can invite the student to feel an existential demand to talk about ideas irrespective of the motivation. The basis for learning is not as important as a teacher's willingness to help a student discover an existential demand that propels him or her to learn and to talk about ideas. It is better to have a student wanting to converse about ideas just to get a better grade, than it is to wait for purity of educational desire, losing many students in the process. In dialogic education, idea discussion is our common center, arrived at from many different routes, similar to the notion of "equifinality" in computer systems.

In summary, the common center on a college or university campus needs to be conversation about ideas. The existential demand that calls us to study and converse about those ideas is of less importance than a willingness to enter the conversation. The task of a dialogic educator is to uncover many different existential demands that will offer various students a reason for entering such a conversation. Such a willingness to permit multiple existential demands begins to model the importance of being respectful of other persons.

Conversation Between Persons

An emphasis on persons is a reminder that discussion of ideas is not initiated in the abstract, but with others, attempting to contribute to human life, aesthetically, emotionally, economically, and practically. One faculty member, when asked why a particular member of the faculty could not attract students into his classes, said what many of us know but are unwilling to state publicly. Students that do not feel mutual respect from a professor will agree with ideas, but when given the chance will refuse to enroll for another course with that professor. Few of us are willing to pay to be abused if another option is possible.

Interaction between persons in dialogic education resides between two extremes: an impersonal orientation that works to put factual information "into" the student, and a personal relationship more interested in affect and feeling of the student than in increasing the knowledge base of the student. Dialogic education cannot guarantee that each student will feel close to a professor or become the finest intellectual in the class. If we cannot guarantee that dialogic education will result in a close relationship with a professor, what can be guaranteed about the nature of the relationship? Perhaps we could suggest that a dialogic educator will meet each student in a civil fashion both inside and outside the classroom as we work together to increase our respective knowledge bases. Being civil to another is simply another way of expressing respect without adopting what Parker Palmer, in *The Company of Strangers,* calls the "ideology of intimacy."[27] Not every relationship can or should be personally close; but one can work at inviting civil and respectful relationships with others. Some colleges, in a tight market for students, have begun to sell the impression that "we care," which implies that a close relationship will automatically emerge between teacher and student. Such a promise cannot always be delivered and in some cases should not even be attempted.

We can, however, emphasize a commitment to civility on the college or university campus, and in a department. The notion of civility is central to how this work envisions education within a dialogic context. A Carnegie report suggests that there is a need to reclaim the importance of civility on the college and university campus. According to the Carnegie Institute, there is general agreement among students, professors, and the administration that there has been a severe breakdown of civility on the college and university campus and it seems we have yet to find its end.[28]

Civility is defined in Webster's as "the state of being civilized; good breeding; politeness, or an act of politeness; courtesy; or kind attention."[29] Civility is an effort to respect oneself, others, and other cultures in a way that permits diversity to coexist, mutually supporting the community.

Granted, civility is not a word that has been frequently used in the last twenty-five years. But if the Carnegie report can be trusted, it may be time for such a notion to be reexamined in the context of higher education. On a personal note, the Carnegie report seems to be in agreement with my own observations and in concert with two of my classes on interpersonal communication. When I asked members of these two classes what was the primary obstacle to inviting quality interpersonal relationships on campus, I received a nearly unanimous statement that it was rudeness. In fact, some suggested the newest "in" thing to do was to deliberately cultivate an image of being rude to others.

Glenn Tinder, in an interesting and thoughtful work, examines the limits of the ideal of human community and the dangers of unchecked rudeness.[30] I am intrigued by Tinder's work, because it offers an interesting complement to my own work on human community.[31] Tinder offers the notion of civility as an alternative to the concept of community and as a way of coping with a less than perfect world where so many value systems seem in contrast or direct conflict. Tinder reminds us that the ideal of community has a tragic history and that civility might be a more realistic way to approach the diversity of subgroups that populate a campus.

The notion of civility may be a significant communication means or process that can keep diverse subgroups working productively with one another. The standard of civility as the rule of the game permits different ideological positions to clash in the marketplace of ideas without destroying a campus. Take for example, a Marxist sociologist, well-published in his academic area, and a professor of economics, a published follower of Adam Smith. Both professors recommend that students take the other's course out of respect for each other's expertise.

Civility permits conversation about ideas, recognizing that as time passes many ideas will prove to be ill-founded and left behind. But civility on the campus requires some ideas to win out in the longer course, rejecting shortsighted efforts at victory that bring personal animosity toward those in contrary ideological camps. Such a notion points to an educational oxymoron, permitting intellectual fighting for the long-range direction of a culture to occur within the short-range agreement of cooperation.

Tinder suggests that the notion of community is too idealistic if it assumes that we will be able to bring together significantly different people committed to different ideologies. He suggests that a more realistic hope is to offer a place of civility to the diversity of viewpoints. I concur with his call for civility, but believe that when such a view is accepted by a critical mass on a campus, a community of learners is being born. The commitment of those interested in dialogic education is to keep the conversation going and inviting inquiry. The dialogic assumption that undergirds this book is that being civil in the midst of different positions is a base line need, otherwise, discussion will be used to ignore, weaken, and ridicule the opposition, moving us from education to the propaganda tactics of a zealot.

Tinder's use of the term *civility* captures some of the positive qualities associated with the notion of community without carrying the baggage of undue optimism that the word community often connotes. He openly admits the difficulty of defining a term like *civility* and suggests a path similar to

Aristotle's definition of *excellence*. Tinder suggests looking for practical examples of civility in action and encourages us to link up with people that personify such virtues, giving us a chance to practice a life of civility after witnessing how the concept can be practiced by another.

Tinder outlines the roots of civility with several guidelines. First, to be civil requires being wary of any ideology that is all consuming. In methodological terms, Tinder is pointing to a participant-observer. Rather than an objective overseer or a subjective interpretation, it is a third alternative to extreme positions. In a sense, Tinder offers a secular version of the theological notion of "being in the world, but not completely of it." One holds back some enthusiasm, being cautious of a true believer status that lessens the possibility for us to discern the limits and contradictions of a given theory, action, or philosophy. Similarly, Michael Polanyi's *Personal Knowledge: Towards a Post-Critical Philosophy* calls us to acknowledge our own biased contribution to an experiment or study, without legitimizing the ignoring of the text.[32] Wayne Booth also reminds us not to ignore the text or the unique questions we bring to the text.[33]

Second, civility applies to the manner of one's action more than historical results. As Gandhi often suggested, "means are simply ends in the making."[34] It is not, however, that a person attempting to act in a civil fashion is unconcerned about what will result. Results are important. The notion of civility reminds us, though, that the way in which we work with others will have an impact as well.

Third, civility is based on giving voice even to our enemies, not necessarily agreeing with them, but trying to understand their viewpoint. Civility is more interested in taking the time to understand another's position than in agreement. "Civility is manifest in Abraham Lincoln's awareness that his enemies in the South were human beings like the people of the North—fallible, but in most cases doing what they thought was right."[35]

Fourth, civility requires exemplary action that paradoxically reflects both the autonomy of detachment and a commitment to community that permits hearing ideas that may be at odds with one's own views and agenda. This action is based on tolerance, and the permitting of multiple perspectives.

Civility requires walking between the extremes of undue optimism and pessimism, radical activism and detachment. It is a manner of living that works to see the humanness in those like us, as well as our adversaries.

The standard of civility calls on us to maintain the integrity of our communal nature even in the face of the communal disasters of our time. . . . Civility is an effort to take part in history while avoiding political ideology, to achieve a universal relatedness that is uncorrupted either by absolutism in theory or fanaticism in action. It means trying to participate in the affairs of the whole human race without either killing in order to redeem the earth from all evil or pretending that established society, with all of its subtle and habitual as well as glaring injustices, is a community.[36]

Education based on the importance of persons encountering ideas together in a civil fashion requires us to hold ourselves back a bit and be willing to examine and discuss important informational and value issues. During a conference discussion of civility, I was asked, "How does this notion of civility relate to marketing a college campus?" My answer was that a college or university has an ethical need to be sensitive to the persons on their campus and to invite a long-term vision. Keeping both these issues in mind, civility can be translated into marketing terms by use of an 80-percent solution.

A college or university might choose to advertise no more than 80 percent of what it believes it can deliver at its best. Civility asks us to hold back some of our enthusiasm, so we market what we are sure we can deliver, not that which might happen for only a small number of students. Such a marketing method is cognizant of long-term market share; as students find out a campus is as good or even better than what they were led to believe, they are more likely to join the ranks of contributing and recruiting alumni than students who felt that a university did not deliver at its declared level of competence. Civil marketing requires holding back, marketing 80 percent of what is possible in hopes of graduating students who believe that they have attended a fine school— one they want to tell others about.

Dialogic education works on the assumption that ideas need to be discussed and people treated humanely if a genuine conversation about ideas is to be invited. A civil environment might keep people focused on the task at hand, learning, instead of having to protect oneself from slanderous gossip. Civility is a practical way to get more done, keeping one's internal communication more centered on the information at hand. Environments where the relationships require people to take time to avoid trouble and be on the watch against the covert actions of colleagues lessen what can be accomplished. Dialogic education accepts civility as a practical way to encourage relationship building and assist productivity and creativity.

Civility in education is an admission that our task is not necessarily to persuade another of our viewpoint or ideological orientation. Rather, the dialogic task of education is to enter conversation about ideas, keeping in mind that human beings can be civil on a campus, even as we contend with one another's theoretical perspectives. In essence, the active detachment that grounds civility needs to be applied not only within a paradigm we accept, but in the clashing of perspectives as well.

The Goals of Dialogic Education

Dialogic Education: Conversation About Ideas and Between Persons is one possible vision of how undergraduate education might be invited. The goals of dialogic education reveal the importance of accumulation of information and a recognition of the following: the importance of having a value base or ground from which to meet and interpret history and current events in one's personal and professional life, as well as in the larger world; the significance of ideas as our common center of intellectual curiosity; the importance that time plays in the nurturing of relationships; and the hope that a student will develop a philosophical foundation open to revision and capable of assisting with the inevitable challenges that will be met in the course of a lifetime.

Value Base

Dialogic education works with the assumption that values do make a difference in the quality of human life and in the way information is processed and applied. Dialogue is made possible by a person having a value position that he or she brings to a conversation that adds to the quality of the interaction. Dialogue does not work if one party refuses to state his or her viewpoint or perspective, because dialogue is the civil exchange of information about various perspectives on a given issue. As Paul Keller, co-author of *Monologue to Dialogue* stated, the true test of dialogue is in disagreement, not in mutual understanding. Dialogic education encourages a student to accept the importance of knowing his or her value base from which information is interpreted and simultaneously be willing to put such a perspective to the test in the give and take of conversation.

Being able to ask value questions about information, ideas,

and relationships recognizes that not all tasks that are technically possible should actually be attempted. There is, however, no prescriptive set of guidelines for how dialogic education can determine whether information and its application will assist oneself and others. As a teacher, one can pose value questions, but as soon as one crosses over the line and begins to dictate answers, one has moved from educator to propagandist.

William Barrett concludes *The Irrational Man* with reference to the mythological "Furies," those bad things we do not want to admit or openly encounter. For some in education, discussion of values has become the "Furies" that are better forgotten. But in dialogic education, values are given a place of overt discussion, in hopes of adding to the quality of education through debate, rather than silence.

> In giving the Furies their place, we may come to recognize that they are not such alien presences as we think in our moments of evading them. In fact, far from being alien, they are part of ourselves, like all gods and demons. The conspiracy to forget them, or to deny that they exist, thus turns out to be only one more contrivance in that vast and organized effort by modern society to flee from the self.[37]

Value discussion in dialogic education is grounded in rhetoric or discussion of probabilities. Perhaps then value discussion can be brought to the explicit level, moving it beyond the tacit level of unknowing approval. Thus, dialogic education brings together a technical "how" (information accumulation) with an ability to ask "why" (value questioning) something should be done.

Ideas as a "Common Center"

Dialogic education works on the premise that conversation about ideas is the underlying fundamental reason for going to a college or university. As stated earlier, holding discussion of ideas as primary does not preclude enjoying the social life of a campus, engaging in athletics, or taking courses in a major that offers opportunity for employment. What makes a campus unique, however, is not its social life, sports activities, or opportunities for job advancement. What may be different from other institutions is the opportunity to discuss ideas with one another, no matter what the motivation for beginning such conversation.

At its best, a college or university offers conversation about ideas as a way of pulling diversity together, offering a chance to engage in a common mission. Muzafer and Carolyn W. Sherif refer to such overarching commitment as a "superordinate goal."[38] A superordinate goal is not mystical, but rather a goal that can pull people together around a common task.

This common center of conversation about ideas is not just the basis of a college or university campus, but from the vantage point of dialogic education, it is the beginning foundation for leadership. "Commitment to ideas and purposes creates 'will,' and widespread agreement produces legitimacy. The combination is legitimate will. And with that, as Lincoln said, everything succeeds."[39] Dialogic education seeks to model the importance of conversation about ideas, not just as the common center of a campus, but as the beginning foundation for creative leadership. A commitment to inquiry may be the only way in which a common vision can be discovered in an ideologically diverse culture.

Time and Relationships

Dialogic educators recognize the importance of human relationships and the value of taking time with students. Working with undergraduates frequently involves contact with eighteen to twenty-two year olds and older nontraditional students making serious changes in their lives. Both need time and relationships, not just to learn about the subject matter, but to sort out the kind of life they want to lead. Perhaps the conclusion to a special edition of *Newsweek* devoted to the teen years offers appropriate advice for teachers, as well as parents.

> The teens of the '90's do emulate the culture of their parents, many of whom are the very teens who once made such an impact on their own parents. These parents no doubt have something very useful to pass on to their children—maybe their lost sense of idealism rather than the preoccupation with going and getting that seems, so far, their main legacy to their young. Mom and Dad have to earn a living and fulfill their own needs—they are not likely to be coming home early. But there must be a time and place for them to give their children the advice, the comfort and, most of all, the feelings of possibility that any new generation needs in order to believe in itself.[40]

This article is a reminder to parents that some college and university professors might need to hear as well. We need to spend time with students, assisting them with the struggles that dominate their lives.

Such a relational theme is not a new one, but is important to articulate when the complaint about higher education is one of lack of content. Teachers will need to take the content question seriously without ignoring the personal and relational needs of the students. Storyteller Hermann Hesse, in *Beneath the Wheel*, reveals the dangers of pushing students too far, too fast, without a holistic understanding that education is more than information accumulation.

Hans, the main character in the story, has been prepared for the intellectual demands placed upon him at an exclusive boarding school. What fails him is lack of knowledge about people and relationships. Even the rudimentary elements of how to invite and nourish a friendship are not part of his knowledge base. The story is a chronicle of failures, based not on lack of information, but a lack of relational knowledge that leads to doom for this fine young mind, both at the boarding school and later back home as a mechanic's apprentice.[41]

Hesse's story is an extreme case that reminds us of the dangers of too narrow of a life. People and the importance of human relationships are an important complement to the drive to know more information. Perhaps the main educational contribution of Hesse's writing is to remind us that knowing about people and relationships is not just a luxury, but a necessary skill for a successful and happy life. The quality and quantity of the information we learn will determine the potential that we bring to a given task. What we learn relationally will determine whether or not we will succeed at what our informational capacity permits us to accomplish.

Dialogic education assumes that involvement in student life is a necessary companion to learning an academic discipline. I. F. Stone contrasts the style of Socrates with that of Aristotle, the former calling for withdrawal from participation in the polis and the latter considering it a noble use of a life. "Aristotle was closer to the classic idea. He developed his politics and his ethics, as we have seen, from the premise that virtue was not 'solitary' but political or civic."[42] Conversation in the classical style of responsibility, not just as a citizen, but in this case, as an educator ushering in the next generation of leaders, is part of dialogic education.

Conversation about ideas is supported by an emphasis on dialogic friendship. Concern for others and one's own learning results in a posture of mutual goodwill. The ideal of dialogic education is a form of friendship that invites an environment where there is concern for self and other, a spirit of mutual goodwill. "I merely point out to you that, as a matter of fact, certain persons do exist with an enormous capacity for friendship and for taking delight in other people's lives; and that such persons know more of truth than if their hearts were not so big."[43] Such goodwill does not imply always liking students. But one can encourage words like tolerance, goodwill, and a recognition that civility of a culture is based more directly on our response to those with whom we do not feel kinship than those who are ideological companions.

A Philosophical Foundation

Dialogic education, as I envision it, develops a philosophical foundation emphasizing three goals. First, dialogic education encourages a recognition that life has a value dimension and that the educated person should be equipped to ask value questions. Such an education cannot give *the* value answers but can reveal *why* asking such questions is important to oneself and the community in which we live.

Second, content needs to be the center of our time together on campus. Continued learning and willingness to discuss such learning needs to be part of a philosophical foundation that guides a person after graduation when the pressure to know and learn may begin to subside in intensity. The willingness to read, listen, watch, and talk about information offers a foundation for continued learning after college life, and provides a way of making contact with other human beings not based on gossip or complaining.

Finally, as one develops a philosophical foundation that embraces the importance of asking value questions and conversing about information, dialogic education reminds us of the reason for our learning—the enhancement of the quality of human life for ourselves and others. Thus, as we learn to ask questions and share information with others, we need to realize the importance of being sensitive to the quality of relationships. A person is more likely to listen to us if we nourish the relationship, even if we ask tough value and informational questions. Concern for relationships not only expresses the value that human beings are important, but, pragmatically, people are more likely to listen to us when the relationship can be trusted.

Dialogic Invitation in Education

Dialogic education offers an opportunity to discuss content, values, and relationships, framing a philosophy about life that can assist in the maturation of one's personal and professional life. Such an educational style cannot be forced, however, on a faculty member or a student. One school, for more than a decade, required a colloquium each semester in a three-year graduate program. One of the goals was to invite conversation about ideas. For some the program worked, but for others the colloquium experience forced an inauthentic form of intimacy and revealed a lack of confidence in the material being studied and an unwillingness to let the material more naturally elicit conversation.

No matter whether one has less than twenty or more than a hundred students in a classroom, dialogic communication can only be invited. A student has the right to ultimately remain oblivious to conversation about ideas, relationships, and value discussion. In such a case, the educator must not force concern for ideas, relationships, and value discussion as a remedy, or the formula is ripe for failure.

Each student deserves the right to presentation of information and to be evaluated. However, some students will not be interested in anything beyond that. Our task is to offer information and evaluation to any student, without condescension for the student who wants no more than that.

The small college that attempts to make every student and faculty member learn in a dialogic fashion will invite a "tyranny of intimacy," interpersonal pressures to conform to a narrow paradigmatic view of education. The large state research campus that offers such an approach to all students might put at risk its long-term research commitment that is designed to assist the next generation of students. Dialogic education can only work when invited and accepted without duress.

Dialogic education is not a panacea, nor is it possible in all environments. Conversation is just that—conversation. It can not be demanded, only invited. My worst classroom experiences as an educator have occurred when this simple fact has been forgotten. We do not control others. We can only invite conversation in hopes that some students will find more to their education than information and evaluation. At some time, all of us are asked to apply information within the real life context of people with consequences to our decisions. When I am able to get some students to enter conversation over issues that offer no one answer, the educational environment for the students and for me is frequently enriched.

Perhaps a reasonable goal is that I will be able to know when an invitation has been taken up, while resting somewhat easy when lack of student interest in conversation about ideas is present. The reminder for me is that the notion of conversation assumes an invitation and an acceptance, both acts presuming that time and circumstance may result in no dialogic invitation or acceptance.

Perhaps dialogic education is based on a philosophy of "hope," hope that concern for values, information, and people can still make a difference. As Buber suggested, "The hope for this hour depends upon the renewal of dialogical immediacy between men. . . ."[44] Dialogic education is viewed as a chance not only to discuss the importance of the above three goals, but to put them into practice, both inside and outside the classroom. Such a form of education involves hope that conversation about information and values with persons can assist the quality of life for ourselves and for others.

> When all choices are gone, hope is abandoned. . . . Hope rises with the number of trustworthy directions envisioned.
> Hope is imagining, choosing, trusting that there is another way.
> Hope opens the options, hope welcomes the future, hope sets us free to choose again.
> Hope offers tomorrow.[45]

Dialogic education is based on a conviction that human beings can be invited into conversation about ideas, values, and relationships, not out of a conviction that one can learn all the answers, but out of a belief that dialogue with others is the foundation of a quality of life for oneself and others. "Let me repeat once more that a man's vision is the great fact about him. A philosophy is the expression of a man's intimate character, and all definitions of the Universe are but the deliberately adopted reactions of human characters upon it."[46]

There is an assumption that educated people need to genuinely grapple with problems of application of information, values, and questions about the type of contribution we might like to leave behind when our lives are concluded. In the novel *Zorba the Greek*, the intellectual, "boss," was asked by Zorba who was right about how to live life, Zorba or an old man. The old man said to Zorba, "'My son, I carry on as if I should never die.' I [Zorba] replied: 'And I carry on as if I was going to die any minute.' Which of us was right, boss?"[47] The question cannot be answered for all time, but conversation about such questions can leave a significant impact, reminding us of the importance of life choices. How are we to use the years given to us? In essence, there is hope that dialogic education, based in conversation about ideas, can make a difference in individual lives and in the larger human community, not just by big leaps and discoveries, but by small steps, one conversation at a time, between student and teacher.

PART 2

A Foundation for Dialogue in Education

3

An Academic "Home"

Members of a home—

I read a massive and engaging novel by Ayn Rand, *Atlas Shrugged.*
In it she made a seemingly compelling case for her philosophy of
rugged individualism and unrestrained free enterprise. Something
about that philosophy, however, bothered me—something I couldn't
quite put my finger on. It kept gnawing at me until one day I finally
realized that there were essentially no children in the book, which
was a panoramic novel of around a thousand pages recounting the
sweep of society and the drama of many lives. But there were virtually no children. It was as if children did not exist in her society; they
were missing. And of course that is exactly one of the social situations
in which rugged individualism . . . falls short: where there are children and others who, like children, need to be cared for.

> M. Scott Peck,
> *The Different Drum:*
> *Community Making and Peace*

We study in—

The locus of study is not the object of study. Anthropologists don't
study villages (tribes, towns, neighborhoods . . .); they study in
villages. You can study different things in different places, and
some things—for example, what colonial domination does to established frames of moral expectation—you can best study in confined
localities.

> Clifford Geertz,
> *The Interpretation of Cultures*

This chapter takes the position that loyalty rests in the academic
home and relationship, not in abstractions about the unity of all

37

humankind, but in one relationship at a time, each in its own particular place. The home discussed in this chapter is the college or university. For many, however, viewing a college or university as a home is not realistic; for some faculty a sense of home might be a smaller entity, perhaps a department, or a cadre of students and faculty.

Christopher Lasch, in *The True and Only Heaven: Progress and Its Critics*, outlines the debate between a commitment to an abstract ideal and a unique particular home. If we want to protect the opportunity to select unique and contrasting educational options from a pluralistic array of campuses, then a distinct flavor or sense of home needs to reflect the unique characteristics of a given place. Lasch quotes Josiah Royce in pointing to a position that embraces the unique and particular as a place of loyalty, and recognizes the importance of a good interlocutor in a democratic culture.[1] "Advocates of particularism challenged one of the central tenets of enlightened ideology, the equation of progress with the eradication of tribal loyalties and their replacement by an all-embracing love for the whole human race."[2] This chapter is about finding a campus, department, or cadre of learners that can offer a sense of home, not claiming it to necessarily be the best, but claiming it as one's own place to belong, work, and learn.

Dialogic education invites a sense of home for a campus, a department, or a small number of persons willing to accept the responsibilities of loyalty and commitment to one another and to the common task of inquiry. As stated in chapter 2, dialogic education cannot be guaranteed for all, just as a sense of home will not be felt by all members of a campus.

The key word throughout this book is *invitation*. Dialogic education is based on invitation, just as the bonds of loyalty to any feeling of home must be if we are to avoid the danger of a totalitarian commitment fueled by demand and fear. Dialogic education is facilitated in homes that invite conversation with students that goes beyond information accumulation, recognizing the importance of relationship and values in education.

I was asked by a group of graduate students why I loved being an educator and I responded by saying that I found myself most at home on campuses working with students. This chapter is an effort to sort out what it means to be at home on a campus, in a department, or with students and colleagues. Such a feeling of being at home cannot be manufactured by a mission statement or official decrees. It will not be felt by all. Some will feel at home on an entire campus, others in a department, and still others with a small cadre of students and colleagues centered on a common objective of learning together.

I have at different times in my career felt both "realities"— a sense of being at home and a feeling of alienation, like a stranger or fish out of water. It is this vague feeling of being at home, however, that has given me the greatest satisfaction as an educator and as a human being. This chapter is an effort to outline the notion of being at home on a campus, and connecting it to an ongoing commitment to dialogic education. As Lasch and Peter Berger suggest, being "homeless" can only be overcome as we commit ourselves to local institutions, working for their renewal within a value system sensitive to the dignity of people and the importance of work worthy of being done.[3]

A Sense of Home

A sense or feeling of being at home includes a commitment to keeping a campus, department, or group strong and full of purpose; a place capable of offering not just shelter, but inviting participation in a meaning structure that enlightens the importance of worthwhile work. Finding and supporting an educational home requires commitment and attitudes that may seem oddly out of place in today's world. Lasch reminds us that love was once defined as sacrifice and commitment, even though today it is more likely to be equated with self-fulfillment.[4] Like Lasch's old view of love, the notion of *home* suggests a commitment that takes one beyond mere employment. Rob Anderson offered an interesting response to the notion of home that assists in understanding the point of this chapter.

> [There may be] . . . significance to the linguistic habit in English of saying "I'm home" . . . or "I'm going home". . . . We don't say "I'm school" or "I'm going church." There are different senses of "place" at work here—a place of "home" is psychologically enveloping, maybe immersing, understood. The "I" is integrated automatically within a "home," while our speech suggests that an "I" simply visits, observes, or attends other places.[5]

Feeling at home is different than simply attending a college or university or being employed within an institution; it means that I feel a part of a place.

Books ranging from Berger's *Homeless Mind* to Lasch's *Ha-*

ven in a Heartless World to Robert Bellah's *Habits of the Heart* all speak of a common theme—a sense of longing for a place where one feels significant, loyal, committed to a common task, or at home. Some college professors and students, like others in the general population, want a haven of support and trust. Perhaps faculty look for a place where inquiry is encouraged and invited and one feels a part of something worthy of passing on to the next generation of students.

For some this feeling of being at home might be part of an overall commitment to a private college. But even on private campuses this feeling of being at home is not always present, particularly as schools move from familiar connections and mutual loyalty to contractual and fiscal obligations. Thus, at small colleges or large universities the search for a feeling of being at home is often limited to an academic department and in many cases to a group of students or faculty.

When we move the notion of being at home from the level of the college or university itself to much smaller groupings, we open ourselves to the division of a campus through the proliferation of subgroups, each with its own agenda. But for a sense of home to be felt as a realistic possibility, we must admit that large organizational structures and small colleges with a contractual rather than familial ethos will be unlikely to provide such a feeling. It seems we are left with taking the risk of inviting a sense of home under whatever circumstances are given to us or eliminating the possibility of finding a place to feel at home, while we work with students and colleagues.

What might separate a feeling of home from simply a campus clique is that the former gains its identity from agreement on a common task, loyalty, and commitment, keeping open the invitation for others to join. A clique, on the other hand, is exclusive; its identity comes not so much from a common task, as it does from opposition to other groups on campus. The test of an academic home might be whether or not there is willingness to permit others to join the conversation and whether the gathering point of conversation is around what can be done, rather than discussion of errors and limitations of other groups and individuals on the campus. Without an invitation to join and willingness to reject conversational complaint as the common theme of interaction, a subgroup or clique on the campus will emerge.

On a college or university campus the notion of home, whether grounded in a department or a smaller cadre of students and faculty, offers a sense of meaning for work that can take one beyond employment alone. In a concrete fashion, a commitment to an academic home offers a reason for going beyond the base norm of acceptable work on a campus or in a department. "[In] Nietzsche's words, 'He who has a *why* to live for can bear any *how*'. ... Woe to him who saw no more sense to his life, no aim, no purpose, and therefore no point in carrying on. He was soon lost."[6] It is possible to become lost on a campus or in a department and ask, Why did I join such a profession? Why am I at this particular school, in this particular department, working with these students? A meaning structure for *why* the work is important might come from feeling at home in one's job and task. Again, we can not demand that such an environment be present. But if dialogic education is invited, so will a meaning structure that goes beyond information and evaluation with at least some students and faculty.

A sense of home offers a meaning structure that embraces a feeling of having a place from which to stand and contribute to education on a campus. Participating within a home environment can provide a feeling of satisfaction for work that cannot be bought or contrived. And, according to research done by Bellah, the search for such havens at home is longed for at least by some.

> [Bellah has discovered that] ... few have found a life devoted to 'personal ambition and consumerism' satisfactory, and most are seeking in one way or another to transcend the limitations of a self-centered life. If there are vast numbers of a selfish, narcissistic 'me-generation' in America, we did not find them, but we certainly did find that the language of individualism, the primary American language of self-understanding, limits the ways in which people think.[7]

Dialogic education begins with the invitation, which will not be wanted by all, to join an academic home where the common center is inquiry. Such a home centers on conversation about ideas, relationships, and values—learning from one another.

Finding a "Home"

The first definitive characteristic of an academic home grounded in a dialogic orientation is that it defines education as more than information. Some social critiques have criticized western civilization for too frequently limiting itself to the question, "Can something be done?" without the accompanying concern, "Should it be done?"[8] An academic home has a sense of character and uniqueness, offering a value context where the question "Should it be done?" can be discussed.

A campus or a department can become a place of critical inquiry, supporting one's work concretely, in daily interaction. In offering a value sensitive education, a home or educational environment, whether it be a campus, department, or a small cadre of students and faculty, invites a willingness to take seriously value discussions. To demand total adherence to a value system of any group results in a "technology of propaganda,"[9] not dialogic education.

Jacques Ellul's critique is similar to William Barrett's theme in *The Illusion of Technique*; it is possible for "how," to become more important than "why," even in the examination of values. Creativity and meaning discovery do not emerge from prescription, but from discovery.[10] An educational home is open to invitation, discussion, and critical reflection, or one violates the mission of thoughtful exploration of ideas and theories essential to the life of a campus.

Dialogic education is nourished when an educator does not impose value answers. Once imposition of values begins, we leave the realm of education and enter the narrow confines of a propagandist, demanding conformity.[11] An invitation to be at home while studying and teaching seeks a middle ground between a value-free education, and a closed value system. Such an effort seeks to avoid the dangers of value neutrality and closed paradigmatic arrogance, walking a tightrope between excess, too much value orientation, and deficiency, too little value discussion.[12]

Excess, in this case, is propaganda, imposition on a student's right and ability to conceptualize and draw his or her own conclusions. Deficiency withholds the opportunity for value discussion. The teacher might present his or her own views as a teacher without requiring the students to comply with that position. Being at home in a dialogic educational setting requires finding a place between the extremes of dogmatism and untempered freedom.

The Jeffersonian tradition of debate and free exchange of ideas and the early roots of academic freedom in Germany both attest to guaranteed intellectual choice as a beginning foundation for finding an academic home. Thomas Nilsen uses the term *significant choice* to define democratic free exchange of ideas. "When we communicate to influence the attitudes, beliefs, and actions of others, *the ethical touchstone is the degree of free, informed, and critical choice on matters of significance in their lives that is fostered by our speaking. We shall call this significant choice."*[13]

Significant choice is necessary if we are to avoid the obvious danger and threat that propaganda poses to academic freedom. The case of Father Curren at Catholic University might be considered an example of excess on the side of value education. His teaching was considered contrary to Catholic doctrine and he was asked to alter his approach or lose his position.[14] Before comparing the way in which this case was approached versus the Maguire case at Marquette, another Catholic university, it is important to note that the charge of the two universities is considerably different, with Catholic University being a land grant university of the Catholic church. In short, a case can be made for why the two schools handled academic freedom issues differently.

The case of Daniel Maguire at Marquette University, however, is more in keeping with the tension that must accompany value education and academic freedom, as envisioned by dialogic education. A full one-page ad was taken out in the *Milwaukee Journal*, the city newspaper, in opposition to Maguire's teaching. The university responded by stating that they did not support Maguire's position, which was in contrast to Catholic doctrine, but would stand by his right to question and present his viewpoint.[15] Marquette University's support of academic freedom embraced values that go hand in hand with an academic institution, permitting openness to question and challenge without falling into the trap of a value-laden education. Without a dual effort to affirm values and offer critique, we are left with an academic community trained to implement *the* truth, not a home pursuing truth in the spirit of a community of scholars.

An academic home invites commitment and is enriched by a sense of tradition. A second major characteristic of an academic home centers around concern for its quality continuation, even after employment. When faculty emeriti believe that the environment which typifies a university, department, or program is worth passing on to the next generation of students and scholars, some will continue to volunteer time, energy, and resources after retirement. Such volunteerism is a barometer of the significance of the home environment.

The sermons of John Winthrop have been quoted by many, from Ronald Reagan to Michael Dukakis, as some in this country have searched for ways of bonding together for the collective good. Various speakers have tried to remind us of an obligation beyond our own lives and careers.

Now the only way to avoid this shipwreck and to provide for our posterity is to follow the counsel of Micah: to do justice, to love mercy, to walk humbly. . . . We must be knit together in this work as one man; we must hold each other in brotherly affection; we must be willing to rid ourselves of our excesses to supply others' necessities. . . . For we must consider that we shall be like a City upon a Hill; the eyes of all people are on us.[16]

Not unlike the time of John Winthrop, we too, long for a world connected between generations; a perception that we are not alone, but one of many carriers of information and values from one generation to another. Various reflections on the "City Upon a Hill" theme provide insight into generational sensitivity—a place where there is concern for the next generation of teachers and scholars.

An academic home, whether a campus, department, or a group committed to a common task, operates within tradition, not just the needs of the moment. Perhaps the following story points to how the faculty of tradition, professor emeriti, and new faculty can function together. A young man who had been lost in a forest finally found an old gentleman deep in the woods. He told the old gentleman that he had been lost for three days. At that point the old gentleman stated "Only three days? I have been lost in this forest for three years." Such a discovery caused the young man to feel great pain and despair. " 'No, no, my young friend, don't despair,' replied the man of the woods, 'It is true that I cannot show you the paths that lead out of the woods, but I can point out to you the paths that do not.' "[17]

People find their way either by following paths taken before them or searching for new routes, at times with the advice and support of the previous generation. Such a view of generational connectedness points to the importance of tradition guiding the mission of an academic home. In a home campus or department, the members need to be able to articulate a tradition without feeling a sense of false marketing or hypocrisy.

Home campuses and departments are not just places that dispense abstract philosophies to their students; the tradition manifests itself in practical workings of life on a campus. For instance, is international education important? Should we develop a graduate program? What is our commitment to the study of foreign language? Such questions are partially answered by the tradition of an institution. If there is a good match among tradition, the faculty, the students, and the everyday workings of the campus, morale is likely to be high.

Tradition provides an educational home with a feeling of energy, purpose, and direction. Belief in the tradition of a campus or department can move actions from the realm of work into the sphere of vocation. Thomas Merton discussed the importance of vocation in *No Man is an Island*, suggesting that life is most meaningful when connected to a tradition of a people.[18] Merton used the term *vocation* to describe such a life, both in religious and nonreligious terms, as Bellah did in a much later work, *Habits of the Heart*.[19] A vocation involves a meaning structure that accompanies work, creating a "calling" to use life for a significant purpose.

Bellah examines, from a secular interpretation, the notion of calling––the placement of one's life within a community committed to a particular set of learnings and practices that shape one's character.

> In a calling . . . one gives oneself to the learning and practicing activities that in turn define the self and enter into the shape of its character. Committing one's self to becoming a 'good' carpenter, craftsman, doctor, scientist, or artist anchors the self within a community practicing carpentry, medicine, or art. It connects the self to those who teach, exemplify, and judge these skills. It ties us to still others whom they serve.[20]

The notion of a tradition, whether a calling or the general atmosphere of an academic home, need not imply an old decaying sense of order and ritual. If traditions do not change, they become a form of totalitarian rule. A tradition is not something to be feared. It is a perspective from which to judge and respond to events. "To stand within a tradition does not limit the freedom of knowledge but makes it possible."[21] We need to know where a tradition has come from, who we are, why we exist as we do, and what events mean for us today. In what ways can and should we apply tradition to a unique present? Without the application of a tradition to the present, the tradition dies, unable to shape the current moment or be of value for the future.

This commitment to a "live" tradition may not encourage many of us to become Trappist Monks or to follow a religious vocation, but we may assist in the maintenance and growth of an educational home. As one faculty member stated, "I teach here because I believe in the institution. I am lucky. Many people just work; I have been able to be part of an important educational task at this school."

Affirming a home campus requires us to recognize the value of the history and tradition of that place. Ernest Boyer has stated the need for more loyalty to one's home campus and community. Boyer understands that an educational home does not emerge out of a vacuum; such a place requires the efforts of many to present a particular world view, while still supporting academic freedom.[22]

Perhaps an educational home can provide an environment more akin to the philosophical understanding that Walter Brueggemann offers of the Old Testament view of "land."[23] The notion of land was not just a literal concern, but a philosophical question of meaning in life. One attempted to find a place to call home, a place from which one could make sense out of the world, and a place to gather and draw a perspective. This same case could be made for Martin Buber's understanding of "blood." He saw the need to be connected, not biologically, but in terms of philosophical perspective; being part of an ongoing story.[24] The philosophical implications of the notions of land and blood are similar to the use of the term *home* offering a place of tradition, a place to belong, work, and to be of service, calling for a thoughtful loyalty from its members.

One of the more controversial books of the late 1980s was Allan Bloom's, *Closing of the American Mind*. He argued that a classical tradition should be known by an educated population. His frequent references to Plato, known for his aristocratic and nondemocratic views of education and society, led some to quickly reject his work. But one of the main points of his book is that education without a sense of tradition is a contradiction in terms. The debate over the breadth and inclusive range of educational traditions needs to continue with the notion of tradition being positive, inclusive, and willing to grow and evolve.[25]

What do we know of our past? How can we learn from our tradition? How can we improve upon it? Without a home, a sense of land, or a tradition from which to operate, we are left with what Peter Berger called the "homeless mind" and what Robert Bellah meant by life without "habits of the heart." The varied traditions at diverse educational homes throughout the world will not all agree with Bloom's call back to the classics, nor should they. But a campus or a department still needs to be guided by an inclusive tradition worthy of passing on to the next generation of scholars and students.

An academic home is nourished by knowing what the institution stands for (its tradition) and why an education at that particular institution is worthy of being passed to another generation. For instance, Manchester College supports a major and minor in peace studies, the first of its kind in the country. This particular college is affiliated with a church tradition that initiated the organization after which Peace Corps was modeled. In this case, there is reason and tradition for a peace studies program; it is not a fad, but a thoughtful curriculum sensitive to the tradition of the campus known for its global perspective.

Although Bloom was critical of interdisciplinary programs such as peace studies, he might find it interesting that the classics are avenues for conversation *and* critique in this particular program. Albert Schweitzer stated that we must know our Western tradition to be able to compare and contrast it with other world views.[26]

Tradition defines what a campus is, has been, and can become. In the example above, it is appropriate to critique the peace studies major. But it is unlikely that peace studies will be banished or destroyed unless the objective is to alter the tradition of this college home. The same could be said of Athenian democracy. It was critiqued, but attempts at destroying the democratic culture were met with fierce opposition.

Tradition is not composed of a list of designated items. We may be able to name some major elements that carve out the tradition of an institution, yet at times the specifics are difficult to enumerate. Often the tradition of a campus or a department remains at a tacit level. We may only become aware of a tradition when someone violates what we have taken for granted. When change happens, we sometimes are pleased by the change and at other times may seek to reinstitute previously taken-for-granted traditions of an institution.

We are often left with an understanding of tradition that embodies the term, *gestalt*. The entire sense of home, is greater than the sum of the individual parts. When this gestalt understanding of tradition ceases to have meaning, an atmosphere of tradition that sets one campus apart from another is at risk.

The notion of home may be one of the most important characteristics for dialogic education. Dialogue begins with our having a ground or home to begin a conversation. An academic home offers an ethos suggesting reasons for keeping an institution strong for the next generation of users and workers. In a transient world, it is no small educational gift to witness commitment and loyalty to a philosophical and practical home.

Nourishing the Home Environment

Erich Fromm's effort to define love is helpful in conceptualizing what is needed to support, protect, and pass on the significance of an educational home to the next generation of students and faculty. Fromm defined love as embracing four different and equally important components: care, responsibility, respect, and knowledge.[27] An educational home needs care in the short and long term, to keep a campus or department strong and worthy of its educational goals. Such an institution encourages remembering that caring must include the immediate student population, without being totally consumed by them; the next generation of students deserve an up-to-date professor as well. One must balance concern in short-term care (availability to students) with long-term care (scholarship time that permits knowledge acquisition), which will contribute to future students as well.

One's responsibility is to work for the common good of an educational home: "We cannot justify political arrangements without reference to common purposes and ends, and . . . we cannot conceive our personhood without reference to our role as citizens and as participants in a common life."[28] Aristotle reminds us of the importance of seeking the common good, not just our own life goals or status. Just as Aristotle nourished the polis for the politician and general population, it is our responsibility to nourish an educational home for the benefit of teachers and students.

Respect for an educational home implies an understanding and a commitment to the mission of the campus or department. For example, while examining a department, one review team discovered that a department chair was teaching an overload without compensation. The chair was over sixty and had a number of younger faculty that could have taught the course. When questioned about the arrangement, the answer was simply, "The younger faculty need time for research and families. I am no longer publishing and my family is now gone. I ask for no additional pay because the institution has been good to me and I need no further income." Such faculty, no matter how small in number, still walk the halls of some educational institutions, offering a model of dedication.

Finally, knowledge is necessary. One must give something to one's home by remaining on the cutting edge of one's discipline. It is not enough to simply have an educational home; one must continue to build that environment with knowledge brought through disciplinary discussion and teaching. When asked why she continues to publish and do research long after her tenure and promotion to full professor, one friend stated what many of us who love education and teaching might say, "I read, write, study, and publish, not to advance, but to learn. I guess I do it because I cannot do otherwise. I love to learn." This commitment to constant knowledge renewal contributes to the future strength of a home campus or department.

Love of an educational home involves a willingness to act out of care, responsibility, respect, and knowledge. Such a commitment may not be for all, but for those wanting to feel part of a tradition, such a campus, department, or cadre of learners can offer a special dimension to academic life. As one of my colleagues reflected at his retirement: "Teaching here was a great life decision. It has been a good way to lend service to others, while giving meaning to my own life."

Do Such Places Exist?

At this juncture you may question whether it is possible to find educational institutions worthy of calling home. In an age of mobility and individual rights, why would anyone want to feel attached to an academic home? Perhaps a faculty member needs to ask: Do I want to feel some commitment and loyalty to the institution at which I teach that goes beyond fulfilling my professional responsibilities? Is there something that should concern me other than learning and imparting information within my disciplinary domain?

Finding an educational home does come at a cost of time and commitment. The cynical position is that there is nothing of significance on a campus or in a department worthy of extra commitment and time. Yet there are faculty such as this colleague who stated: "I will retire in five years, but I am still concerned about the future of the college. Teaching here has been more than a job; it has been a vocation, a calling. My life and my identity have been tied to this institution." Job satisfaction and commitment to a college or university can and still do motivate many faculty. Not all faculty will find a home on a given campus, but for those that do there are at least four major elements that seem important in the overall morale on a campus: commitment to the mission of a school, involvement in decision making, a sense of community, supportive leadership, and an environment where work and creativity are rewarded. Dialogue requires a ground from which to speak, philosophically and in a concrete sense on a campus or in a department.

It is still possible to find people and places where loyalty to the tradition of the home campus or department guides the interaction. One report, *Community, Commitment and Congruence: A Different Kind of Excellence,* also revealed the importance of identification with one's place of employment. The findings described the following as frequent contributors to morale in academic settings: distinctive organizational cultures, participatory leadership, organizational momentum, and identification with the institution.

Identification with an institution reveals a feeling of home as an appropriate metaphor for some campuses.

> This inordinately strong identification with the institution begins with the way faculty are initially recruited and screened for appointment to the college. . . . Faculty are recruited not merely into an educational institution, but into a community with definitive values and goals. . . . Joseph Katz, the leader of that case study team (examining the University of Notre Dame), reports:
>
> Several faculty with whom we talked described their joining the college as faculty as "coming home." The team did not get the impression that so large a percentage of graduates among the faculty led to intellectual or social inbreeding. It seems instead to have infused fresh vitality into the spirit of community, and the graduates bring back to the college the fruits of their lives, work, and studies in other settings in other parts of the country.[29]

Two points from the above quotation deserve further attention: hiring graduates committed to a particular tradition can assist a home campus; and hiring others, although new to the ethos of a campus or department, can affirm the tradition while making a unique contribution. The notion of home implies that there are faculty and students with values consistent with the ongoing workings of the campus or department.

In general terms, for a faculty member dedicated to undergraduate instruction to feel at home and to experience good morale on a campus, the following seem to be important. First, teaching is a high priority, with scholarship translating into classroom enthusiasm and excellence. Second, there is a close match between the mission of an institution or department and an individual faculty member. Third, faculty need to be willing to be part of the community, participating in some campus activities beyond personal interest. Finally, there is a feeling of ownership and responsibility in the maintenance of the institution or department.[30]

If a faculty member joins an undergraduate campus only for employment with little regard for the tradition of the institution, problems may arise. On the other hand, if one is willing to genuinely encounter a tradition centered environment, an interesting set of learnings might happen.

A faculty member new to a tradition can judiciously critique and question from the eyes of an outside agent, even gaining stature on the campus. Practically, it is important to know when one has gone too far in questioning a tradition central to the heart of the campus. Any group will not respond well to a threat to its fundamental identity. Peter Berger, in *The Homeless Mind*, points to the importance of institutional affiliation. "Man's fundamental constitution is such that, just about inevitably, he will once more construct institutions to provide an ordered reality for himself. A return to institutions will ipso facto be a return to honor. It will then be possible again for individuals to identify themselves with the escutcheons of their institutional roles, experienced now not as self-estranging tyrannical roles, but as freely chosen vehicles . . ."[31] The key terms to a possible commitment to the tradition of a campus or department are "freely chosen." A student or faculty member needs to make a choice and follow through on actions of commitment that tie him or her to a tradition and offer a sense of uniqueness that might contribute further to the life of a campus or department.

Community

An educational home calls for commitment to a campus or departmental community,[32] acting out the Greek notion of *Koinonia*, where the common good is held at an even higher level than individual success. There is danger, however, that one might translate such an orientation into martyrdom for the community. Such a view is at odds with Aristotle's notion of the common good. The common good of *Koinonia* involves both the rights and hopes of the group *and* an individual's right to be heard and respected.

Taking the common good seriously in no way underplays the importance of individual excellence. The good action of one person reflects on an entire community. The notion of the common good calls us to recognize heroes, heroines, and talented persons. Their good work reflects on all of us, because the community has encouraged, shaped, and permitted such excellence to arise. For instance, at one campus a teacher was presented the national "Teacher of the Year" award. The acceptance speech reflected the best of the notion of the common good. "I accept this award on behalf of my students, family, and colleagues. They have provided the context and the encouragement for my continuing commitment to teaching." This national teaching honor reflected well on the faculty member, but also on the community—the context from which excellence had sprung.

As one places a high value on a common good or a *Koinonia* understanding of community, excellence is encouraged. Such a view of excellence has interesting implications for understanding the notion of arrogance. It is arrogant to believe that individual achievement emerges out of a vacuum. The community deserves respect and reward for its work in shaping an environment that permits the development of a successful person. In addition, it is arrogant for a community to fail to applaud those who go beyond the norm of performance. The success of one person enhances the opportunity for the success of others as a campus or department gains in stature. Creative individuals and competent communities provide a context for excellence when they work in mutual respect and support. In short, to view a place as an educational home is to take pride in its achievements and the quality work of individual members. This perception of home is significantly at odds with an individualistic way of comparing success. Let's examine a far too common response on college campuses.

One professor was invited to spend a year as a Fulbright professor. Yet not one person on the faculty offered congratulations or best wishes. Unfortunately, the other faculty were concerned that the success of one member of the department might reflect negatively on them. In reality, however, the Fulbright professor's success actually brought more attention to the department and aided the entire staff. When there is more commitment to image than one's "home base" of intellectual activity, competition for recognition guides the interaction. Concern for the common good is then exchanged for shortsighted attention for "my" career and "my" advancement, which can limit individual recognition as one attempts to minimize the importance of another's work.

Faculty who are part of an educational community need to encourage one another's achievement while working toward their own. All of us have met faculty who fail to offer such encouragement. In fact, it is possible to frame one's entire professional identity around the act of criticizing others. This action is like living with mirrors; one tries to keep the reflection, the focus of attention, on another's inadequacies in order to keep people from noticing one's own lack of achievement.

From a practical standpoint, a dialogic commitment requires us to rub shoulders frequently with one another. Therefore, we need to keep attention on what we *can do* and minimize attention focused on the limits of others. Communities and people improve by stretching one another into action and productivity rather than by detailing their shortcomings.

Early in my career, I heard one faculty member, who was a devoted Catholic, explain why he had returned to his alma mater. His comment reinforces the need to be part of a supportive community. He wanted to be part of a community that rallied around the successes, as well as the pains, of one another. The old adage "all for one and one for all" had special meaning to him as he returned home to a campus propelled by a tradition he affirmed.

Such an understanding of excellence conceptualizes one's own "good" as dependent on both one's own work and the success of others. Such a viewpoint results in a special understanding of what it means to be a colleague. The term *colleague* has an interesting beginning. "Middle French *collègue*, learned borrowing from Latin *collega* one chosen at the same time . . . *com*- together + *lēgāre* send or choose as deputy."[33]

Colleague is a combination of "one chosen at the same time" and "deputy." *Colleague* is a term suggesting co-concern or taking care of one another. Dietrich Bonhoeffer used the notion of "deputyship" to describe our responsibility to one another. A deputy is concerned about the good of another. Life is to be lived not just for oneself, but for mutual service.[34] Granted, such a view of a colleague may not be the norm. But to live life for the good of an academic home puts high priority on the value of giving to others. Recognition and appreciation of colleagues are important parts of giving.

We discover this form of communication in Aristotle's description of friendship. Friendship, according to Aristotle's definition of the "best" case, requires affirmation of another's values. Most of us would correlate friendship with liking and affect. We like a person because he or she suits us emotionally, or we are attracted to him or her. We usually affirm people because we like them. Aristotle suggested that a person's virtues are more important than likability.[35] For the faculty member at an educational home, this suggests that it is more important to appreciate another's contribution to the tradition of a college or department than it is to have affection for them. A community centered around tradition has a friendship base grounded more in common values than in affection.

At one college a business manager was asked why he did not give the library the amount of money they had been allocated. The response was: "The President can give the library funds, but I do not have to sign the requisition forms. I do not like the director of the library, so I am withholding funds from him." The business manager was guided more by feeling and affect, in this case a mean streak, than by a classical definition of friendship.

Genuine friendship revolves more around a common value system and a willingness to speak honestly in agreement or disagreement than fondness. Friendship requires a habit of hard work, assisting the conditions for another person, and affirming the importance of working for the common good.[36] Such a friendship centered on the common good does not come easily; it requires an active commitment. "For though the wish for friendship comes quickly, friendship does not."[37]

The value of a home work environment is that colleagues care enough for an institution or department to see that individuals who contribute are rewarded, even when not liked. The tie to a common home is more important than affect. As one colleague stated, "I do not like her, but she does great work for this school. I will do everything in my power to support her because of that fact." An educational home is not a place where all get along, but it is a place where commitment to an ongoing tradition is alive and well. It is a place where another's success is applauded out of support for the community, even when affection for the successful person is absent.

To discuss the notion of an educational home or tradition in a world geared to change, a fast pace, transience, and mobility, may seem anachronistic. But when one finds a place where faculty turnover is low and retirement ceremonies recognize the contributions of people with thirty or more years of service, then perhaps one has found a place to call home.

A final warning, however, is in order. As one pursues a commitment to home on a college or university campus or in a department, one must not look to have all emotional and psychological needs satisfied. Such a view of a home is contrary to the view of friendship outlined above and to Bonhoeffer's understanding of *Life Together*. Bonhoeffer stated such a dreamlike state is not a part of a constructive view of a home. When such a dream is destroyed, a cynical and desperate picture of the community and one another will emerge.[38]

A campus or department home is not ideal or perfect. It is not without need for change. But it is a place where the tradition is steady and where one can say, in spite of the flaws, "this place is a worthy place to invest a life."

The Significance for Dialogic Education

Great education can occur anywhere. But I am suggesting that having a sense of home on a campus or in a department offers a foundation for reaching out to others that can significantly enrich the dialogic educational experience. Abraham Maslow stated that the person most capable of giving of themselves comes from a supportive environment, a good home.[39] Perhaps some of our "best" teachers find themselves in a good university home— a place where they fit with the mission of the school.

The confidence and assurance of a home offer a foundation for faculty and students. In gestalt terms, having a good academic home is the background that permits focus on the foreground of new information and new ways of viewing events. Even for educators, having the security that one belongs is no matter to take for granted—ask any new instructor without tenure.

The connection between this sense of home and teaching can best be described with a reference to mental health. If one has the security of a home, then the risk of reaching out to others exploring new ideas is minimized and one's energy is less likely to be drained. A home functions as a psychological battery charger, giving one the energy to carry on the task.

Martin Buber discusses the fundamentals of dialogue as requiring, first and foremost, a place from which to stand and speak. Before one can listen and engage in dialogue with another one needs a place that undergirds us.[40] Buber reminds us that there is still importance in speaking from a place that can be counted upon as we explore new terrain and make contact with others. An educational home offers a philosophical support system for the practical task of being open to conversation about ideas and between persons.

An educational home offers a base for reaching out to students and faculty with new ideas. An educational home serves a paradoxical function: out of security can come the opportunity and resources for meeting the risk of change.

The first step for a campus or department interested in conversation about ideas and between persons is to invite an atmosphere that feels like home. Such a task is no small effort. But such a tall order seems worth the effort. If we take seriously the work of Robert Bellah in *Habits of the Heart*, and Christopher Lasch's discussion of "havens of trust,"[41] perhaps the task of inviting places called home on the campus is not just an old fashioned effort at sentimentality, but a way to encourage creativity, productivity, and a sense of meaning.

4

Teaching with a Vision

Testing a vision—

But how is one to realize this Truth. . . . By single-minded devotion. . . . however, of such devotion, what may appear as truth to one person will often appear as untruth to another person. . . . there is nothing wrong in everyone following Truth according to one's lights. Indeed it is one's duty to do so. Then if there is a mistake on the part of any one so following Truth, it will automatically be set right . . .

Mahatma Gandhi,
Selected Writings

Constructive criticism—

What we can say, even those of us who do not think that all meaningful life depends on what professional critics do, is this: Wherever understanding is maimed, our life is threatened; wherever it is achieved, our life is enhanced. The world of critical and artistic achievements lies before us in all its dappled grandeur.

Wayne Booth,
Critical Understanding

Teaching with a vision is part of an intellectual and philosophical base that reaches out to others. The base is flexible, but situated within four major guidelines: commitment to conversation about inquiry; a modeling of lifelong learning; a willingness to entertain constructive criticism that seeks to question, modify, and refute evidence; and a recognition that people, not just ideas, are involved in disputes. Teaching with a vision ties the educa-

tional journey more closely to inquiry and continual learning than
to fixed answers.

Three basic questions guide this discussion of what I describe
as teaching with a vision. First, how does the notion of vision
relate to a department or a campus? Second, what kind of vision
might a dialogic teacher require? And finally, what is the connection between dialogic education, breadth of education, and understanding of the "good life?"

Institutional Vision and Debate

The word *vision* often suggests a mystic attempt to foretell
the future; such an effort goes well beyond the scope of dialogic
education. However, I do use the word *vision* as "something sup-
posed to be seen otherwise than . . . the ordinary . . ."[1] The notion
of vision calls attention to what might go unnoticed in everyday
looking. For example, a teacher may envision a potential for excellence in a mediocre performing student. A coach may be able to call
out greatness in her players, who otherwise would only function at
an average level of achievement.

The test of a vision is in performance, the carrying out or
execution of an idea or task. In essence, I use the term *vision* not
as a dream or a glimpse of a definite future, but as a picture of what
might be; a future powerful and significant enough to capture the
imagination and commitment. A vision is a picture of possibilities
that shape and guide collective action, played out in the praxis of
everyday living.

A vision for a campus or department is the result of an
interplay among the historical mission of an institution, the future
direction, and the debate about history and future direction. A
vision unites a group of people and motivates them to practical
action. A good story in an organization tells its history, value
system, purpose, and future direction. An educational vision is
the end result of knowing our roots and rejecting inflexible answers, while being guided by a framework or mission statement
that is more than a statement in a college catalogue. In classical
terms, the notion of vision is tied to a teleology and a knowledge
of where one is going. Such a direction or vision emerges out of a
story that outlines a history capable of capturing our imagination
today.

A vision captivates us not just because of the information
provided, but out of the moral power it stirs in its listeners. The
words of John F. Kennedy in the early 1960s caught our moral

imagination, as did those of Franklin D. Roosevelt, Winston Churchill, and contemporary speakers such as Ronald Reagan and Jesse Jackson. They moved us with their ability to speak for many. Successful leaders articulate a moral vision that some choose as worthy of their participation. Such leaders tell stories of which we want to be a part and to which we want to contribute.

> The story provides good reason to accept . . . truth . . . . Life is fullest when one loves and is loved; and maturity is achieved by accepting the reality of death. We learn these truths by dwelling in the characters in the story, by observing the outcomes of the several conflicts that arise throughout it, by seeing the unity of characters and their actions, and by comparing the truths to the truths we know to be true from our own lives.[2]

Stanley Hauerwas illustrates the notion of vision in his examination of Richard Adams' novel, *Watership Down*. Though the book portrays animal characterization, its message is fully intended to address the human condition and our need for stories. Life is best lived when there is a vision that includes tradition, goals for the future, and courage to listen to challenges of taken-for-granted assumptions. Hauerwas states the following about Adams' novel, *Watership Down*.

> Adams suggests that society can best be understood as an extended argument, since living traditions pre-suppose rival interpretations. Good societies enable the argument to continue so that the possibilities and limits of the tradition can be exposed. The great danger, however, is that the success of a tradition will stop its growth and in reaction some may deny the necessity of tradition for their lives. The truthfulness of a tradition is tested in its ability to form people who are ready to put the tradition into question, or at least to recognize when it is being put into question by a rival tradition.[3]

For Hauerwas, the notion of vision underscores the importance of a trinity of elements needed for a healthy story: tradition, future aspirations, and debate. A healthy vision is one that propels people, and is public and tested, not blindly protected. Hauerwas suggests that a quality vision is forged when a story connects people's past and future needs, while being open to constructive criticism. Such an understanding of vision recognizes "truth" as constituted with a small "t," based on the willingness of people to enter into conversation with one another and to look for the best options available at a particular juncture in the life of a community.

The importance of a vision for a group of people is prevalent even in common circumstances. I was once asked to comment on a feud between two groups in a small town. One group wanted to start a new chamber of commerce. The current chamber was asking how it could keep another chamber from being formed. My answer was that one seldom invites long-term goodwill by forcing a group into submission. The old chamber would be better off offering a vision that others could accept, rather than trying to stop a grassroots movement that did not fear them.

Without a living, healthy vision, it is unlikely that extra effort will be given to an organization without additional compensation for one's time and effort. A vision calls for some sacrifice for the collective good, as we also benefit ourselves. The infamous words of John F. Kennedy suggested that we ". . . ask not what your country can do for you—what you can do for your country."[4] These words reminded a people of the importance of others and of service to the world, which the Peace Corps represents in a practical fashion.

A collective vision that binds people together can move an average sports team to above average performance. It can make a good college into a great one. In psychological terms, a vision is the gestalt, larger than the sum of the parts. A vision is the web that pulls people together, generating a sense of organizational uniqueness. But even as we recognize the value of a collective vision, we are reminded of the importance of questioning and testing. Such challenges are necessary to protect us from the dangers of a Third Reich, a Jim Jones in Guyana, and on the campus, threats to academic freedom posed by "McCarthyism" from the right or the left.

The testing of a vision, as suggested by Gandhi's quotation in the chapter opening, is only possible as we risk living a vision that may or may not be "truthful." In the case of Woodrow Wilson and the League of Nations, one must ask if the historical time was appropriate for the forging of such a vision, or if Wilson's failed effort was necessary to pave the way for the United Nations? As we commit to a vision for future action, there needs to be a willingness to test and challenge not only other visions, but our own as well. The test of a leader's or group's vision is whether or not people begin to assist in the project. A tested vision moves the action to the collective arena.

Dialogic education encourages acceptance of a vision after

doing the following: knowing the tradition or literature so well that one understands the issues, and understanding the main points of positions contrary to one's own position. Testing one's own vision, particularly in the presence of others, requires some courage. Courage is central to any honest testing and fundamental to the process of charting and recharting a new direction.[5]

I suggested in chapter 3 that we might benefit from being part of an academic home. I offer this chapter as a counterbalance asking, "Does the college, university, or department do what it says it will do according to its articulated mission or vision?" Blind loyalty cannot be the foundation for any educational vision hoping to pursue ideas and truth. Loyalty to any institution without criticism is a form of servitude, not a home of dialogic education. Catherine B. Burroughs speaks to this issue, as she defines "the new professionalism" on the campus.

> Most of us have known someone from the 1930's who "sold his (or her) soul to the company store;" and either grew older resenting the servitude or, when fired, discovered he or she lacked the skills to find another job. This way my grandfather, and his lessons of loyalty instruct one to guard against obsolescence by becoming both an expert and a neophyte [constant learner]. It seems to me that combining teaching with research provides the greatest defense against such a scenario.[6]

I acknowledge the danger in blind attachment to an academic home. There is a significant difference between loyalty to a campus and loyalty to the vision and mission of the school or department. This differentiation can, however, be viewed as disloyalty by some. For instance, on one campus a distinguished scholar worked very hard as a faculty advisor assisting a doctoral program at the institution; she then wrote a critique of small doctoral programs like the one at her institution. She was unmercifully chided by the administration and colleagues.

This faculty member's defense of her article is at the heart of my concern—loyalty needs to be given to a vision of an institution, not survival at any cost. The faculty member believed that students need to know the limitations of an academic program. The educational task is the pursuit of truth, not institutional survival. This faculty member contended that success cannot be found through any shortcuts; students and the program are more likely to grow in an atmosphere where quality improvement is more important than hiding flaws out of blind loyalty.

Perhaps the faculty member described above would be in good stead with Warren Bryan Martin, author of *The College of Character*. Martin states that a good college or university must have a vision that transcends mere survival. He contends, as I do, that a clear vision will not only give direction and integrity, but is central to marketing an educational institution. One needs to be wary of an administrator that purports the following.

> The Board of Trustees hired me to keep this ship afloat. I accepted their challenge. Survival is the goal and good management is the means to that end. I will, therefore, introduce programs that pay and cut out those that don't. Good intentions will no longer in themselves be good enough. Sentimentality pays no bills. We will produce in response to market demand. From now on, "He who pays the piper calls the tune." We will not only survive, we'll prosper.[7]

Constructive criticism of the campus or department vision may be the only practical way to ensure the absence of administrative "survival" speeches offered as substitutes for a unique vision of an institution. Faculty have the right to criticize an institution when the publicly stated vision has been violated. Institutional idolatry cannot claim one's actions; loyalty needs to be motivated more by agreement with the vision of a campus or department.

If the vision of a campus is to pursue truth, one may have to risk calling a campus or department to accountability. For instance, one should not have to assume a political position in one's scholarship or teaching just to remain in agreement with those in power at an institution. The following excerpt reveals the chilling effect of scholarly orthodoxy.

> A young medical researcher in the last year of his probationary period, who had discovered toxic qualities of a drug distributed by a company which was supporting his university with generous research grants [had to ask the following]. Should he publish the report on his findings? Would he risk non-renewals of his appointment if his publication angered the donor and the chairman of his department? As it was . . . the young man decided to publish and he lost his post. . . . To get such candid discussion by all who can contribute . . . it is necessary that the unpopular, allegedly unpatriotic "rabble-rousers" be protected. . . .[8]

A college or university gathers its uniqueness from its agreed upon mission statement. But the mission of an institution is only half of the vision that propels a campus. The vision includes the mission statement of the institution as well as the operational, everyday fashion in which that mission is enacted. To test a vision of a campus necessitates examining its stated mission with practical implementation of that organizational philosophy.

It is difficult to challenge a mission statement of a college or university without a major revolution regarding what a campus or department is and does. It is more feasible to challenge the practical or everyday manner in which a mission is followed or ignored. For any campus, the vision of an institution is operationally played out by the way in which the administration and faculty work with one another and the students, as they address issues of relevance to education and the culture.

Philosophically, the mission statement of an institution provides a vision of education accepted by that particular university or college. If one can not accept the mission statement of a campus, it is better to go elsewhere. It is possible, though perhaps not easy, to hold a campus accountable when its everyday operational way of dealing with people and issues is at odds with the mission statement. But it is virtually impossible to alter a mission statement when the everyday actions of the campus support such a view of the world.

One institution had in its mission statement the importance of the student feeling like a global citizen. A faculty member worked hard to remove the section in the general education list related to a required course in "non-western civilization," but lost the battle and some credibility. The assault on the non-west courses was a direct hit on the mission of the institution. If the faculty member had been successful, a gulf between the mission and the operational practice of how that mission is to operationally influence the institution would have been opened.

The congruence between the mission statement and the everyday operation of the institution permits the vision of a campus to be strong and clear. It becomes the backbone of an understandable image of an institution. The mission of an institution is where a campus or department gains its identity. It takes consistent commitment to keep a mission statement contemporary, relevant, and connected to the everyday life of the institution. Individuals on campus need to live out the advertised mission statement in a congruent fashion through everyday operations of the campus. Otherwise, the mission statement becomes a public relations document for external marketing purposes only.

It could be said that the civil rights movement of the 1960s was a debate about a vision of America in which the mission statements of the Constitution and the Bill of Rights for all citizens were at odds with operational practice. The changes that emerged from that era attempted to lessen the disparity between the power of America for "all people" and daily living. It would have been more difficult to alter the mission statements of the country. In short, if change is to take place it is more likely to succeed when operations are upgraded to fit the mission than when the mission of the institution is altered through a revolution. A mission can be altered, but the price paid by those wanting such a change will be significant.

A vision for a campus or a department is the result of the congruent interplay of a mission statement and everyday operations, laying the groundwork for dialogic education. For a dialogue to be invited, one needs to lead out of a position open to conversation, but nonetheless from a stance. Recent communicative displays in some leadership circles represent what a friend has called "positionless leadership." The appearance of openness should not be confused with an act of dialogue. Positionless leadership is an effort to find someone else to take the heat for an idea or direction pursued, or, worse, it is the result of having no idea or position worth trying to save or implement.[9] Dialogue requires us to know our own position as we enter conversation with another. Educators interested in dialogic education need to keep the vision and mission clear, if for no other reason than to remind a campus or department of what has been promised to students.

Clearly, a book on dialogic education cannot address all the particular visions represented on different campuses and reflected by the merger of mission statements and everyday actions. But it is possible to articulate one general vision to guide dialogic education: a commitment to lifelong learning. This vision encourages an ongoing conversation about substantive issues long after graduation. The teacher interested in dialogic education needs to offer a vision of *why* a commitment to lifelong learning is a key to a productive and quality life of thinking, questioning, and action. Students continue conversation about ideas, values, and relationships throughout life. A dialogic educator needs to model, while inviting students to catch the "bug" of lifelong learning, a willingness to continue conversation about ideas long after graduation.

A Vision of Lifelong Learning

Lifelong Learning/Tentative Commitment

Lifelong learning is essential if we believe that "new" information, insight, and interpretations will make some basic information, now considered contemporary, obsolete and limited. Dialogic teaching is an act of conversation about content and between the extremes of absolute certainty and subjective imposition of one's own will on the information being studied. The goal is to bring to the text or content questions from the learner without ignoring the importance of the text.

Teaching without blinding a student requires us to be committed to education, see multiple sides of issues, and avoid propaganda, by not limiting teaching to one perspective alone. A colleague has suggested that the time honored effort of offering a two-sided message, one that at least acknowledges an opposing position, keeps an audience alert to our perspective and to the fact that other views are available.[10] The vision of such a commitment to education is that inquiry and continuing conversation are more important to a teacher than a student adopting a perspective isomorphic to that of the instructor.

Opening eyes of students to the importance of lifelong learning requires a teacher to offer an alternative to the extremes of an objective, value-free discussion, and a subjective, propagandistic portrayal of material.[11] Dialogic education invites participants to take informed positions on the subject matter under discussion, permitting those of contrary perspective to outline positions or cases for hearing. A professor can ask a student to remember his or her viewpoint, but must caution against the claim that the information learned is the only perspective available, now or in the future.

For example, one professor arranged to sell tickets in class for a peace rally concert in opposition to a particular federal government action. When a group of faculty, who were also going to the concert, were informed of this decision, they encouraged the faculty member to let students know about the concert, but to sell the tickets outside of class. The line between letting one's perspective be known and propaganda is a thin one at times, requiring us to find symbolic ways to reveal the difference.

Teaching with vision requires taking a stand, while simultaneously being open to counterperspectives. Such a view of education involves what Martin Buber calls walking the "narrow ridge" between the extremes of relativism and an authoritarian contention that only one perspective is worthy of consideration. Teachers can openly guide as they describe not only their own perspectives, but other views, permitting the student to be a choice maker, not a recipient of propaganda.

Through the Eyes of a Stranger

The theme of the book *Teacher as Stranger* is relevant to this chapter on teaching with vision. The book posits the teacher as a stranger in a strange world—questioning, learning, and observing what generally is taken for granted in the world around us. The teacher as stranger probes ideas with the insight and vision of a thoughtful and inquiring new person in a community. Such a teacher walks with open eyes, helping students see and discover what may be missed in casual everyday looking.[12]

The vision of teacher as stranger recognizes the unseen significance of everyday actions. A stranger makes us aware of our eagerness to accept such phrases as "We have always done it this way."[13] Such a teacher offers tools for seeing the world in new ways, appreciating and apprehending the wonder and mystery of all that we encounter and attempt to accomplish.

This emphasis on the stranger "seeing" differently and recognizing what is missed by causal observation, is at the heart of anthropological investigation. However, a word of warning is appropriate at this juncture; the stranger must not only share information that his or her new eyes can discern, but must also manifest a willingness to understand the common perceptions of people living in the environment. Clifford Geertz points to this dual function of giving novel insight from new eyes in the community and receiving from veterans of a given group. Geertz suggests that "experience-near" is the common compilation of everyday information shared by the cultural participants, and "experience-distant" is a result of insights brought by the person "new" to the community trained to see the symbolic implications of actions.[14] In short, the vision of a teacher can not be arrogant; such a teacher not only helps students to see (experience-distant), but is willing to have his or her own vision broadened by the students (experience-near) through their common perceptions. Dialogue between the parties signals a commitment to mutual learning and growth.

Teaching that embraces the value of both "giving" and "getting" is a pragmatic effort to model a vision central to lifelong learning. Take, for example, the vision offered by a superb teacher we will call Paul. Paul was known for his extraordinary teaching style and depth of knowledge as a scholar. In fact, his career was a reminder to others about the real life possibilities and excitement that emerged from the integration of conversation about ideas and a valuing of the student in the classroom.

Paul consistently opened the eyes of students to topics they had not previously considered important. He was successful because he functioned as a stranger, not only in exploring theory, but in listening to the ongoing lives of his students. He modeled a commitment to lifelong learning and the students responded by encountering material that they would not have attempted to understand if anyone else had made the request. Paul was able to inspire students to learn as he learned from them. Opening the eyes of others, while allowing one's own eyes to be opened, is central to teaching with a vision committed to lifelong learning.

The significance of Paul's teaching style and the implications of a teacher as a stranger emphasize that interaction between faculty and student is a major cornerstone of a dialogic education. Paul was willing to learn from students as well as offer a model of lifelong learning, both within his discipline and beyond his subject matter expertise.

Breadth of Vision—Specialist/Generalist

A vision of lifelong learning embodies another educational assumption fundamental to dialogic education: "What is the breadth of one's knowledge and continuing commitment to learning?" To be in dialogue with another requires us to know more than our field of specialization; good conversation is dependent on our ability to ask questions relevant to a given topic and to know some information that fuels examples of our main conceptual points from a world closer to the student's immediate life.

The sixties and the seventies moved us into interdisciplinary study; today such study is less popular. From a dialogic perspective, a highly specialized education is not as helpful to the goal of carrying on conversation beyond one's area of study. This book contends that only when the faculty and graduates embrace a vision of education beyond their respective areas of specialization is dialogic education invited and nourished.[15]

Before one misunderstands this emphasis on learning beyond one's major, it is important to acknowledge that excesses occur in both disciplinary and interdisciplinary study. Neither the extreme of interdisciplinary study nor the opposing extreme of rigid adherence to an academic discipline are productive dialogic models. During the 1960s and 1970s, the interdisciplinary degree was used in an academically appropriate fashion by some professors and students, but in some cases it was a catchall for students unable to commit themselves to in-depth inquiry. On the other hand, narrow professional training on a university campus at the undergraduate level is questionable from the perspective of dialogic education.

A dialogic alternative to overemphasis on interdisciplinary study or the other extreme of a credit heavy disciplinary major with a professional emphasis, is a vision of the *specialist/generalist*. In a time when majors have become increasingly more specialized,[16] the student and the faculty member need to model a vision of lifelong learning both in their disciplinary domain as a specialist and outside their chosen area of study as a generalist.

On any campus one will discover specialists but few of them are without other interests. We need to encourage and support the generalist component of learning for faculty and students. For example, on one campus, a chemistry professor known for his fine teaching was also rewarded for his study of Spanish. This professor is well traveled and conversant on numerous subjects beyond chemistry. Another example is a college librarian who has also pursued his interest as a classical pianist. Such diversity of activity needs to be openly applauded and rewarded if dialogue is to be invited beyond one's narrowly focused specialization. A vision of lifelong learning based upon a specialist/generalist model recognizes that decision making in a complex society cuts across disciplinary lines regularly. "The capacity to judge rightly in a choice of both means and ends cuts across the specialties and the technologies, and it is, I dare say, the hallmark of a liberal, as distinguished from a utilitarian or vocational education."[17]

Basic educational skills of critical thinking, reading, writing, speaking, and listening are required in our complex personal and professional culture. Such knowledge comes not from one course, but largely from an education of breadth that embraces basic information acquisition and creative application. It is this commitment to both specialization and breadth that propels dialogic education. As Ernest Boyer suggests, it is breadth after specialization that makes for a quality education.[18]

Although a number of factors contribute positively to dialogic education, I contend that the breadth of an instructor's knowledge and his or her interest in the student are important elements in keeping the vision of lifelong learning of the specialist/generalist vibrant. It is my subjective hunch that the breadth of the faculty and their varied interests often lead to success in teaching undergraduates. Perhaps such breadth partially accounts for the following statistics about teachers on campuses that have stated their first and principal mission as teaching: 73

percent of students interviewed felt their teachers cared about the learning progress, 81 percent of the students felt encouraged to discuss the material and their reactions. It seems that students are more satisfied with the teaching on such campuses, than in other settings.[19]

The specialist/generalist educator might have a greater chance to facilitate conversation about subject matter with an undergraduate student if she or he can relate the material to multiple areas outside the formal classroom. Breadth makes for better conversational partners who are able to engage students with examples from multiple realms of life.

Placing value on the breadth of knowledge assumes that concentration on one topic without the diversion of other interests narrows one's vision and ability to do creative thinking and decision making. Victor Frankl uses the term *hyper-reflection* to define what happens when one becomes too focused on the task at hand.[20] In a well-known popular culture book of the 1970s, *Zen and the Art of Motorcycle Maintenance*, Robert M. Pirsig discusses the ability to discover insights into problems and issues as we engage in other activities as well.[21] Dialogic education works under a premise that a singly focused life may not always contribute to health and quality decision making. Breadth of knowledge lays a foundation for creativity and a basis for examining issues from different orientations.

A colleague of mine expressed the need for breadth in this cautionary paraphrased statement. Beware of zealots of any kind. Breadth insures, as best we can, that the decision maker recognizes that most good ideas are partial and require a counter from another perspective, in order to not be misled into simple black and white thinking. My colleague's warning is consistent with Hoffer's *True Believer*. We need competing loyalties to keep us from acting foolishly and with unnecessarily excessive passion, or with the blindness of a "true believer."

Herman Hesse, in *The Glass Bead Game*, offers a warning that any academic might want to consider. The learner in this novel gave himself totally to the acquisition of knowledge. His time was spent doing one thing: learning more and more from books. All that learning came to a quick end, however, when he fell into a pond and being unable to swim, drowned.[22] It is possible to become so focused on a single topic that we can drown. We need specialists, but dialogic education envisions that general knowledge will add to the quality and productivity of our work and our lives as well.

The Practical Benefits of Breadth

The vision and mission of dialogic education includes more than a romantic love of books motivating a commitment to lifelong learning. Two major practical benefits of such a vision are the effects on democratic participants, and implications for a classical understanding of the good life.

A foundation for democracy. Educational breadth is vital to the health and longevity of a democracy. Alexis de Tocqueville, in his study of American life, made it clear that the knowledge of the nonexpert will contribute to the quality of life in a democracy. "It depends upon themselves whether the principle of equality is to lead them to servitude or freedom, to knowledge or barbarism, to prosperity or wretchedness."[23] De Tocqueville, who had some questions about the wisdom of democracy, recognized the need for broad-based knowledge in order for such a system to work well.

It is the capacity for breadth that makes possible the strength of a democracy in everyday living. Karl Wallace, well known for his work in communication and free speech, provided a summary of what must be protected for a democratic culture to continue to prosper and survive. The following paraphrase of Wallace's work offers a minimal agenda of what a broad-based dialogic education might offer in a democratic culture:

1. affirmation of the worth and value of the individual person,
2. equality of opportunity for both success and failure, and fairness in evaluation,
3. freedom *limited* by sensitivity to the freedom of others, and
4. recognition of the importance of making controversial and new ideas public.[24]

Breadth of knowledge and a model of lifelong learning cannot ensure the continuation of a democracy, but such attitudes can support actions necessary to keep a democracy strong. The willingness to search for information, to permit others to do the same, and to learn from one another is a key to quality decision making. Democracy has been called a procedural ethic in need of conversation in order to function.[25] Learning that frames a dialogic vision of lifelong learning, affirming people and ideas contrary to our own, and encouraging civil conversation and debate is necessary for a democracy and on college campuses.

One of the pioneers of educational breadth for a democratic culture was John Dewey. Dewey believed that involvement in the social process of a democratic culture required an ability to move through various disciplines with at least a minimal level of understanding. "Democratic society is peculiarly dependent for its maintenance upon the user in forming a course of study of criteria which are broadly human. Democracy cannot flourish where the chief influences in selecting subject matter or instruction are utilitarian ends narrowly conceived. . . ."[26]

The work of Dewey is still relevant if we believe in the importance of faculty and students participating in public policy debates. More recently Ernest Boyer has made a similar case. "For those who care about government 'by the people,' the decline in public understanding cannot go unchallenged. In a world where human survival is at stake, ignorance is not an acceptable alternative. The full control of policy by specialists with limited perspective is not tolerable."[27] Sidney Hook, well known for his work on the democratic tradition, suggests that we correlate the health of a democracy with the breadth of information available to a people and their desire to encounter that information. Hook speaks of Dewey's commitment to giving voice to the nonexpert or the non-technocrat as a fundamental element of a democracy.[28]

Hook, like Dewey and Boyer, recognizes the importance of general information and a willingness to participate in decision making and questioning in a democratic society. For a democracy to work, one must know enough to ask important questions, which requires general knowledge outside one's area of specialization.

To leave discussion and debate about major issues to those with technical expertise alone is to stop conversation. If one were to find an objection to *Walden Two*, the utopian society described by B. F. Skinner, it may be reliance on experts for decision making and governance.[29] A democracy, on the other hand, requires those with technical and general insight to join in decision making. Walter Fisher reminds us to be wary of the expert unwilling to put his ideas out for questioning by those with less knowledge and expertise.

> The problem posed by the presence of experts in public moral argument [is that] . . . One [the average person] is not a judge but a spectator who must choose between actors [technical experts]. . . . [It would be better to consider] the proper role of the expert in public moral argument . . . [as] that of a counselor . . . [or] . . . storyteller. His or her contribution to public dialogue is to impart knowledge, like a teacher, or wisdom like a sage. It is not to pronounce a story that ends all storytelling. The expert assumes the role of public

counselor whenever she or he crosses the boundary of technical knowledge into the territory of life as it ought to be lived. Once this invasion is made, the public, which then includes the expert, has its own criteria for determining whose story is most coherent and reliable as a guide to belief and action.[30]

It is necessary for a democratic culture to encourage conversation among those with breadth of knowledge, as well as those with specialized information on a particular topic, facilitating input from a variety of perspectives.

A vision of the good life. A second practical benefit of a vision of broad-based, lifelong learning is tied to the quality of life one lives after graduation. Subjects such as foreign language are valuable for travel and understanding of other cultures. Love of literature and the arts offers aesthetic enjoyment and knowledge of the world beyond provincial boundaries. Knowledge of the sciences permits one to understand current issues, from questions about environmental use to the manipulation of human genes. The quality of life in a civilized culture is based on the assumption that breadth of knowledge is necessary to understand oneself and others in the global community.

Dialogic education encourages an understanding of the good life, as a value laden notion calling for contribution to the human community. The good life, resulting in "happiness" for Aristotle, involves the following: a life of virtue, paraphrased as honor, justice, and bravery; education that encourages virtue through knowledge of one's culture and its modification through participation; and the ability to put that virtue into action for the "common good,"[31] defined as concern for oneself *and* others in the community. As Paul Weiss indicates, the good life involves a concern for the common good of self, others, the society, and larger world. "The best of men is a public being who lives a private life alongside others. Near the center of a civilized world, he is also somehow at its periphery, directly or indirectly involved in the making and use of means. His work makes leisure possible, and his leisure makes his work worthwhile. A wise man, his knowledge sustains and is sustained by practice."[32] Such a vision of concern can be viewed as the bedrock of dialogic education, preparing students for leadership in a world in need of broad-based perspectives.[33]

The good life calls us to action and to service to others, not just because it is a good thing to do, but out of a conviction that life is better lived when concern for self and others propels our actions. The book *Habits of the Heart* is a summary of interviews with diverse people across America. Many are dissatisfied with life centered around individual concerns. They desire a sense of community where others are also important.[34] Such a life comes from participation in the activities of an ongoing community and a willingness to be of service to others and the larger group.

As Paul Weiss stated, the good life involves not only others and oneself, but how leisure time is used. A broad general knowledge base permits us to make spare time into leisure time, with creative, active, and freely chosen recreation.[35] The vision of lifelong learning and breadth of knowledge encourages leisure time open to a wide range of learning from physical activity to the arts.

Can overspecialization in any career add stress and strain to a life and limit its quality? Dialogic education works on the assumption that life needs breadth to complement our specific competencies. After-work activity that is centered on other projects assists the general quality of life, while at times, offering insight into one's area of specialization at unexpected times. Perhaps one of the ways to understand another human being is to observe how his or her leisure time is used.

Dialogic education accepts a vision of breadth and lifelong learning as our best defense against inflexible and narrow ideology. As educated people, we need to keep the conversation going about significant issues. The answers come from interaction of knowledge of the past and the needs of the present, requiring us to remain alert to the changing needs of society. Like the poet Homer, we need to continue to grow through conversation and change, not just with others, but with ourselves. Continued learning permits a richer sense of self-talk; dialogue with oneself is only possible when knowledge of multiple perspectives exists.

> Homer is a creator, a man who could actually see new figures so as to see what a son was after the time of the *Iliad* and to see what a son had come to be under changed conditions . . . he had to have a very fundamental understanding of the matter. And that means he conducted conversation with himself. That dialogue of the soul, the conversation of Homer with himself, would be a formidable book.[36]

One need not love Homer to appreciate dialogic education. But one does need to understand the link between the general quality of one's life and the commitment to lifelong learning. As one of my teachers used to suggest, "Life is great, yea!" It is great as we meet new challenges and take in more of the wonder that surrounds us. For the dialogic educator, the love of life is tied to a lifelong commitment to learning, by both the student and the teacher.

Vision—What Could Be

The vision of lifelong learning, so central to my understanding of dialogic education, can be supported by motives as diverse as desire for professional success, family values, love of learning for its own sake, a large array of unspoken and at times unknown hopes and aspirations, and even by a desire to give something back to the world, a hope to be of service, a commitment to the common good.

In a time of cynicism, me-ism, careerism, individualism, and other self-centered "isms," dialogic education accepts the premise that others are important to the quality of one's own life and that of a community. While one's own success is important, the hope is that one's efforts might make a difference, not only for oneself, but for others as well.

Jacques Ellul theorizes that in the latter part of the twentieth century there has been an eclipse of the person. The power of the individual, or at least the perceived power of the individual has dissipated.[37] But dialogic education offers a perception that people can potentially make a difference. The possibility of making a constructive difference is important to a dialogic educator.

In my experience, I have met many faculty who believe in such a philosophy. One faculty member takes students to do service work in Appalachia during college breaks; another faculty member takes January term off to donate work to a project in a poor economic region of the world; and still another donates one evening a week to be of service to a local hospital. When asked why they do such work, their collective response seemed to echo, "If we have a vision that others are essential in the human dialogue, it is important to model and expose students to such values." In the midst of contemporary careerism, these people reach out to make a difference.

An environment in which the individual can and will make a contribution to the human community offers a vision of hope, less cynicism, and a picture of possibilities for the future. In a time in which many feel without power, the lifelong learner continues to move ahead with confidence that "we" can make a difference. In short, if asked "Why teach dialogically?," perhaps the answer may relate to the belief that people *can* make a difference in the world, not only with their specialized knowledge, but with their breadth of information and concern for others.

PART 3

The Ingredients for Dialogic Teaching

5

Conversation About Ideas

Personal merit through conversation about ideas—

Our traditional social goals were unforgettably renewed for us by Martin Luther King, Jr., in his 'I Have a Dream' speech. King envisioned a country where the children of former slaves sit down at the table of equality with the children of former slave owners, where men and women deal with each other as equals and judge each other on their characters and achievements rather than their origins. Like Thomas Jefferson, he had a dream of society founded not on race or class but on personal merit.

E.D. Hirsch,
Cultural Literacy:
What Every American Needs to Know

On the importance of telling the story—

When the great Rabbi Baal Shen Tov saw misfortune threatening the Jews, it was his custom to go into a certain part of the forest to meditate. There he would light a fire, say a special prayer, and the miracle would be accomplished and the misfortune averted.

The story tells us that, with each successive generation, the rabbis forgot how to light the fire, then how to say the prayer, and finally they no longer knew how to find the place in the forest.

Then it fell to Rabbi Israel of Rizhyn to overcome misfortune. Sitting in his armchair, his head in his hand, he spoke to God: "I am unable to light the fire and I do not know the prayer; I cannot even find the place in the forest. All I can do is tell the story, and this must be sufficient." And it was sufficient.

Peninnah Schram,
Jewish Stories One Generation
Tells Another

E. D. Hirsch has earned a reputation as a critic of contemporary education's disregard for the cultural literacy of its students. The rationale for the inclusion of a quotation by Hirsch is that dialogic education requires a commitment to scholarship tied to learning and knowledge through personal merit, not aristocratic expectations of entitlement. Dialogic education encourages students and faculty to link expertise to the merit of the scholar's work, not race, birthright, or political position. Conversation about ideas rooted in personal merit requires faculty and students to continue to acquire expertise as a specialist and a generalist.

I assume that success based on information, not just being connected to the right people, requires us to be concerned about the knowledge base of our students and ourselves. A lead article in the *Chronicle of Higher Education* suggested that there is ill health in the liberal arts education of American students today due to fragmentation and lack of sufficient breadth and depth knowledge in subject matter.[1] Again, dialogic education is based on a commitment to others and the conversation about and beyond one's own academic discipline. Depth and breadth of scholarship are needed to enhance the possibility of conversation with those outside one's specialized area of interest.

Perhaps the following story can illustrate the point that dialogue begins with knowledge of one's own home and then reaches out to others. I listened to a lecture suggesting the importance of tearing down all walls that separate people. The lecture, not surprisingly, came on the heels of the reunification of Germany. The speaker suggested that separation is not healthy for the human community.

In this instance I agreed with the speaker, but I also wonder what would happen if we had *no* walls that separated us? Walls do not have to suggest total separation, but can also be signs of difference and uniqueness. Are there some walls we might decide to keep, but install *doors* within them, in order to reach out to others? Some walls should be torn down—the walls of racism, sexism, and religious bigotry. Other walls help us to know and understand who we are. Walls with doors can be viewed as a way of reaching out to others while maintaining a sense of uniqueness.

Dialogue requires us to bring our own perspective to a conversation, not as the *only* perspective, but with the knowledge that new insight comes when both parties bring their uniqueness to the conversation. Dialogic education is based on knowledge; it is content centered. Faculty interested in dialogic education need to commit themselves to scholarship both inside and outside their academic disciplines—not necessarily for publication, but for the fuel or background knowledge that can propel conversation with students.

I contend that a commitment to dialogic education does not begin in analysis of the curriculum or the student body, even though the quality of courses and students is very significant. The starting point for dialogic education is the scholarly commitment of the faculty, both in breadth and depth of knowledge.

The American Association of University Professors has stated that the first commitment of a professor must be to uphold the advancement of knowledge and scholarship, detailed in the "1966 Statement on Professional Ethics."

> Professors, guided by a deep conviction of the worth and dignity of the advancement of knowledge, recognize the special responsibilities placed upon them. Their primary responsibility to their subject is to seek and to state the truth as they see it. To this end professors devote their energies to developing and improving their scholarly competence. They accept the obligation to exercise critical self-discipline and judgment in using, extending, and transmitting knowledge. They practice intellectual honesty. Although professors may follow subsidiary interests, these interests must never seriously hamper or compromise their freedom of inquiry.[2]

The AAUP's emphasis on information renewal and update as the primary task of a college professor is consistent with the theme of conversation about ideas. Such an overt uplifting of the importance of scholarship may not totally coincide with the conventional image of a teacher committed to interaction with students both inside and outside the classroom. However, if one is aware of the specialist/generalist orientation of the lifelong learner outlined in chapter 4, an understanding of scholarship consistent with the dialogic theme of this work is present.

Chapters 2, 3, and 4 of this book describe the importance of having a foundation, an academic home, and a philosophical vision from which the educational dialogue can be invited. This chapter assumes that faculty members not only have a foundation from which to begin the conversation, but bring a high degree of expertise and substance to the exchange. Dialogic education encourages and assumes the competence of faculty in their respective disciplines and in the liberal arts.

An understanding of institutional mission dependent on faculty excellence in scholarship can prevent a church affiliated college from becoming what I have called "a church where you can get a college degree." I support both private and public education, but a private school with a value mission has an equally important task of pursuing the best information one can discover, research, and present as a faculty member. The emphasis on breadth in scholarship is necessary as a counter to overly narrow research agendas that will limit dialogue to a few interested colleagues. Maurice Friedman critiques such a group as a "community of affinity" unable to make contact with the "otherness" of people with different ideas and perspectives.[3]

We all bring a particular value perspective to the subject matter, but knowledge of basic information is imperative, both currently and historically. Dialogic education is based on the assumption that it is possible to do both—have a value mission of commitment to others and simultaneously support a vigorous intellectual climate where people pursue truth in scholarship and teaching.

A commitment to faculty excellence through scholarship is consistent with the vision of lifelong learning. This commitment to continued scholarly growth makes the model of teacher/scholar appropriate for dialogic education. Educational excellence involves teaching and scholarship; it is possible to be a good scholar and not succeed as a teacher, but a good teacher must manifest a commitment to lifelong learning.

The term *teacher/scholar* is certainly not always a reality. Not all the teachers on a small liberal arts campus or at a research university bring scholarly dedication to the classroom, but such commitment is needed to invite conversation about ideas. An emphasis on scholarship as breadth, growth, and the beginning of conversation is consistent with John Dewey's model of "education as growth."

> Active habits involve thought, invention, and initiative in applying capacities to new aims. They are opposed to routine which marks an arrest of growth. Since growth is the characteristic of life, education is all one with growing; it has no end beyond itself. The criterion of the value of school education is the extent in which it creates a desire for continued growth and supplies means for making the desire effective in fact.[4]

Dewey's connection of education with continued growth is fundamental to the life blood of a campus. It is this commitment to growth that the faculty member from such an environment must personify in daily action and habit.

Scholarship appropriate for those interested in a close scholarly connection to teaching was detailed by Kenneth Eble and Wilbert J. McKeachie. They discussed the conflict that can emerge between teaching and research, and offered an outline of how to reconcile the tensions between these two important responsibilities.

First, dialogic education assumes that whatever model of faculty development pursued should be appropriately connected to the mission of the institution. In order to implement this first suggestion, the mission of the college or university needs to be clearly understood by the administration and key faculty members. It is the task of this group of key leaders to socialize new faculty into the particular academic environment. For instance, at one small college, a first year faculty member refused to teach a course in his discipline, stating that he lacked graduate training in the course needed by the department. The departmental chair and head of the division sat down with the discontented faculty member and explained that on a small college campus, one needs to continue to learn beyond formal graduate training, not only in disciplinary depth, but in breadth.

The departmental chair and the division head suggested that disciplinary scholarship cannot be limited to what one has previously learned. The faculty member then had to decide if such a place, where breadth is not only affirmed but expected, was going to suit his career aspirations. The unfortunate aspect of the above situation was that the faculty member should have been informed of the type of demands necessitated by the philosophical and practical needs of such a campus before a contract was ever offered.

Second, scholarship central to dialogic education needs to have some connection, either directly or indirectly, to the teaching of students. An administrator at one college stated: "Here many professors are involved in scientific research and extra-academic activities such as serving on boards of important associations or writing for national journals. But their discoveries are brought back to the classroom for the students' direct benefit."[5]

Dialogic education thrives on an excited faculty member willing and able to discuss issues both inside and outside the chosen field. This connecting of scholarship and teaching sounds good in the abstract. But in the daily operation of a college or university, interpretation of what is meant by "connection of scholarship to undergraduate teaching" is clearly debateable.

Eble contends that scholarship connected to undergraduate teaching needs to encourage the synthesis of broad-based information.

> Highly specialized research in a general-purpose college is not likely to have a very good fit with the actualities of teaching. Such research in a research-oriented university may have a better fit, but draw away from the teaching program. There is no argument that teachers should not have a command of their subject matters. . . . Scholarship, in this loose sense, is a requisite for professing.[6]

The reasons for the specialist/generalist as the scholarly core of dialogic education in undergraduate education are both philosophical and pragmatic. The specialist/generalist is the philosophical cornerstone for the ability to make contact beyond a narrow band of believers and experts. The pragmatic support for such an assertion centers around the premise that an educated democracy must have people capable of understanding conceptual issues important to the culture, society, and the global community, as well as their specialized domain.

Eble contends that a faculty member who claims that he or she cannot do research at an institution because the library does not have a complete selection of the papers of a little known historical figure is probably at the wrong institution. From a dialogic perspective, one needs to find satisfaction in a broader research agenda that will keep one satisfied and pedagogically current within the teaching situation. Highly specialized research is important, but not all educators need to do such work to be valuable. Dialogic education supports the value of a general scholarly agenda as the teacher reaches out beyond his or her specialization.

Finally, scholarship that invites dialogue and intellectual discourse can include publication. The term scholarship is used to emphasize that publication is not the only key to achievement on campus. Taking additional classes in one's discipline or in subjects outside one's discipline, working on foreign language acquisition, traveling to enhance cultural diversity, and reading within and beyond one's discipline are some of the breadth elements of scholarship appropriate to dialogic education.

Appropriate scholarship for a faculty member is defined by asking the conventional question, "Is the scholarship related to the discipline the person teaches?" and a second question of breadth, "Is the scholarship part of the general mission of one's particular undergraduate college or university?"

One physics professor at a small liberal arts college wanted to take his sabbatical to study theology. After much debate the request was approved, because the college is church related and the administration saw an opportunity to increase dialogue between the humanities and the sciences on the campus.

On a state university campus where faith and interdisciplinary conversation are not central to the mission of the institution such a request might appropriately be denied. A faculty evaluation committee can make an assessment of appropriate scholarship by asking whether or not the scholarship contributes to the type of dialogue called for by that person's academic discipline or the particular mission of a college or university.[7]

One note of caution is needed here as we accept a vision of scholarship that extends beyond publication. We cannot penalize those that do publish. Scholarship is tied to conversation, especially when we define it as more than publication. I reject the extreme position of discouraging those that publish; such a viewpoint is as inappropriate as equating scholarship solely with publication. Many nonpublishers contribute well to scholarly dialogue on campus and many publishing faculty will be able to publish and carry on dialogue with specialists in their own discipline, as well as general conversation with others.

As I discussed my position on scholarship, two of my valued colleagues suggested an even stronger position. They stated that those who do not submit work for publication review by colleagues might be open to a form of hypocrisy—asking students to be open to evaluation without following a similar course themselves. It is possible to form a distorted picture of one's own understanding of an academic area when collegial review is ignored. In short, a clear case for publication review can be made.

We need to support the "star" faculty member who engages in scholarship in both a specialty and in a general liberal arts sense. Quality teachers whose ideas are shared in book or journal form also deserve support and encouragement. It is possible for some to excel at multiple levels of the profession. When asked why she left a particular college, one young faculty member stated: "I love to teach, but I could not stand the jealousy. I had to keep quiet about my publication efforts. A group of departmental chairs even got together and agreed to deny secretarial support to those of us attempting to publish."

When an academic dean spoke to the faculty, she articulated a motto of not fearing the success of another. At any college or university, it is important to applaud excellence in our students and in our colleagues, not fear it or become absorbed in it. In short, scholarship need not be limited to publication, but those that do publish should not have to experience bitterness or disconfirmation from colleagues.

In summary, the following definition of scholarship is central to dialogic education: scholarship needs to embrace depth and breadth, the importance of conversation with others, and a commitment to lifelong learning in one's discipline and in the liberal arts in general. This broad and flexible view of scholarship is consistent with the description supplied by Jacques Barzun in *Begin Here: The Forgotten Conditions of Teaching and Learning*.

> The best means of rescuing research in the long run is the steady encouragement of solid, manifestly useful undertakings. In the modern infatuation with research, these are at a disadvantage: they look regular, not innovative; they call for sober work, not fancy techniques; they promise utility along recognized lines, not amazing revelations and upside-down revisionism. With common sense in charge . . . the genuine investigation of great subjects might once more give to research and its products the value and the praise they used to deserve.[8]

Scholarship that is broad-based and consistent with the mission of one's academic discipline and the college or university can be translated into classroom stimulation and learning.

Conversation of Ideas

The type of dialogic scholar being called for above is capable of inviting conversation about ideas nourished by scholarship that values depth and breadth. For instance, what is the connection between individual rights pointed to by Carl Rogers, the importance of public policy debates affirmed by Sidney Hook, and "capitalism with a conscience," to quote one of my accounting colleagues? There is, of course, no one answer. But such a conversation can only take place when people know something or are willing to learn about the issues.

Rorty uses the term *informed dilettante* to discuss the kind of person needed to generate conversation between specialists.[9] Dialogic education attempts to nourish an environment for the "informed dilettante." Let us examine two such examples of this type of scholar. On one university campus, a music professor has a Ph.D. in music, followed by a M.A. in art history, and multiple languages at his command, including Hebrew. He also teaches a course in Judaism and Christianity. He presents papers and does some publishing at a periodic rate. However, he is often too busy reading and providing a connecting link between the humanities and the fine arts on the campus to find publication outlets for all his work.

On another campus, a chemistry faculty member is studying intermediate Spanish and is also known as the personal computer expert on campus. The faculty member links the sciences and others on campus to new and appropriate technology. The breadth of his knowledge, like the music professor above, moves the campus to conversation about ideas.

On college and university campuses the conversation about ideas that embraces scholarly breadth should be upheld by the campus leaders: chairs of significant committees, department chairs, division heads, deans, and the president. Ideally this group of leaders should personify scholarly breadth. They are required to make decisions on issues outside their formal training. Without a commitment to breadth, both in their own disciplines and in the liberal arts, these leaders cannot properly facilitate the conversation about ideas necessary to invite dialogue between narrowly trained academic specialists.

The above philosophy connecting scholarship to campus leaders and administrators is in contrast with the current mood of the higher education industry, where some administrators might be encouraged to cease scholarly activity. The dialogic education philosophy does not fit this current mood. It is important not only to orally support scholarship, but to manifest a personal commitment to such lifelong learning. Just as the term *scholar/ athlete* should match the reality, so should combinations such as *scholar/administrator* or *scholar/chair*.

The person committed only to administration and not to lifelong learning of liberal arts breadth may be a handicap for the operational implementation of a scholarly environment. Ideally, a commitment to scholarship in depth and breadth permeates the campus—faculty, students, and administrators. Each academic component of the campus needs to be held accountable for knowing more in ten years than is known today. A concrete model of living the commitment to lifelong learning makes a difference to students and sets the tone of a campus.

The selection of leadership on a campus wanting to invite dialogue needs to include a commitment to scholarly breadth. The danger for any campus is when it searches for leaders without giving first and foremost consideration to a commitment to scholarship appropriate to the mission of the school.

The theme of *The Last Intellectuals: American Culture in the Age of Academe* by Russell Jacoby is a reminder of the need to be well-read, broad-based and able to synthesize diverse amounts of information. Jacoby challenges writing only for specialized journals, and he suggests that scholarship needs to include public conversation.[10]

Jacoby describes what he considers a missing generation in America—one interested in serious public discourse that requires breadth of knowledge. He laments that we have lost a public eager to read a pamphlet by Thomas Paine or willing to stand in line all night waiting for a debate between Abraham Lincoln and Stephen Douglas. We have entered a time of limited attention span and decreased patience. We have academics well known in their own disciplines and unknown in the common culture. Writing is done for other professionals in the guild of one's discipline, not for a general public.

Jacoby laments the professionalization of scholarship, as it limits the ability to speak to those that are not part of the inside group. Intellectuals seem to have lost the desire to write for a larger public. And who can blame them? Academic rewards are seldom given for articles in the *New Yorker*, but more often for publication in *The Quarterly Journal of . . . .* The push for publication leads to more and more subfields within an academic discipline in which one is deemed an "expert." Perhaps the theory of dialogic education supports Jacoby's call for places where breadth of scholarship and conversation about ideas can still take place. A campus committed to dialogic education needs faculty willing to read, write, and enter conversation with others about ideas relevant to current issues. Such persons are crucial to a strong democratic culture. I hope they can find an educational home with an enlarged view of scholarship, where an intellectual can not only flourish, but discover himself or herself as central to the mission of the campus. But the old adage that we make time for those things we consider important is very true. Conversation about ideas requires us to consistently increase our own learning base. Scholarship is a practical commitment to the next generation of students. Teachers, like any leaders, must be encouraged to refuel their engines.

The notion of teacher/scholar can be understood as a continuing tradition. Such a value is transmitted to students through a person-to-person transmission of a love of scholarship if the faculty keeps the joy of learning at the heart of the campus.

> My commitment to a teacher/scholar model of education was formed as I sat in the classroom with such teachers as. . . . Their enthusiasm for the subject matter encouraged discussion and in-depth study. They were fellow travelers with the class as we worked together in the learning process. . .
>
> The vitality of a college is largely maintained by teachers who through their lives pass on an infectious love of learning to their students. . . . college is a place where the learning bug can be caught for a lifetime—not because our students are told that learning is an ongoing process, but because they witness the fruits of such a commitment in the lives of our faculty.[11]

This scholarly conversation about ideas does not just enrich the lives of the faculty; it can dominate an entire campus and inspire the students and faculty. Learning comes not just from knowledge, but from an environment that models the importance of scholarship.

Barriers to Scholarship as Conversation

When one accepts a view of scholarship based on disciplinary and academic breadth, the question is, What can and does get in the way of actualizing such a commitment? This section examines three barriers that must be broken down in order to promote a scholarly understanding of teaching and scholarship within a dialogic framework: careerism, commitment to students, and institutional survival.

Careerism

It is possible to move a healthy commitment to a career to excessive preoccupation. The rewards for scholarship in most academic disciplines come not from breadth, but from specialization. Disciplinary journals are based on the assumption that incremental knowledge assists the academic field of study; an assumption I do not refute. My suggestion, however, is that an incremental approach to knowledge enhancement is not the *only* way to contribute to scholarly education. Tying careerism to specialization results in fewer rewards for the specialist/generalist; credit and attention is more likely to be given to the specialist.

The risk for a faculty member who pursues a career of breadth is potentially forfeiting higher recognition in a specific field of study. Syntheses, summaries, interpretations, comparisons, and critiques are possible contributions that the specialist/ generalist can make to scholarly inquiry. Dialogic education encourages commitment to an area of specialization in addition to perspectives and viewpoints beyond one's formal training.[12] Scholarship grounded in specialized expertise that simultaneously embraces breadth is often more publishable in journals and books. But the most important criterion for dialogic education at the undergraduate level is that the scholarship enliven the classroom by enriching dialogue between teacher and student.

Take for instance, two faculty members who did their graduate work together. One went to a major university to do specialized research. The other went to a university interested in the scholarly dialogue of teacher and student in the classroom. At the end of their careers, these two friends were honored for their outstanding work in teaching and publication. The specialized one was honored at the national level of the discipline and the other regionally.

The nonspecialized faculty member, in the acceptance of his award at the regional level, had not made the same impact on the discipline as had his friend. But he stood surrounded by nine of his former students, each with a Ph.D., indebted to the scholarly inspiration he had given them.

It seems that a sacrifice had taken place in the life of the specialist/generalist as he gathered his honor at the regional level of his discipline. There had been a sacrifice of time and energy given to his home campus; he could have focused his energies more narrowly at an institution that was a place of work rather than a home. The sacrifice was not one that he regretted or perhaps even recognized. Somewhere along the way, the faculty member had made a decision similar to the one articulated by Martin Buber in "Books and Men."

> If I had been asked in my early years whether I preferred to have dealings with men or only with books, my answer would certainly have been in favor of books. In later years this has become less and less the case. Not that I have had so much better experiences with men than with books; on the contrary, purely delightful books even now come my way more often than purely delightful men. . . .
>
> Here is an infallible test. Imagine yourself in a situation where

you are alone, wholly alone on earth, and you are offered solitude but that is only because there are still men somewhere on earth in the far distance. I knew nothing of books when I came forth from the womb of my mother, and I shall die without books, with another human hand in my own. I do, indeed, close my door at times and surrender myself to a book, but only because I can open the door again and see a human being looking at me.[13]

The faculty member described decided to join a campus where dialogue between teacher and student had a high priority. The nine students standing beside their former undergraduate professor were living monuments to a special view of scholarship that personified this faculty person's commitment to his discipline and the liberal arts. He was honored at a regional conference for a life well spent, a model of what dialogic education has to offer. Ideally, dialogic education offers not just information to students, but invites conversation about how to live as human beings interested in leaving behind something of value to others when one's work is completed.

Commitment to the Student

A major premise of this book is the importance of relationship with students. Such a commitment, however, cannot become an excuse for sacrificing future knowledge for immediate recognition from students. Some may get more satisfaction out of working with students than from scholarship. A quality commitment to students is essential for dialogic education to occur. But one cannot sacrifice future generations of students by limiting one's service to those currently on campus. A faculty member needs to close the door to read and write. Constant availability of a faculty member is not a positive sign, but an indication that students a few years from now may not be taught the most current information available in a discipline.

A faculty member committed to a dialogic view of scholarship should be wary of an institution that just counts publications. But one also needs to question the slogan "we teach on this campus" when it is offered as a defense against scholarship. Higher education is different than a traditional production business that has some people doing sales and others conducting research and development. Using business language, I explained to a Board of Trustees member that each faculty member is engaged in sales, quality teaching, research and development, and the scholarship for the future.

A dialogic view of scholarship should not attempt to emulate a narrow specialized understanding of research, but neither should it assume a model based solely on teaching. Granted, for many faculty *teaching* suggests work inside and outside the classroom with students and an active life of scholarship. But for some, teaching might be a way to justify presentations based on past learnings, not current scholarship.

An exaggerated emphasis on teaching may represent an entrepreneurial model of education. The entrepreneur sells teaching time without a long-term commitment to research and development or renewal. The following quotation on professional ethics affirms the importance of the immediate student generation with the realization that more knowledge must be learned in order to service future students.

> A reciprocity . . . of giving and receiving is at work in the professional relationship that needs to be acknowledged. In the profession of teaching to be sure, the student needs the services of the teacher to assist his learning; but so also the professor needs his students. . . . The professional's debt, moreover, extends beyond direct obligations to current clients. . . . Humility. . . .is essential to professional self-renewal. No teacher stays alive if he or she does not remain a student.[14]

The contribution of a teacher is best judged over his or her career. The performance of one or even ten years may not tell the final story. A Ph.D. recipient can coast on information learned in a graduate program for the first part of a career. A teacher can become a buddy to students, making it difficult for students to judge the teacher's actual knowledge base. The above are but two ways in which a faculty member can avoid doing scholarship and engaging in renewal of the information base.

Take for example a faculty member well loved by students for ten years, who found it increasingly difficult to attract students over the last two years. This faculty member was well grounded in a humanistic approach to communication, now considered dated by some professors. When students began to question the approach he had learned in graduate school by comparing it to other approaches discussed by updated and younger faculty members, he became defensive and angry at the new faculty. It was as if his religion, not an academic theory, had been challenged. Had this faculty member kept pace with the discipline, he could have placed the humanistic approach within a spectrum of various theories and then defended his case. In essence, without a commitment to professional renewal through scholarship, future generations of students are slighted for the gratification of servicing those currently on campus.

Institutional Survival

Keeping an institution healthy and growing is vital to any organization and has been an issue of considerable discussion in the last twenty years. The concern for survival can be carried to an extreme and begin to interfere with faculty teaching and scholarship. The changes in the life of a faculty member in higher education during the last twenty years have been significant. Some faculty have been involved in recruiting and fund-raising as threats to budgets have been experienced. To a degree such involvement can be helpful if one accepts commitment to a home campus as outlined in chapter 3. Thus there is benefit in faculty having knowledge of the fiscal and recruiting challenges facing a campus.

But the danger is that this emphasis can be overdone. A campus that begins to reward recruiting and fund-raising by faculty more highly than the scholarly impulse begins to wager the future out of desperation for the present. If a faculty member accepts these new responsibilities as additive to current duties in teaching and scholarship, more hours are assumed outside his or her primary focus. Worse yet, but more likely, the responsibilities are substitutional for some of the hours better spent on teaching and scholarship.

The administration on any campus must bear in mind that faculty are set aside in a society to learn and to pass on information. This charge needs to be protected; we must be cautious as we involve more and more faculty time in activities other than teaching and scholarship. Even the best intentioned faculty members can get caught in the vocabulary of institutional survival as the "noble" and "important" mission, missing the fact that survival in the long run will be dependent on basic fundamental issues, scholarship and teaching. Dag Hammarskjöld cautions us against too much reliance on a "glorious mission" form of commitment. "The 'great' commitment is so much easier than the ordinary everyday one—and can all too easily shut our hearts to the latter. A willingness to make the ultimate sacrifice can be associated with, and even produce, a great hardness of heart."[15] Sometimes the best one can do for an institution is to just do one's job as well as possible, taking the risk that quality teaching and scholarship can and will in the long run assist the strength of a college or a university.

The Scholarly Impulse

My hope for those interested in dialogic education is that a scholarly impulse can motivate the learner throughout life. Today we might lament the lack of scholarly depth in everyday discourse both in personal and professional settings. "My father used to write business letters that alluded to Shakespeare. These allusions were effective for conveying complex messages to his associates, because, in his day, business people could make such allusion with every expectation of being understood."[16] To engage in such communication today would likely cause puzzled looks and questions regarding how such material relates to the subject at hand. We have become more technical, linear, and direct in our conversation. Today we are more likely to quote computer phrases than we are to refer to Shakespeare. Such a warning about the overuse of "technical communication" is consistent with messages from Martin Buber and Jacques Ellul.[17]

But there is also need for an ability to be conversant about different cultures and perspectives. The rise of the Third Reich demonstrated to us that knowledge without awareness of the rights of other people and cultures is indeed dangerous. One colleague stated, "Knowledge without heart is dangerous."[18] Dialogic education cannot ignore changes in technology; we must help students compete in a technological market. We need, however, an environment that is not only supportive of technology, but asks creative and critical questions about its use. When facing a difficult hiring market, students and faculty need to define the task of learning more clearly than ever, including both technical knowledge and breadth.[19]

We need to be sold on the idea that a college is a place where ideas are to be exchanged. It is first and foremost a place of intellectual activity. A college or university committed to conversation needs to be a place where the "University of Utopia," detailed by Robert Hutchins, can take place. Hutchins called attention to the following ideals which point to a scholarly environment centered on conversation about ideas. First, a specialist/generalist needs to walk the academic corridors willing and able to engage in conversation both inside and outside his or her own discipline. Second, discussion of ideas needs to have a high place of value on

the campus. And third, one must not give in to the illusion that
all ideas are equally good. Debate and conversation need to filter
out ideas which do not stand up to examination.[20]

Dialogic education has the potential to bring people together
from various disciplines for intellectual discussion. One campus
has a "professional studies" meeting six times a year in which
interdisciplinary issues are discussed. The majority of the issues
are philosophical in nature, but touch on multiple areas, such as
science, art, and education. The effort encourages faculty participation on panels and invites discourse across the various academic
areas.

Dialogic education offers an opportunity to invite conversation that goes beyond small talk and enters into issues of substance. It may not be easy for such conversations to naturally take
place with the large number of students entering college and with
jobs, money, and just getting through taking higher priority than
the love of learning.[21] Students need to witness a scholarly environment that sows the seeds of scholarly impulse, takes pride
in the discussion of ideas, and recognizes the value of clashing
viewpoints. It is only when the environment of scholarly conversation is the norm rather than the exception that the ground of
dialogic education is nourished.

The Discipline of Scholarship

As I conclude this chapter, it is important to emphasize a
basic foundation that undergirds the commitment to conversation
about ideas. Scholarship, a scholarly attitude, does not emerge out
of a vacuum. It is the result of long and painstaking work. When
Thomas Edison stated that success is 1 percent inspiration and 99
percent perspiration, he was very much on target.

To establish a scholarly environment, we need to admit that
work is involved in learning. Faculty members who attempt to
retrain or stay up with national trends in a discipline are faced
with a challenging task. One encouraging note is that, as Frankl
discovered, meaning often results from pursuing the difficult, but
worthy task.[22] A scholarly environment also requires people to
make tough choices on time management. Sometimes one may
have to choose study instead of recreation, or close one's door in
solitude rather than be open to the spontaneous conversation.
Like anything else in life, a priority needs to be given to what one
considers central. In dialogic education, learning through reading,
writing, and experimenting is essential.

We all have heard many excuses that limit scholarship. Perhaps the most important way to end this chapter on scholarship is to paraphrase a friend who stated that it is wrong to require or request all to publish. Much that is written is poor quality. But we cannot claim the abuse of publication as a defense. It is still a misconception to think we can continue to teach well without engaging in conversation about ideas.[23] Dialogic efforts at scholarship can be envisioned as a vehicle for reaching out to others, contributing to them and learning from them—the passing on of the love of inquiry through conversation.

6

The Two Sides of Caring: Hope and Disappointment

The interplay of contraries—

Since all opposites are interdependent, their conflict can never result in the total victory of one side, but will always be a manifestation of the interplay between two sides. In the East, therefore, a virtuous person is not one who undertakes the impossible task of striving for the "good" and eliminating the "bad," but rather one who is able to maintain a dynamic balance between the two.

> Young Yun Kim,
> "Intercultural Personhood:
> An Integration of Eastern
> and Western Perspectives"

The limits of utilitarian relations—

The persistent cultural tendency to conceive all social relationships in the languages of utilitarian or expressive individualism also inhibits our capacity to make moral sense of our complex interdependencies. Without a morally meaningful comprehension of the relations that bind us to other individuals, groups and institutions, the ideals of citizenship that animated the nation's founding have little chance of realization.

> Robert N. Bellah, et al.,
> *Individualism and Commitment
> in American Life*

Dialogic education views learning as an ongoing discussion of information between persons in hopes of making a difference in the quality of life we live with one another locally and globally. Both idea discussion and relational concern guide dialogic education. A colleague asked me to choose which is primary, ideas or people, and after a number of efforts to skirt the question, I said that conversation about ideas is central to my view of education, but without relational concern to support an emphasis on inquiry, dialogic education is impossible. In short, conversation about ideas is one-half of the process and relationship completes the second half, together constituting dialogic education. This chapter brings relationships and ideas together in the process of caring as a dialogic educator.

I was introduced to Mayeroff's *On Caring* more than twenty years ago. It is this form of caring relationship that makes dialogic education possible. Mary Field Belenky and co-authors in *Women's Ways of Knowing: The Development of Self, Voice, and Mind* point to a view of education that is consistent with the theme of dialogic education. Belenky uses a number of helpful metaphors that point to a caring relational view of the educator: "connected teaching," "sharing the process," and "teacher as midwife." Each metaphor is an effort to provide an alternative to an authoritarian view of education called the "banking concept" by Paulo Freire. She offers a "portrait of a connected teacher":

> She had to trust each student's experience, although as a person or a critic she might not agree with it. To trust means not just to tolerate a variety of viewpoints, acting as an impartial referee, assuring equal air time to all. It means to try to *connect*, to enter into each student's perspective. . . . A connected teacher is not just another student; the role carries special responsibilities. It does not entail power over students; however, it does carry authority, an authority based not on subordination but on cooperation.[1]

Dialogic education views caring in educational relationships as the act of reaching out and connecting with another's experience.

The theme of this chapter is caring. Two equally important foundational sides of caring are *hope* and *disappointment*. I listened with surprise to a colleague say to a student that she cared for her very much, "I hope we will stay friends of goodwill, but you and I will feel pain as I read your dissertation and make comments. Having something so close to us critiqued and parts even rejected will not be easy." The professor cared and wanted goodwill between them, but she was wise enough to remind both herself and the student of the difficulty we all have in hearing what we do not want to hear, even when it might be true.

The two sides of caring, hope and a realistic view of disappointment and pain, invite both parties to work for a common good. In the case of education, this is the best insight we can muster together. As Sissela Bok suggests: "For the sake of our children and our children's children, we now have direct and practical reasons to further what has long been called 'the common good,' a vision that links philosophies as different as those of Confucius, Aristotle, and Thomas Aquinas, and that echoes in most later philosophies of equal depth and scope."[2] The two sides of caring, hope and disappointment, both call for acts of support for the common good, that will help teacher and student. Hope is only possible when one is prepared to meet disappointment. Otherwise a false sense of optimism guides our action.

Alva Myradal has stated, "It is not worthy of human beings to give up."[3] In the two sides of caring we do not give up—both are part of our common agenda together. As unreal as the notion of caring may sound in the increasingly businesslike environment of higher education, it is central to what it means to be human. As we reach out to one another in dialogic education, we shape and alter the lives of those around us as well as our own. In the words of Ashley Montagu, the fourth *r* in education is human relations, the ability to care for others in constructive and appropriate ways. "In our schools we teach the three *r*'s; the fourth *r*, *relations*, it has been said, we do not teach."[4] Dialogic education centered on conversation about ideas is supported by a foundation of caring, including a willingness to walk with another in moments of joy and hope for the future, as well as to continue the journey in the depths of disappointment.

The Foundation of Caring

Just as it feels like part of the world is given another chance each time a child is born, a university begins anew each fall. Caring for a new life, in the form of a child, or new ideas as we read and write, requires energy. To a degree the needed energy emerges from a *hope* that our caring might make a difference. The teacher manifests hope in learning, hope in young people growing, and hope that ideas being shared will be more likely to implement *care* in action. Caring is action supported by a sense of hope that education can and will make a difference. Each birth offers hope that novel ideas, energetic leadership, and a concern for others will guide the next generation of decisions. No matter how cynical we may become, the sight of a child offers a sense of hope in the future. New possibilities are manifested as a child is given the opportunity of life. In the child we sense hope for the world and all its wonder, a perception that often seems dim for those of us grown old and battle weary. Hope enables us to see something worthy of being done and the act of caring attempts to bring life to that hope. When I asked my neighbor why she seemed to care so much for the neighborhood children, she simply said, "I hope for them a good life. This is my way of helping them on their way."

Hope in the birth of another generation is a common response as we envision our own life extended; the next generation carries on in our stead. The child becomes the concrete carrier of values, a family name, and hope for yet another chance at life. Caring is the action that implements our hope for the next generation.

Such hope for family is a major theme in the Biblical stories of Abraham and Jacob, built around genealogy. The philosophical significance of these stories can easily be overlooked as one tries to keep all family connections in the correct order. One interpretation of such statements of blood connection is the importance of caring for the next generation in order for life to be most meaningful. This interpretation moves the story from a biological connection to a story-laden generation—one is connected by the "blood" of a given story, not by birthright. Weighing the significance of our life means that we ask what impact we have had on others that are left behind; how much and in what ways we have cared.

This generational view of caring, the passing on of the baton to the next generation, is a significant part of dialogic education. Teaching is a concrete expression of concern, not just for the current generation, but the following generations as well. Quality of life is determined by both the information passed to the next generation and a hope that such knowledge will be critically examined, adapted, and even rejected, as that generation works to assist the next.

If one is not appreciative of the child metaphor, perhaps a lighter, but similar point can be made with the sport of baseball. Spring fever, baseball style, comes with hope that "this year may indeed be our team's year." A prime example of this hope rings familiar in the hearts of Chicago Cubs fans. "Maybe this year!" is the cheer heard at spring practice for Cubbies fans, some of the most diehard believers in the world. This team has not won the

World Series since 1908, but hope is somehow present each spring when the Cubs begin to hit, pitch, and field.

Even the *American Scholar* had an article on Ed Roush, who at the time of the article was the oldest living member of the Baseball Hall of Fame with a .323 lifetime batting average and known as one of the finest defensive players of all time.[5] Why would a scholarly journal care about baseball? Perhaps one of the major interests in the game is that each spring it offers another chance; like the seasons, it can be counted upon. As a child I remember watching the 1949 movie "It Happens Every Spring." The title reminds us of enthusiasm and excitement generated by a powerful voice yelling, "play ball!" The sound of such a voice signaled that, no matter how the team or individual failed last season or even in the last game, there is another chance to succeed, another opportunity to drive in the winning run.

The 1988 World Series of the Oakland Athletics and the Los Angeles Dodgers was classic fare. The pitching of Orel Hershiser, the hustle of Mickey Hatcher, and the heroic home run of Kirk Gibson realized the dreams of many. In the bottom of the ninth inning of the first game, Kirk Gibson walked to the plate to pinch hit with the Dodgers trailing. Barely able to walk due to injuries, he pushed the count to three balls and two strikes and then drove the next pitch into the right field seats for a home run, winning the game. Then in 1990, the Cincinnati Reds beat the mighty Oakland Athletics in four straight games against 300–1 odds. Again in 1991, unexpected hope emerged for another set of baseball fans; the last place American League team of 1990, the Minnesota Twins, won the 1991 World Series. Indeed, baseball may be a metaphor of hope each time a new season begins.

The birth of a child, like spring training, brings yet another opportunity. Diehard fans and new parents have in common a significant element that makes life very much worth living—hope personified by another beginning. George Will suggests that the athletic and human excellence of Jackie Robinson offered hope to a whole race of people eleven years before Rosa Parks refused to take the back seat of a bus in Montgomery, Alabama.[6]

This hope that leads us to new beginnings is the foundation of caring and central to dialogic education. Without hope, there is little reason to care. Caring is based on the assumption that there is something to hope for—a person or an institution. Without hope, there is little chance that faculty will care enough about a campus or department to go that extra mile to make it a vital and unique educational home. It is the feeling of hope and acts of caring that made the movie "Field of Dreams" so powerful, and Donald Hall's *Fathers Playing Catch with Sons* so convincing. We care because we hope to be linked to something worthy of continuing.

I can think of no other job or task more akin to the seasonal hope of baseball or the feeling of newness brought on by the birth of a child than that of teaching. As in the metaphor of birth, teaching begins with a hope of helping others learn, which requires active care. Enthusiasm for teaching, a feeling that "It happens every fall!" points to the acceptance of a vocational calling. As one of my colleagues stated, "I am very lucky. I have been paid to read, write, and talk about ideas, while helping others learn. When I cannot get excited about such an opportunity, I should give up my right to usher in the next generation of leaders. It will then be time to let someone else do the teaching."

The Teleology of Hope

In philosophical discourse over the last thirty years the notion of teleology, being pulled by a vision or direction, has not been significantly emphasized. Chapter 4 touched on the importance of teleology in terms of educational vision.[7] This discussion of the rediscovery of the importance of teleology is consistent with the current philosophical willingness to reexamine Aristotle's writings and the focus on "practical philosophy."[8] Dialogic education is essentially a particular practical philosophy about education. By definition, teleology requires the hope that some task or project is worth pursuing. Richard Johannesen, as well as Toulmin, has reexamined the tradition of teleology and character development as it applies to our leaders. He suggests that a vision or teleology that brings together both the best of male and female virtues needs to guide our leaders. "What Gilligan describes as the male moral voice of rights, rules, justice, and fairness and female moral voice of care, compassion, relationships, and responsiveness *both* must be legitimized as encompassing virtues necessary for the moral conduct of politics broadly defined."[9] Seeing the need for political candidates to be moral provides a teleology that limits and guides behavior in decision making.

Alasdair MacIntyre, in *After Virtue*, made the case that life without telos results in a relativism without direction. Some direction is needed if one is to pursue a life of virtue or service. One does care about making a contribution to better the world without being propelled by a vision of what such a world might look like.

MacIntyre laments the de-emphasis on telos, that calls us to be more than we are at a given time.

> The moral scheme which forms the historical background to their [Athenian] thought had, as we have seen, a structure which required three elements: untutored human nature, man-as-he-could-be-if-he-realized-his-telos and the moral precepts which enable him to pass from one state to the other. But the joint effect of the secular rejection of both Protestant and Catholic theology and the scientific and philosophic rejection of Aristotelianism was to eliminate any notion of man-as-he-could-be-if-he-realized-his-*telos*. Since the whole point of ethics—both as a theoretical and a practical discipline—is to enable man to pass from his present state to his true end, the elimination of any notion of essential human nature and with it the abandonment of any notion of a *telos* leaves behind a moral scheme [that is quite] . . . unclear.[10]

Dialogic education rests on the hope that students and teachers can be more; such a telos brings together both sides of caring.

Some philosophers of the human being have gone farther and equated a lack of direction with an evil impulse. They questioned the wisdom of action without a plan, direction, or a teleology.[11]

An educational home committed to dialogic education assumes a teleological commitment consistent with the mission or vision of the campus or department. For instance, a regional state university may have a focus or direction emphasizing preparation for a career and life in a democratic culture.

This sense of hope undergirds caring in dialogic education and is captured in the following description of the direction of one particular campus.

> Unlike most of today's colleges and universities. . . [our campus] is not an institution to produce value-free and assumption-free knowledge to establish expertise and to satisfy the interest of apprentice experts. . . . [such an education] requires teachers who use the subjective devices of dialectic and rhetoric, and the combined intellect, character, and emotion, to persuade people to avoid ignorance and immorality, and to seek wisdom.[12]

A campus or department based in care finds a reason to hope as faculty assist students with their educational journey. Life that has caring as a foundation is fundamentally tied to hope. David Augsburger reminds us of the basic connection between life and hope: "The longer one lives, the more deeply one feels, the more whole one becomes, the fewer the hopes. But those few become all important. For hope is the first and last breath of life."[13] It is this hope of potential for the future that has made it possible for some teachers to state that they had never met a young person without merit and promise. It is this sense of hope that directed the caring actions of educators such as Martin Buber.[14] It was hope for the development of a more civilized person that led Aristotle to discuss education of character.[15] In short, there can be no education of character without a teleology of hope that the human is educable *and* that there is something worthy of being learned.

The Standard-bearers of Hope

Hope does not appear out of some act of magic; it comes in concrete form as people attempt to live guided by particular ideals and principles. Such persons can be viewed as standard-bearers. Claude Brown, in *Manchild in the Promised Land*, offers autobiographical insight into movement out of Harlem; his life is an inspiration and an example of a standard-bearer of hope. Brown describes relationships with significant people in his life, who consistently remind him to consider how his life was being spent and how it *might* be changed for the better. At crucial junctures, his mother, teachers, wardens, and even people on the street saw abilities in him that he only slowly began to claim as his own.[16] The "Hawthorne" studies indicated that students can sense whether a teacher has an attitude of hope about their abilities.[17] One of my colleagues was asked what the crucial ingredient for student success was. He replied, "A parent, friend, teacher, or someone significant offering a sense of hope that the young person is worthwhile and can and will succeed." In short, there needs to be a standard-bearer of hope that life can be better and times of disappointment are worth the effort. A mentor helps interpret both success and disappointment; learning comes from the meaning we attach to both the positive and negative life events.

A standard-bearer of hope might invite a student to glimpse the "good life" as hope is modeled both personally and professionally.[18] Who will demonstrate what hope can do for a life of caring in a professional and personal life? Aristotle's suggestion is to find people of virtue that we admire and permit them to be standards of what is "excellent" and central to the "good life."[19]

The primary excellent person or standard-bearer on a college or university campus is the faculty member. In a U.S. Department of Education booklet on "moral education," research findings suggest that the teacher model is *the* major contributor to character development for the student.[20] It is the teacher who embodies a foundation of caring and a sense of hope that education can make a difference. Most of us can name faculty who have changed the very life and hopes of a student for the better. Caring for students is primarily shouldered by great teachers who give more than information. They give part of their own lives and an attitude of hope that gets passed on to their students.

One of my colleagues was known for her quality time spent with students. She was known to visit students when they were sick and when they had been absent for more than two days in a row. When asked why she spent so much time with these students, she simply stated, "I had teachers do the same for me. I have hope for almost all my students. The attention they get from me reminds them of that hope. I believe in education and in just about all my students."

In dialogic education, the faculty of a campus or department need to reflect hope that ideas and tasks, when well presented and researched, will get a genuine hearing and invite conversation. One faculty member stated that interpersonal skills of negotiation through one-on-one, small group, and faculty meetings require a commitment to pragmatic and humane negotiating skills and a hope that important ideas can be discovered in our work together.[21] Another faculty member stated that sending a child to a school where the teachers model hope for what intellectual excitement can offer is important in the selection of a college.[22]

Even without state-of-the-art facilities on a campus, the faculty member can still make a difference in the education of a student. In an essay "Inspiring Teachers to Revitalize Teaching," Zelda Gamson stresses the importance of the teacher as a standard-bearer. "In their own ways, faculty members become aware that 'the medium is the message'—that teachers educate as much by *how* as by *what* they teach. This principle has a symbolic level: Teaching style becomes a metaphor of an attitude toward human relationships."[23]

In dialogic education, the teacher is the standard-bearer of hope. The most important resource on the campus is not the quality of the buildings, curriculum, or even the scholarship. All of these elements are very important, but the key to education that offers direction for a student is still the faculty member. The teacher in the classroom has the opportunity to direct a student and offer a sense of hope that information, values, and relationships are to be taken seriously in whatever vocation one pursues.

An Alternative to Cynicism

Some would contend that as a culture we have become too cynical. Cynicism lays the foundation for looking out for number one. A university committed to caring needs to be a place where cynicism about life can be combatted. If a campus does not offer an alternative to cynicism, then one of its potential gifts to the students and leaders of tomorrow will be lost. Betty Siegel, in a call for "knowledge and commitment" on campus, states: "Arthur Levine in his book, *When Dreams and Heroes Died*, gives a detailed and chilling portrait of our students. Bringing together information from national surveys of 95,000 undergraduates during the 1960s and 1970s, he reveals that students today are overwhelmingly materialistic and extremely cynical about society and its institutions, including higher education."[24]

One of my former teachers stated that he did not see how one could remain a teacher interested in passing on the love of inquiry to the next generation if cynicism is one's primary disposition. An institution run by a mission cannot be combatting cynicism at every turn. Institutional support is necessary for an education grounded in hope to continue; constant cynicism about the institution, administration, faculty, or students will hurt a campus. Just as Aristotle, Aquinas, Mill, and Kant hoped that the individual is educable and can be motivated by a vision of courage, honor, and justice,[25] a dialogic teacher believes that the student can learn and that there is something worth learning that might, in a small way, make the world a better place.

If cynicism, in terms of unreasoned negativism, has captured the dominant attitude of the professor, it is unlikely that the student will be able to combat such an environment. Cynicism in education can also be promoted by professors who assume an unbending moral virtue that they force on others. Such a stance fits the actions of the narrow-minded propagandist interested more in brain washing than mind expansion. As Sidney Hook observed: "He [Lincoln] feared the fanaticism of virtue, the idealism focused only on one value or program pursued at any cost to other values violated by the means employed to achieve the ideal goal."[26]

Cynicism emerges not only when there is no hope, but when

there is a narrow single view of hope as "my way" that ignores and rejects contrary positions. One national periodical ran an article questioning people of continual good cheer and joy. The article reminds us that even a good thing can be overdone. Similar to the fanaticism of the true believer in Eric Hoffer's warning, even those of good cheer are likely to lead us too quickly from optimism to cynicism.[27]

For realistic hope for the future, one needs to walk the narrow ridge between extremes of despair and blind hope motivated by intellectual rigidity. Buber saw the narrow ridge as a willingness to live life in the midst of controversy, being open to criticism, and encouraging hope that is not an arrogant confidence closed to question and modification. Closed, narrow ideologies can backfire, causing us to question hope, feeding the seeds of cynicism. Cynicism has been defined as "undue optimism" that cannot possibly be fulfilled.[28] It is this excessive or unrealistic view of hope that we must guard against. The irony is that as one offers hope as an alternative to cynicism, the latter can be nourished by unkept promises and unfulfilled optimism.

An unrealistic understanding of hope, or what I would call "false optimism," is the breeding ground of cynicism. Cynicism is so prevalent today that the suggestion of hope as a major foundation for caring and the teacher as the embodiment of such a value is seldom discussed. Recently I presented a paper which discussed the work of Christopher Lasch, who conceptualizes hope—as opposed to optimism—as fundamental to life. I was intrigued to hear a critic call me a "humanist" in a way that made the word seem dirty. My colleague had become vulnerable to cynicism as he spoke, unable, at least in that meeting, to differentiate hope from false optimism. He wanted to reject false optimism, but was too quick to lump optimism and hope together as unrealistic components of what he called "humanism."

[Lasch states that] if we distinguish hopefulness from the more conventional attitude known today as optimism—if we think of it as a character trait, a temperamental predisposition rather than an estimate of the direction of historical change—we can see why it serves us better, in steering troubled waters ahead, than a belief in progress. Not that it prevents us from expecting the worst. The worst is always what the hopeful are prepared for. Their trust in life would not be worth much if it had not survived disappointment in the past, while the knowledge that the future holds further disappointments demonstrates the continuing need for hope. Believers in progress, on the other hand, though they like to think of themselves as the party of hope, actually have little need of hope, since they have history on their side. But their lack of it incapacitates them for intelligent action. Improvidence, a blind faith that things will somehow work out for the best, furnishes a poor substitute for the disposition to see things through even when they don't.[29]

Optimism is part of the inevitable view of progress that is rejected by Lasch, as well as myself. Hope is grounded more in tenacity of spirit and optimism than in the demand for immediate results consistent with one's vision.

Hope is a teleological direction worthy of being followed, with the end result being unknown. An undue sense of optimism is likely to generate cynicism when ideals are not met. Hope is an alternative where strife, difficulty, limits, and unforeseen components of life are accepted as one strives for a worthy project. Hope is realistic; the outcome may not match the initial vision, but the journey seems worth the effort.

I was a member of a campus committee meeting when a case from a particular student was brought to our attention. The student had not enrolled in a course for academic credit at the proper time and wanted to receive academic credit after completing the course. Such a case is normally easy to resolve with a simple no. But in this instance, there was some confusion as to whether or not the student actually thought she had enrolled for credit, and it was unclear whether the faculty member in charge of the class had encouraged the incomplete enrollment.

The committee examining this academic issue decided to question the student in order to facilitate their deliberation. The committee first offered the following forewarning, "Your answer will determine our decision as well as contribute to the development of your own character." Then they asked, "Did you actually believe you had signed up for this course for academic credit at the appropriate time or did you decide to request a letter grade after seeing how well you had done in the course?" After a long pause, the student stated that after completing the course she was sorry she had not taken it for a grade and then applied for credit through a letter grade instead of a pass/not pass option that this course carried.

The committee denied the request *and* made sure the student understood that the committee respected her honesty when she was directly confronted. Four points are of interest here. First, it is unusual to warn a person about the potential consequences of an answer. Second, it is uncommon for a committee to request an honest answer that might be detrimental to the person giving the answer. Third, the committee was not deterred by the pain or inconvenience that the loss of the course caused the student. Finally, the student's choice of character development over her accumulative grade point average in itself is noteworthy. The student's request resulted in the committee members and the student examining issues of honesty, character development, and the protection of academic standards.

The above example reflects a choice about the type of campus that is shaped by daily decision making. It is a risk to trust a student's ability to be honest and it is a risk to distrust such potential. A campus willing to risk erring on the side of trust, at least until proven wrong in individual cases, is grounded in hope that honest decisions are still possible. Dialogic interaction expects honesty, at least until proven otherwise. Such action must be weighed with the knowledge of the extent of student cheating on campuses today.

Without contrary evidence, the committee decided to trust the student. Such a communicative style sets the tone for dialogic education. Consistent distrust of students without evidence sets a negative campus tone. It is not naive to have hope in another's trustworthiness unless significant evidence is given to the contrary and one still continues to be falsely optimistic about that person's truthfulness. Fundamentally, dialogic education suggests that it is possible to shape the future through leaders of character. Hope, according to Stanley Hauerwas is our primary weapon in the combatting of cynicism.[30] One writer suggests that hope motivated by moments of success is what determines a feeling of self-worth.[31] Leaders need to be people with hope, good ability, and feelings of self-worth. After ability, hope may be the next most important ingredient. Without hope there is little reason to initiate projects.

Martin Luther King, Jr.'s speech, "I Have a Dream," left a mark on race relations in the United States. The speech revealed hope about the future. In spite of the trials he had experienced and the struggles of a people for one hundred years after the Emancipation Proclamation, the civil rights movement he represented called for hope that one could make a difference.

And when we allow freedom to ring, when we let it ring from every village and hamlet, from every state and city, we will be able to speed up that day when all of God's children—black men and white men, Jews and Gentiles, Catholics and Protestants—will be able to join hands and to sing in the words of the Old Negro spiritual, 'Free at last, free at last; thank God Almighty, we are free at last.'[32]

King offered a convocation address on a small campus only months before he was assassinated in 1968. That speech reflected the tone of his life, calling people not only to recognize problems, but to embody a hope that energizes us with the courage and conviction needed to tackle the tough issues before us.[33] Such hope in the midst of realistic struggle was the foundation of King's oratory and actions. As we remember the hope of King, we are asked to place it within a realistic context of vision, legal efforts, and a broad-based struggle of many asking for a new agenda for America.[34] Hope within a context of support can have realistic and concrete changes in direction for a people or a campus.

Disappointment

Hope may be the major foundation for caring, but realistic perception dictates that we understand that not all hopes will, can, or even should materialize. In short, any effort to care for students needs to accompany hope with the reality of *disappointment*. Disappointment is the result of unfulfilled hope. Dealing with disappointment as a result of a destroyed hope is a necessary life skill.

Disappointment can strike anyone on a campus, from the freshman wanting to go to medical school, only to discover a lack of potential in math, to a faculty member buying a house and then not being granted tenure, to a president of a university wanting to change the mission of a school being unable to find an equally powerful substitute mission. Each of us within a campus community needs to be prepared for disappointment.

Only by giving up on hope can we save ourselves from the all too often feeling of disappointment. Not everything one hopes for can happen; if we hope, disappointment is potentially just around the corner. One professional I admire lost his wife and later his daughter to early deaths. Yet he lived life by being hopeful and recognizing the need for grit. Life will permit pain more than once on the walk through uncharted paths. Pain is a certainty. How one meets that pain will determine the quality of one's life. Not only must we be careful that our hope not be unrealistic, fueling cynicism, but we need to make sure that a view of caring and embracing hope is open to the reality that life can bring disappointment as well as good tidings.

The two sides of caring, hope and disappointment, require that dialogic educators see educational possibilities in future projects *and* failed tasks. As a little league and soccer coach, I remind parents that learning comes from the hope of getting better and working through disappointment. If disappointment is seen as an inevitable result of having hope as a foundation of caring, then assisting a student with disappointment needs to be the second half of the foundation of learning. People of constant good cheer can lead others into the trap of discomfort, frustration, and cynicism. The managed smiles on the faces of the registrar, advisors, and secretaries are often an effort to please the customer. But the task of dialogic education is not to please the customer; we are charged with educating and shaping students, requiring us to ask, "What educational value might frustration offer?" Dialogically, frustration and disappointment that have educational value presume conversation about what has occurred and possible implications.

Education involves learning how to cope with disappointment, not just eliminating all of it; we need to give students the intellectual and professional resources necessary for meeting unexpected challenges. A caring campus does not eliminate frustration, but offers guidance and help in dealing with life turns that are contrary to what is hoped for or desired.

Caring about students is not always easy. Such work, however, seems more palatable if hope is accompanied by a realistic understanding of disappointment. Thus, disappointment and even pain are not without merit if discussed and interpreted. Since this chapter began with the emphasis on the hope of a new child, the following story is an important reminder of the difficulty of caring for a child, in a humorous, but nevertheless real life situation.

> I was walking toward my car outside a shopping center a few weeks ago, when I heard a loud and impassioned howl.
>
> "Auggghh!" groaned the masculine voice.
>
> I spotted a man about fifty feet away who was in great distress (and for a very good reason). His fingers were caught in the jamb of a car door which had obviously been slammed unexpectedly. Then the rest of the story unfolded. Crouching in the front seat was an impish little three-year-old boy who had apparently decided to "close the door on Dad."
>
> The father was pointing frantically at his fingers with his free

hand, and saying, "Oh! Oh! Open the door, Chuckie! They're caught . . . hurry . . . Chuckie . . . please . . . open . . . OPEN!"

Chuckie finally got the message and unlocked the door, releasing Dad's blue fingers. The father then hopped and jumped around the aisles of the parking lot, alternately kissing and caressing his battered hand. Chuckie sat unmoved in the front seat of their car, waiting for Pop to settle down.[35]

Not only is there hope when a child is born, there is pain and disappointment as that child grows to maturity. The parent does, at times, find the child unknowingly slamming doors on his or her fingers, literally and figuratively. We are hopeful each time a new generation of students arrives on campus. But some will cause us disappointment and pain in their maturation process. The close association of faculty member and student in dialogic education invites relationships that can be significant and on occasion, disappointing.

Meeting the inevitable pain of working with people, ideas, and institutions will be a part of caring in dialogic education. Working with undergraduate students is not only exciting, but it is also hard work. A college needs to be clear about both elements of the caring process and be forthright in articulating these concerns as part of the mission of the college.[36] Without both elements of caring a campus can move into an entrepreneurial effort of attempting to placate instead of educate a student. Caring requires us to be more concerned about a student's education, including how to handle both hope and disappointment, than with the appearance of being a nice place to study.

Dialogic caring must be strong enough to do what is necessary for a student, even if that student does not necessarily appreciate it at the time. As an undergraduate, I recall two students who stated their dislike of the work required of them by the instructor. Only after the students had completed their graduate work did they write the disliked professor and offer appreciation. Had the faculty member attempted to be a buddy and ease the work load, the two students might not have been as prepared for their graduate programs. Being liked as a faculty member is a potential by-product of good teaching, not the aim. Dialogic educators need to be willing to do what is necessary for the education of the student, even if there is a lack of uniform appreciation.

Because caring involves assisting with disappointment as well as hope, we must be careful that we do not eliminate either from a student's education. When I began teaching, I was deeply committed to the student's right to evaluate faculty. After I joined administration, I became increasingly opposed to student evaluation of faculty; too often the scores were used to encourage faculty to conform to a narrow perception of a "good" faculty member. Such a vision does not take into account the change of heart described above, where the "bad" faculty member suddenly becomes "excellent." As an administrator, I was skeptical of student evaluations of faculty because the student is in a better position to judge style than competency. My position on such evaluations is that they should be used with great care, trying to work between two extremes: ignoring all student input and encouraging faculty to teach to please the customer.

Steven Cahn, Provost and Vice-President of Academic Affairs at the Graduate School of The City University of New York, goes further than my position, calling student evaluation of faculty a disgrace. He reminds us that by definition the teacher knows more than the student. The student can judge style, not reliability of content. Cahn cites the classic study of an actor who was given enough information to get good ratings as a mathematics instructor.

> It is not coincidental that the increasing use of student evaluations occurred at the same time as grade inflation. If teachers' livelihoods depend on the degree of their popularity with students, self-interest dictates that they award their students high grades. After all, which of us is not inclined to take a more favorable view of those whom we know take a favorable view of us? And are we not likewise apt to be less than enamored of those from whom we receive cool treatment? To be blunt, it is hardly likely that students who fail a course will award the teacher their highest accolades.[37]

My concern is that we need to make it less likely that a university or a faculty member could sell a caring environment grounded in optimism and comfort instead of hope and conversation about the inevitability of disappointment. I believe that some efforts to empower students can lead to later cynicism; we need to make sure students are well educated, not just happy with each instructor. Faculty need to be lifelong learners concerned about quality of relationships with students. But the caring needs to be motivated by authentic concern, not by an effort to placate the customer. Caring for students needs to permit opportunities for discussion of both hope and disappointment. If we rid the campus of technically competent faculty members who do not conform to a particular set of interpersonal relationship skills, we may open the door to momentary comfort and fewer chances to learn from realistic hope and disappointment.

The marketing of painless hope or undue optimism is not caring; it is vulgar manipulation of the student. Dialogic education needs to give students the resources to counter stress and frustration. An educator does not have the right to eliminate a major part of maturation and take away the opportunity to learn coping skills for dealing with disappointment and pain. In short, caring is the offering of hope and conversation about inevitable disappointments.

Take for example, a college known for its quality graduates, many of whom have been historically educated in the professions of teaching and ministry. This school has not sent many people into professions earning a great deal of money. The college therefore, has a small endowment from alumni and has learned to do much with little. Ironically, this has given it strength. The college has modeled a life of service and quality use of resources. The sufficient but limited resources became a strength, not a weakness. Perhaps the key to mental health and growth is the ability to take a difficult situation and work with it creatively.

Caring as a Practical Philosophy

Dialogic education involves two sides of caring, and learning not only from books, lectures, and labs, but from the faculty member as a person willing to talk about hope and disappointment. Such action is an example of "practical philosophy." In this case, the practical philosophy is that of educators assisting students with hopes and disappointments, and encouraging learning from each. It is not enough just to know abstractly; one also needs to put knowledge to use for the common good.

How can students learn about caring that involves hope and disappointment? A teacher interested in dialogic education may or may not use materials that point to such learnings. Some classes lend themselves to discussion of the trails of Job, questions about life and death, Old Testament scriptures, or the importance of art in Western and non-Western cultures of the world. In addition, outside of class, a teacher can listen and respond to students' concerns and struggles. Even discussion of how a democracy works as one wins and loses in an effort to get one's ideas accepted points to the importance of hope and the need to understand disappointment. A teacher who recognizes that the grading system offers a chance to learn from hope *and* from disappointment offers students a lesson in the practical philosophical arena of organizational survival. Dialogic education is based on the assumption that philosophical knowledge is practical if played out in the everyday life of faculty and students.[38]

The writings of William James describe the practical nature of philosophy and a liberal education. The liberal arts are not just niceties, but are central to the education of leaders who need to have a perspective that is broad-based, informed, and not limited to one discipline. "We think that for a general about to fight an enemy it is important to know the enemies' philosophy."[39] James reminds us that philosophy is practical and impacts how we approach people, education, and the world.

Hope and disappointment compose a sort of practical philosophy that calls for an education that can make a difference while offering a realistic warning that pain and disappointment will need to be met and dealt with creatively along the way. Caring is not just something that emerges spontaneously. It can and should be part of the practical education on a campus or department. When Aristotle detailed the importance of a practical philosophy, he was concerned about the education of virtues. The virtue of caring that embraces both hope and disappointment is fundamental to dialogic education.

As Aristotle suggested, virtue needs to be invited and encouraged by "habituation," or practice. A campus is an ideal place to practice caring. The rapid changes in personal and professional lives offer much opportunity for learning. Dialogic education suggests that humanitarian and civic values are nourished by interaction that permits discussion and reflection on subject matter and the trials of life—conversation about what one is learning, both theoretically and practically.

Dialogic education works with a dialectic understanding of caring. Somewhere between the extremes of undue optimism and too much focus on difficulty and disappointment rests an education that prepares us for lifelong learning.

An essay written in honor of Professor Robert E. Park of the University of Chicago captured him in the midst of the sides of caring. Park was evidently so hard on one student that the student could barely stand the pain. But the student knew all the while, "He was as interested in them [his students] as he was interested in their subjects."[40] Perhaps Park is like a friend and colleague of mine. She is the finest example of a dialogic educator I know.

My friend has hope that education and people can make a

difference and she fights attempts to placate students, allowing them to learn from disappointment, frustration, and pain. But most students know that if they are in trouble and need a teacher to walk with them in disappointment, helping them once again find hope, that they must knock on my friend's door. The people who might be called purveyors of a managed smile, who offer an unrealistic sense of optimism grounded in expectations of ease and comfort, not work and commitment, are nowhere to be found when intense pain enters a student's life. Dialogic education is grounded in a realistic sense of caring—one in which hope and the tools for meeting pain and disappointment can assist the life of a graduate.

7

Between Persons

Importance of relationship—

I would like to share with you in this paper a conclusion, a conviction which has grown out of years of experience in dealing with individuals, a conclusion which finds some confirmation in a steadily growing body of empirical evidence. It is simply that in a wide variety of professional work involving relationships with people—whether as a psychotherapist, teacher, religious worker, guidance counselor, social worker, clinical psychologist—it is the *quality* of the interpersonal encounter with the client which is the most significant element in determining effectiveness.

> Carl R. Rogers,
> "The Interpersonal Relationship:
> The Core of Guidance"

Relationship through conversation about ideas—

Socrates collected opinions, asked questions, clarified terms and ideas, and indicated commitments. That is all he did. All that was required of those who took part with him was that they should try to think and to understand one another. They did not have to agree with Socrates, before or after. They did not have to agree among themselves. If they came to conviction, they did so by their own free will.

> Robert M. Hutchins,
> "The Socratic Dialogue"

In American education few have emphasized the importance of quality relationships more vigorously than Carl Rogers, and in Western culture few are associated as directly with discussion of ideas as Socrates. The legacy of Rogers' work is a reminder that there is more to a college education than the accumulation of information. Rogers stressed the invitation of quality relationships between student and faculty; he advocated education that went beyond information accumulation and embraced the importance of a supportive relational environment. The quotation on Socrates also reminds us that relationships can emerge as a by-product of conversation about ideas.

If a faculty member considers the dialogic method of teaching, but cannot invite relationships with students or does not consider concern for the student as part of the teaching task, then his or her view of education may be incompatible with dialogic education. There may be a mismatch between the faculty member and one of the basic values of dialogic education—the importance of persons coming together in relationship around ideas. Those who believe that undergraduate education is facilitated through interaction both inside and outside the classroom are attracted to an opportunity to engage in conversation about ideas with students and colleagues. This commitment to interaction is consistent with the reminder that interaction in the education process shapes the intellectual and personal character of the student.[1] As Kenneth Eble, well known for his writing about undergraduate education, suggests in *The Craft of Teaching: A Guide to Mastering the Professor's Art*, any form of education that purports to have an impact on the student's life must take relationships seriously.[2] Research findings have documented the commonsense importance of effective educational leaders being student centered and nurturing as they work to offer the "best" information available.[3]

Dialogic education is facilitated by a relational sensitivity; achievement and aspiration levels of students are influenced by the accessibility of faculty and the importance they place on interaction with students.[4] Such a relational emphasis is more than good will; it is central to providing an invitational environment for learning. Both conversation about ideas, and a relational concern for students make up the foundation of dialogic education.

A highly motivated undergraduate student interested in graduate school or a particular type of job can be assisted from a relational environment. But the student likely to benefit more from such a teaching style is one who is unclear about his or her undergraduate direction. A relational environment can invite talking about future goals and working out possible plans, which might not be discussed in conversation with parents and other students. A teacher who interacts extensively with students has two advantages: first-hand knowledge of and insight into the student and information about the professional demands that await. Students are capable of learning in almost any setting. I found, however, as a first-generation college student with average preparation, that relational concern encourages a willingness to take risks in learning unfamiliar academic material. Dialogic education works to provide a relationship base that makes taking risks seem more viable, offering a supportive environment from which one can reach into new and unexamined territory.

A Supportive Relational Environment

When we discuss the importance of a relational environment, the obvious question is, What might such a teaching style look like? In order to answer that question, one must first ask, What assumptions are basic to such a view of education? Jack Gibb has documented a commonsense assumption that a supportive relational environment is more likely to promote growth than a defensive posture. A defensive environment keeps one's focus away from the work at hand and centered on speculative questions and anxiety. A campus where conversation is possible, faculty are accessible, and students feel support can focus attention on learning, both inside and outside the classroom. Relational attention is offered with a purpose of keeping energy and conversation centered on the prime reason for attending a college—learning.

The following categories of behavioral climates suggested by Gibb illustrate the consequences invited by particular relational styles.[5]

DEFENSIVE CLIMATES	SUPPORTIVE CLIMATES
1. Evaluation	1. Description
2. Control	2. Problem orientation
3. Strategy	3. Spontaneity
4. Neutrality	4. Empathy
5. Superiority	5. Equality
6. Certainty	6. Provisionalism

A relational emphasis encourages a supportive environment requiring description as ideas are discussed with students. Weaknesses and strengths are reviewed, but in a way that is problem-centered—how can we maintain and increase learning for students and faculty? The focus is on the problem of finding ways to invite the student to learn more; such a stance does not approach a student's lack of knowledge with ridicule. As students come to us with less academic preparation than we might hope for and with less of a will to get the job done,[6] the temptation is to blame the student. Instead of blame, a problem orientation encourages us to find ways to encourage underprepared and poorly motivated students to learn.

A dialogic learning environment needs to embrace some spontaneity, making it possible for people to meet in conversation with one another without planned agendas. Such an atmosphere is relaxed enough to permit spontaneous encounters over ideas and notions learned in the classroom setting. Empathy for the student's struggle to acquire knowledge permits listening and assistance in learning. A faculty member does not become a scholar overnight, and many of us never obtain this status. The difficulty of the learning task should be a good reminder that patience is necessary as we try to introduce students to learning. In addition, we need to bear in mind that it is the faculty who should work to become scholars. Students are in the classroom to acquire information and perhaps to enjoy the learning whenever possible. It is the faculty who should devote a major part of their lives to the study of a particular subject, not the average student.

Equality suggests that both the teacher and the student are important and worthy of being heard, even as both realize that the teacher possesses more information and expertise. Treating persons as equal should not be confused with responding to them in the "same" fashion. Aristotle differentiated the two terms by discussing "proportionate equality," suggesting that equal positions and equal ability are to be dealt with similarly, but different positions and different abilities call for different responses. In essence, to treat all the same, regardless of position and ability, is not equality. Equality respects difference and questions reliance on sameness.[7]

Finally, a supportive academic environment needs to invite a perception of provisionalism, permitting "maybe" to be an appropriate response to much of our learning and allowing us to question ideology and encourage a spirit of inquiry. A relational teaching style is facilitated by an environment of openness, accessibility, and concern.

Let's examine a case where some students and faculty wanted to promote a good cause, but in a fashion that limited inquiry. A group of students wanted to require a pledge at spring commencement saying that graduates would accept employment only at companies or institutions sensitive to environmental issues. The pledge was not endorsed by the administration of that particular university with a long-standing major in environmental studies. In this case, two social goods were at odds: statement on employment and the environment, and the need to keep campuses free of pledges. Time was spent explaining these two concerns to students.

An alternative was agreed upon that did not call for an official endorsement from the administration. Students wore ribbons to indicate their personal position, permitting the university to be a place of academic freedom where such important issues could be discussed. The administration opposed the pledge to protect a provisional response or attitude in hopes of keeping academic freedom alive and well on campus. The goal was to use this controversy as a teaching opportunity to recall the damage done to academic freedom on many campuses during the 1950s. The students asking for support for the pledge had no memory of the aftermath of McCarthy and the fight against pledges on college campuses. Whether a pledge originates from the political right or left, it is dangerous when the provisional attitude necessary for academic freedom is substituted with a firm statement of belief that all must accept.

Without a doubt not all the students were convinced of the merits of the compromise. They wanted an official endorsement. What they received was an opportunity to voice their view without requiring agreement from all. A provisional perspective opens channels of conversation and is wary of positions that view all the opposition as misguided.

Dialogic education recognizes the importance of mission and values for any educational home. Danger to academic freedom, however, is invited when we move from value inquiry to value solidification. A mandatory pledge solidifies and stops value inquiry and conversation about ideas. A supportive relational teaching style should make value options known, but be careful when any one set of values becomes mandatory.

The supportive relational environment provides a good place for students to venture out and take intellectual risks as they learn. A supportive campus environment encourages open discussion of ideas without fear of reprisal. Thus, dialogic education ties the quality of its relationships to a willingness to take risks in learning new ideas and developing more depth in what one already knows.

This supportive teaching style is exemplified by one professor known for his ability to invite students to explore tough and demanding material. Without teacher enthusiasm, constant support, and encouragement, these students would have rejected the material. I asked a student why she was willing to take such a demanding elective course. She responded, "The professor loves the material and supports us in our learning. He does not make us feel stupid as we learn. In fact, each day he learns from us as we learn from him. He is a teacher willing to learn along with us while remembering how important encouragement is when students encounter complicated material."

Limiting Defensiveness, Encouraging Questions

A supportive relational environment invites an attitude of inquiry and questioning as the foundation for the learning exchange. When students work with a minimum of defensiveness in their educational environment they focus more fully on their academic work. Students already bring a number of obstacles to the learning environment from lack of skill to disinterest.

Dialogic faculty and students offer an alternative to defensiveness while still affirming the need for some anxiety in the learning process. Exploring new terrain is not always a comfortable journey. A professional relationship with no anxiety or tension may be sustained by unambitious expectations. An environment without some tension can also breed destructive behavior; some members of a university might be tempted to neglect teaching and find more interesting political work to keep themselves occupied. Frankl, reviewing Freud's notion of tension reduction, suggested that human beings do not live by tension reduction alone. In an environment without enough tension, we begin to create tension to meet our own stimulation needs.[8] Sometimes family vacations without demanding schedules of work result in arguments generated more out of boredom than genuine disagreement.

A supportive relational environment with workable levels of tension helps to nurture a rich intellectual life for the student. For undergraduates the importance of a supportive relational environment is that it lessens the risk of venturing into the unknown. Anxiety needs to be centered on learning, not on self-defense.

The following is an example of a learning environment that combines tension and support. My ten-year-old daughter has a spelling test each week. Tension is needed to get her to study, and support is important in helping her study and manage her time well. She is expected to do well, but not alone. She needs to feel concrete and practical support for her work and for herself. After a test, she needs to know that she will have a home of support, no matter what the results of the test. This combination of manageable tension and support makes it possible to learn information and to ask questions.

Questioning is also an essential part of an educational environment that provides a support base for scholarly inquiry. The following quotation from Hans Gadamer points to the importance of questioning. Gadamer, well known for his work in interpretation of texts, sees questioning as the key to new insight.

> The essence of the question is the opening up, and keeping open, of possibilities. . . .
>
> We cannot have experiences without asking questions. The recognition that an object is different and not as we first thought, obviously involves the question whether it was this or that. . . . This is the famous Socratic *docta ignorantia* which opens up the way . . . to the superiority of questioning.[9]

The importance of relational concern is that it increases the willingness of students to ask significant questions and to engage in intellectual examination before they may feel ready to make a significant contribution. Relationship concern can invite a more open and challenging academic environment as learners work in discussion and in needed memorization of significant data.

A relational, supportive environment is helpful in churches, in social agencies, and at a university or college. However, the motivation for inviting such an environment determines if the institution is more a church, a social agency, or a university. A teacher offers a supportive atmosphere in order to invite scholarly exchange and questioning in hopes of lessening defensiveness that keeps students unfocused on the task of learning.[10]

An observer of the works of sculptor John Baldwin noted an interesting contrast between the gentleness of the man and the cruel and senseless violence in his later work. A colleague suggested that Baldwin wanted us to recognize that "pain, justice, oppression, self-sacrifice, and honor are common to all mankind and go as far back as we can remember."[11] He suggested that the gentleness of the man permitted people to examine the darker side of life more honestly. Such vivid work calls us to have conversation about ideas within an environment made safer by the relational gentleness of the artist. Also, a relational environment of support can encourage us to face the harsh realities demanded by texts that require our attention and time. A supportive relational environment offers a foundation for a learning environment that permits tension to assist us, rather than stop our exploration of ideas and issues.

A Unique View of Relationship

I am interested in a somewhat unique understanding of the importance of relationships involving what happens between persons and the meeting of ideas. One can have relationships with people and ideas. The relationship of persons and ideas forms an organizational web that offers character and identity to an educational home, providing a common center around which people can gather.

Martin Buber recognized the importance of a common center that bonds relationships.[12] The common center in dialogic education is conversation about ideas, the exchange of ideas with persons. Talking about ideas together forms relationships as by-products. The discussion of ideas permits relationships to mature naturally through common commitments.

The work of Dietrich Bonhoeffer offers an examination of the term *relationship* consistent with the focus of this chapter. Bonhoeffer, a theologian interested in the importance of community, reminded the faithful that relationships with one another need to be motivated by loyalty to God. Even people that one dislikes must be included when contributing to God's human community.[13] Bonhoeffer envisioned God as the common center of our conversation and life together as Christians.

Bonhoeffer rejected a view of relationship based solely on affection or feeling. His common center pulled people together and permitted them to work with one another, even in the presence of psychological strain and dislike. Similarly, I have described conversation about ideas with a relational concern as the common center of a campus. Such a common center is fundamental to a university as Bonhoeffer's notion of God is to the Church. Even though the specific common centers are quite different, there is a common purpose; a common center pulls people together even when it may be difficult to like or appreciate one another.

Too much intentional relationship building is sometimes phony and tries to bypass time needed for relationships to grow. A faculty member learns about students the same way an expert craftsman learns to know the people he works with: by discussing the craft. Dialogic education encourages the development of relationships centered around conversation about ideas. Close relationships will sometimes develop as a by-product of such discussion.

In essence, dialogic education builds an academic home where the notion of relationship is uniquely understood. If someone is contributing to the pursuit of truth, we need to remain open to relationship with them even if we do not like them. Affection should not be the primary motivator of our relationships together on a university campus. Our common center needs to be a commitment to learning.

Unsure of the dialectical nature of responses about a young faculty member, I asked the chair of the young faculty member's department to evaluate his discipline and the institution. The chair had been in a number of curriculum and academic discipline arguments with this faculty member. She told me the young faculty member was a fine scholar, a good teacher, and a qualified and committed professional adversary. She said, "I do not like him, but I respect him. We both are committed to learning. Without a doubt, I would support him for tenure." Relationships centered on contribution to conversation about ideas were more important in her evaluation than her personal dislike of an arrogant faculty member. Such a view of relationships may be unusual, in sharp contrast to relationships based on popularity.

As a consultant in organizations, I find it interesting to witness the high priority placed on likability. It seems that relationships in an organization that are primarily based on this theme signal a decline in a mission, purpose, or common center of commitment. Relationships centered on an agreed upon task allow persons who do not like one another to still work together. When the desire to engage in conversation about ideas has dissipated, we are left with the question of who likes whom instead of who contributes to quality discourse on a campus. This level of communication fits what I call the junior high syndrome of concern for self-image. Relational likability becomes too important as we move out of the common center of conversation about ideas needed to keep the diversity of ideas alive. The primary question for a campus is not do you like a particular person, but what does that person contribute to the learning conversation on campus.

A student and a faculty member need to know that professional judgments will be made on competence and achievement, not interpersonal affection. This relationally supportive environment needs to give clear messages that achievement through competence is adhered to as much as possible on the campus. As

Warren Bennis has stated, the university must forgo the temptation to allow charm or interpersonal likability to be primary, holding out as a place where competence is valued most highly.[14] In essence, this unique view of relationship centers people around inquiry and projects to be done, offering a supportive, but not tensionless home in which to work.

Persons Making a Difference

As we affirm our primary task on campus as discussion of ideas, we recognize the importance of teachers being known for a thoughtful knowledge base.[15] Additionally, as we invite a campus to maintain a common center of conversation about ideas and between persons, we need to remember that real people, not information machines, make such a commitment possible each day on the campus. Dialogically, the more we are committed to discussion of ideas, the more we need to respect persons.

It is possible to use information as a weapon when we interact with undergraduate students. A basic assumption of dialogic education is that the classroom is a place to offer information, insight, and interaction with students; it is not a place for faculty members to enhance their own self-worth while interacting with people who have studied the material only a short time. One faculty member, known for caustic comments to students, had one student in tears, deeply doubting her own ability. This A student began to question her own worth to the extent that she needed assurance that the professor might not have all the insight. The evaluations of her other professors and my own were validated when her "near perfect" G.R.E. scores returned. Indeed, we have all met the professor whose self-worth is tied less to learning or teaching than superiority over his best students. My contention is that this competitive style of interaction results in harm to both parties.

If people are abused in the process of learning, discussion will be stilted and curbed. Respecting persons on a campus of higher learning is a practical way of assuring a willingness to enter conversation with experts, risking the revealing of what one does not know. In other words, an environment where the person is recognized and viewed as significant is more likely to invite discussion than a place where persons are put down because their ideas may not fit some ideological formula or the general nature of a campus.

A relationship is invited when a teacher is able to call out the personhood of a student. The most important resource in dialogic education is the quality of teachers. Faculty need to be able to call students into a commitment to excellence by recognizing what those students are capable of accomplishing in the future. Dialogic education invites persons to be more than they may have originally thought possible. It is possible to work with good students and graduate great leaders when teachers model and demand hard work, discipline, and solid preparation.

The key to success with students, no matter what teaching style, is to urge students to be better than they themselves thought possible. Take for example, a dean who worked closely with students. He was able to actually change the life course of many students through his conversation with them. He did not tell them what to do; he listened, helped students search, and talked about some of the questions in his own life. He led not by telling, but by conversation about the difficulties and joys of a life journey. Such a teacher encourages ideas and discussion about ways people can still make a difference. It is not just what you learn, but also the quality of the person from which you learn. We are often inspired by interaction with a faculty member, whether inside or outside the classroom.

Relationships are built by teachers willing to meet students as persons capable of learning and offering insight. Several factors make a difference between an average learning environment and a great one—the quality of knowledge possessed by the faculty member, student willingness and ability to learn, time for conversation, and a willingness to call out the best in the persons in the classroom. All these factors contribute to the nurturing of relationships between student and faculty. The engine that propels this relational gathering around ideas is the individual person. It is the commitment of that person to conversation about ideas with students.

John Stewart defines the notion of person, suggesting that persons are unique and noninterchangeable; each person makes a difference in a conversation. Persons are unmeasurable and complex. We need to respect the mystery of others, recognizing that there is more to a person than the obvious public persona. A person needs to be given the opportunity for choice; when people consistently feel commanded they sense being manipulated as objects. Finally, persons are addressable, meaning a person needs to be talked to, not just about, and given the opportunity to respond.[16]

Treating students as unique, addressable choice makers is central to dialogic education. If we want a broad-based conversational circle, we need to treat people as persons who can make a difference and offer access to conversation about ideas. As Paulo Freire suggests, we need to call one another out as persons in education, for the hope of finding our humanity rests with our ability to recognize our interdependence in attempting to unfold or become more than we were before we entered the learning exchange.[17]

The Hebrew word *kabod* lends itself to a fuller understanding of the notion of person. *Kabod* is used to describe the power and presence of Yahweh. The term implies a sense of weight, presence, bearing, and dignity. A person with *kabod* makes a difference when he or she enters a group environment.[18] *Kabod* can be viewed as a nonadditive factor that enters an organization. A person of *kabod* makes a difference beyond the expected addition of one more person.

Another way of expressing the need for calling out a person in education is pointed to by Jacques Ellul. Ellul states that the latter part of the twentieth century has resulted in the eclipse of the self. Individual responsibility has been lessened—people no longer feel as if they can make a difference. He calls for people to try and make a difference without falling prey to unrealistic idealism.[19] Dialogic education still encourages people to make a difference with their unique abilities, but in order to make such a difference a person must work hard to continue to learn, understand, and implement information.

This notion of making a difference was present in an exchange between a first year faculty member and a chair with thirty years of experience. The chair denied the new faculty member professional studies travel money to a conference. The denial was based on concern that there was not enough direct connection between the faculty member's work and the conference. The faculty member challenged the decision based on the assumption that one person can and will make a difference. After much conversation between the faculty member, the chair, and the dean, the new faculty member received the professional travel money. At this concluding point, the chair made a suggestion for the future about the need for more clarity regarding the scholarly connection between conventions attended and research interests. The final decision between the new faculty member and the chair resulted in a commitment to encourage all to make a difference, even new faculty, and for the university to be more clear and public about some of its objectives. In spite of a painful process, the conclusion revealed that one could still make a difference on that campus.

One final example of making a difference centers on the *kabod* of Tom. Tom was hired by a department after the death of a long-term chair and leader. He kept before the department the importance of scholarship, commitment to students, and appreciation of the department's tradition. Tom's energy and confidence were gradually picked up by others. Publications, student evaluations of faculty, and departmental morale increased. When Tom discovered the department had just been ranked twelfth in the nation by an undergraduate evaluation agency, his response was, "I am lucky to be here with these people. Together we have made a difference."

Dialogic education offers an environment where *kabod* is respected and where people are encouraged to make a difference. Perhaps *kabod* can not be taught, but it can be invited and respected. Dialogic education is based on the premise that people can be invited to make a difference and that leadership looks for opportunities to encourage such action. Dialogic education is based on a hope that persons treated as unique choice makers can still make a difference in the advancement of learning and education.

Communication on Campus

Talking with one another about ideas, hopes, visions, and personal issues is a major component of dialogic education. James Lynch's book, *Language of the Heart: The Body's Response to Human Dialogue*, provides a vivid reminder of the importance of communication between people. "Human companionship does affect our hearts, and . . . there is reflected in our hearts a biological basis for our need for loving human relationships, which we fail to fulfill at our peril. . . . The ultimate decision is simple: we must either learn to live together or increase our chances of prematurely dying alone."[20]

A campus or a department not interested in dialogue may begin to die as the desire to go beyond perfunctory conversation with students is lost. A place where relationships are nourished by conversation both inside and outside the classroom permits persons to talk about the direction of their lives both personally and professionally. One might discover a direction for life through discussion of information, values, and relationships.

Quality of life is dependent on the interaction and communication that one initiates. Norman Cousins, well known for his work on communication and health and for editing *Saturday Re-*

view, makes an interesting point. When a physician can offer bad news in a way that encourages a personal challenge to beat the odds, the patient takes up the challenge and recovery or extended life beyond predictions is frequently possible. Quality of life is tied not only to hearing good news, but hearing bad news placed in a perspective that offers some chance of making a difference. The quality of communication between the physician and the patient is truly a matter of life and death.[21]

Perhaps we can view the success of dialogic education as dependent on the quality of communication between students and faculty; even the sharing of bad news has the chance of making a substantial impact that can assist growth if the student is willing to respond to the challenge. For example, one student was asked to leave a university because of low grades. The student stated his anger to a faculty member about his dismissal, only to be met with a final bit of education. The faculty member told him he had the ability to succeed if he wanted to put in the necessary time. What the student needed was the desire to stick to a task long enough to succeed. The student left the school, enrolled in a less demanding institution, and eventually completed his Ph.D. Upon acceptance of his first teaching position, the student called his former professor and offered thanks for a talk that gave him a chance to assume responsibility for his own education. Dialogic education can offer a sense of hope even when bad news is received. We must learn from all of life, the painful and comfortable experiences alike.

We need time and space for relationship building to take place. The dialogic educator needs to resist being just another hurried and busy person without enough time to think, talk, or dream together.

Time

As we attempt to provide time for building relationships with people and ideas, we need to be wary of ways in which the time of faculty and students is spent. Most of us who have taught for an extended period of time have seen students questioning how to use their time. They are sometimes tempted to be at so many of the evening and weekend activities on campus that they feel overextended and too tired to study.

Being involved in extracurricular activities is a worthy goal and should be encouraged. But like any good activity in life, it needs to be weighed against what is lost. Each day on a campus we place our time on a trading block; use of the limited resource of time in a frenzied effort to be relationally involved may end up being counterproductive for quality relationship development as well as study responsibilities.

Each day students and faculty alike might ask, Why am I on this campus? What is my task? It is possible to fall into an ironic trap of lessening time for study and relational learning as too much time is given to committee work and collective gatherings. Reinhold Niebuhr reminds us to keep a critical, somewhat detached, but not hostile stance to many activities. This avoids the irony of becoming so involved in activities that learning is less possible.[22] His philosophical warning is similar to advice that it is better to have had few experiences and to have learned from each, than to have had so many varied experiences that time for learning from them was not as possible.

All of us have met people who try to make relationships happen very quickly. Buber has called such behavior "the lust for overrunning reality."[23] Dialogic education encourages people to get to know one another over time, discouraging instant relationship development. Regardless of the size of a campus, one needs to recognize that time is needed for the stages of a relationship to mature.

Kathleen Reardon suggests that most of us go through typical stages of relationship development. First, people *initiate* relationships by engaging in small talk. One builds relationships by listening to others. Second, there is the *experimental* stage in which the partners begin to discover different things about one another; one begins to discover novel and interesting bits of information that encourage further exploration.

Third is the *intensifying* stage, when people discover similarities and differences between them. The new ideas can then be compared and contrasted with notions known before. Fourth, *integration* involves the development of a sense of "we-ness." The relationship begins to take on a character of its own, unique to the partners involved.

Finally, there is *bonding* when two people go through rituals and begin to develop a long-term relationship. These steps might suggest that a professional educator needs to go through a ritual which introduces her or him to an academic field of study. Being knowledgeable about ideas in a given academic area requires various steps of approval, from the granting of a degree to response to teaching and scholarship, as one enters not only into information possession, but professional responsibility.[24] In essence, it takes time to develop a relationship with a person and with ideas of merit.

In an early article, I wrote about the danger of the "hurried professor."[25] It is possible to want to move so fast in the building of a career that quality time to think and reflect becomes less of a priority. This same danger can occur as we push students to learn too much too quickly. Take for example, the professor who proudly requires undergraduate students to read fifteen books in a course. But the students actually only skim the material in order to keep up with other classes. It is possible to support standards with significant demands on students without confusing quality with quantity. A philosopher, when asked how much he had read, stated that he had not read a great deal, but he had thought about each work he had read. Education cannot be measured solely by the quantity of work demanded. We need quality time that permits us to understand the material.

At many universities, honors students are required to do more work than other students. I have sometimes questioned the wisdom of such requirements. An honors program that requires more quantity does not necessarily provide a better educational environment. As one student remarked, "I want to think and talk about the material, but the professor seems more intent on setting a record for how much quantity he can cover in one semester." More time might be devoted to questioning and scholarly discussion if quantity was not such a major motivator, at least in the case of this particular professor. In the honors setting, we should expect a higher preparation level and assignment completion level, which should encourage more discussion of ideas in the classroom, but the demand for more quantity can be debated.

The importance of time to converse with one another about the significance of ideas, the value of a particular theory, the mission of a college, or one's role as a future professional is central to the fundamental core of dialogic education. To think and talk about ideas together requires good stewardship of time by the faculty, the students, and the administration.

Each year departments are asked to submit their budget requests, then stay within the approved limits as they make purchases the next year. Would it not be interesting if a similar request could be made for faculty time? The administration could budget a year in advance what committees will be needed and what issues will need to be explored, leaving room for genuinely expected problems and issues that require committee participation. This protection of time would necessitate an estimated budgeting of how much time would be spent on committee work the next year. It is unfair to ask the faculty to budget fiscal resources and not be sensitive to budgeting time.

Bertrand Russell reminds us that "philosophers, accordingly, have sought, with great persistence, for something not subject to the empire of Time."[26] An environment that encourages conversation about ideas and relationship development needs to provide the time to discuss ideas with one another. Paul Ricoeur, in his three volume examination of time and narrative, discusses Augustine's threefold view of time. In analyzing a quotation from Augustine, Ricoeur suggests the following: "The theme of this entire paragraph is the dialectic of expectation, memory, and attention, each considered no longer in isolation but in interaction with one another."[27] To have an expectation, to reflect on a memory, and to focus on an idea all require time, an expensive commodity. Ricoeur reminds us that time is not just a linear measurement, but a quality that permits the interaction of attention, expectation, and memory. Without such an interactive combination, we do not have time, rather we have quantities of moments. Time, as pointed out above, has both a quantitative and a qualitative dimension.

Let us take some liberty with Ricoeur's material and adapt such a view of time (expectation, memory, and attention) into a discussion appropriate to what can happen in dialogic education. Expectation is set by the learning environment present on campus. What signals do we give that quality communication and relationships are important for the encouragement of faculty to talk to students about ideas? Such a goal may be accomplished by protecting time to reflect on ideas together. A student and a faculty member should not be made to feel guilty about taking time to talk about ideas. Work at a university is not just tied to teaching, committee work, and research. The total environment is affected by what people talk about and how they interact together with available time.

Memory can be tied to what Robert Bellah in *Habits of the Heart* calls a "community of memory."

> We can speak of a real community as a 'community of memory,' one that does not forget its past. In order not to forget that past, a community is involved in retelling its story, its constitutive narrative, and in so doing, it offers examples of the men and women who have embodied and exemplified the meaning of the community.

> These stories of collective history and exemplary individuals are an important part of the tradition that is so central to a community of memory.
>
> The stories that make up a tradition contain conceptions of character, of what a good person is like, and of the virtues that define such character. But the stories are not all exemplary, not all about successes and achievements. A genuine community of memory will also tell painful stories of shared suffering that sometimes creates deeper identities than success. . . . The communities of memory that tie us to the past also turn us toward the future as communities of hope. They carry a context of meaning that can allow us to connect our aspirations to a larger whole and see our own efforts as being, in part, contributions to a common good.[28]

A community of memory is a tradition whose past continues to guide its future. We invite students into a community of memory as we offer conversation, relationship, and our time. Memory is built on concrete learning and moments together. In addition, an earlier theme in this work, knowing the mission of a campus or department, is applicable here. Knowing who we are and where we are going takes time. No community of memory is developed by osmosis; only through long involvement with one another can such a memory guide, direct, and offer a base from which change can be considered.

The final notion involved in time is attention. To be attentive requires a reflective environment where people are encouraged to think and consider consequences before acting. Alasdair MacIntyre critiqued the notion of emotivism as a danger in the twentieth century. In brief, emotivism involves making judgments from individual affective standards.[29] Emotivism moves us away from standards that are public and open for others to discuss and attack into privatized standards of excellence. Bernstein makes the point that a major contribution of the Enlightenment and objectivity was to bring standards into public view. Even as Bernstein critiqued the notion of objectivity, he applauded the effort of bringing standards into the public arena of debate.

Attention requires us to bring standards into public view and to question privatized efforts of emotivism or other individual efforts at decision making. Attention is needed as we bring issues into public debate and conversation. Time on a campus committed to dialogic education requires us to have an expectation about a learning environment, a community of memory, attention, and a commitment to relational support of one another.[30]

Space

Teaching within a dialogic education framework is facilitated not only by a willingness to take time to meet people, but by places that make meeting for conversation possible. Russell Jacoby, in *The Last Intellectuals,* offers a lament that can be taken as an indictment of many campuses where physical places to meet and discuss ideas are not readily present. "When Henry Pfachter, a refugee from Nazism and once a devotee of Berlin cafes, taught college in the United States, he bemoaned that 'there were not coffeehouses—and college cafeterias are notoriously unconducive to talk.' "[31] Quality relationships with people and ideas generated outside the classroom need to be nurtured by structures that invite conversation. Coming together over coffee to discuss ideas not only encourages an intellectual environment, but invites relationships that can bond together faculty and students.

Ernest L. Boyer states that buildings and space utilization reflect our priorities. He reminds us that "life is made tolerable by the shared remembrances, and sense of community on campus."[32] He discovered that on undergraduate campuses only 20 percent of the faculty feel a sense of loyalty to the campus, and 70 percent professed more affinity for their own academic discipline. A majority of the students said they felt like numbers in a book, and one faculty member summarized the feeling on one campus as follows: "My community is the WATS line, not my colleagues down the hall."[33]

Certainly an emphasis on space cannot solve the problem of lack of community on campus. But without places for people to gather, the creation of a supportive environment is less likely. How space is used and made available on campus is both a symbolic and practical result of resource allocation. Taking time and finding spaces for conversation can actually alter the functional result of the time spent together. Edward Hall, known for his intercultural work in nonverbal communication, discusses the difference between monochronic and polychronic time. In brief, monochronic persons are governed by schedule and one issue at a time, while polychronic persons are interested in people and have an ability to get more than one task completed at a time.[34] Space to converse with students can permit polychronic use of time in which relationships, idea development, professional modeling, and at times even friendship can be worked on simultaneously.

When I was asked what was significant about my own undergraduate education, I stated that conversation with my professors and fellow students outside the classroom was central to my overall education. Time and space are not just luxuries in dialogic education; they are foundational components for a teacher interested in educating both inside and outside the classroom structure, permitting relationships between students and teachers to naturally mature and develop.

Rubbing Shoulders

Dialogic education is not for all people. Some of us do not want to invite a conversational and relational form of education; it is important to respect moments of solitude. When we put a high priority on relationship, we need to also give opportunities for distance.[35]

The former University of Chicago president, Robert Hutchins, offered a reminder of the importance of talking with others at the university that is still on target today.

> The task of intellectual leadership now is to bring about a genuine communion of minds . . . . One of the things most often proposed as a step toward communion of minds is international co-operation in science, art, and scholarship. Although such co-operation should be promoted, it would not do much to establish a community within a university, or within a country, or throughout the world. A scholar in one country can now communicate with another scholar in the same field anywhere in the West. He is usually incapable of communicating with a scholar in another field on his own campus.[36]

There are varied opinions on what Hutchins' career meant to higher education, but even some who question the extent of his contribution affirm that he was able to generate enthusiasm, interest, and a willingness to learn among students. He communicated that education was important and worthy of reflection and talk.[37] Hutchins dreamed of and tried to implement a form of dialogic education where scholars could talk to students within and across disciplines. A relational, supportive environment lessens the risk level for a student encountering unknown faculty and new ideas, as well as other students. The relational orientation of a dialogic educator needs to pass a commonsense test—does the relationship between student and faculty assist the learning?

Dialogic education involves a notion that some have called "personalism."[38] Persons are central to the process of such an education and fundamental to why we learn. In answer to Ellul's concern stated earlier that people do not feel as if they can make a difference, dialogic education offers a contrasting vision. One of the major values of dialogic education is that it signals the importance of students as persons, pointing to a hope that learning and working together can make a difference in the human community.

PART 4

Dialogic Leadership

8

Dialogic Influence: Persuasion and Choice

Democracy in America—

If there is a country in the world where the doctrine of the sovereignty of the people can be fairly appreciated, where it can be studied in its application to the affairs of society, and where its dangers and its advantages may be judged, that country is assuredly America.

> Alexis de Tocqueville,
> *Democracy in America*

A dialogic ethic of persons—

[We need to] . . . relate to each other as persons (unique, capable of choice, having feelings, being of inherent worth, and self-reflective) rather than as objects or things (interchangeable, measurable, responding automatically to stimuli, and lacking self-awareness).

> Richard L. Johannesen,
> *Ethics in Human Communication*

Dialogic influence requires us to relate to others as choice makers, offering a relational context for influence and persuasion. A dialogic educator takes a position and works to get others to follow, while permitting ideas to be tested, modified, and even rejected. Dialogic influence is a communication approach more interested in the other's personhood and in finding the best solution for a given problem at a given time than in personal winning of an argument. Such a view is consistent with the pursuit of truth, not the propagation of a particular ideological position.

139

Dialogic influence works to nourish conversation between opponents, making conversation possible after an argument has ceased. Dialogic influence has a long-term bias; success or failure on a single issue is not as important as facilitating conversation with an opponent now and in the future. When this long-range perspective is forsaken, we open the door to the clashing of personal agendas and narrow ideologies.

Sissela Bok warns of the danger of partisanship in decision making. Working from an ideological position that has clear boundaries around one's own camp or position and excludes other thinking is dangerous.[1] One of the goals of democratic decision making is to limit the influence of partisanship by bringing multiple positions into the public arena. Partisanship can give way to a revolutionary ethic, where people matter little and the cause is primary,[2] unless concern for people as well as ideas guides action.

Dialogic education seeks a blend of democracy and a dialogic attitude of concern for persons. As we have witnessed in recent local and national campaigns, a democratic election can be based on personality assassination and misleading use of information about an opponent. Opponent bashing has become so prevalent that it is hard to decide what positive ideals some candidates actually uphold. In some cases the campaign is based on the inadequacies of one's opponent, not one's own ideas and positions. However, a democratic environment with a dialogic thrust seeks to discover what is best by vote, while working to maintain relational connections with the opposition. The key to understanding dialogic influence is the combination of democratic and dialogic values of personhood. In an earlier work, I referred to democracy as a procedural ethic that offered a structure that would guarantee voice, at least through voting. "The following concepts and metaphors are representative of this approach: democracy, self-determination, linking democracy and conscious rational choice, debate and open discussion, freedom of dissent, cooperative controversy, democracy as a methodology for discussion, and recognition of the value of diversity of opinion."[3] The notion of dialogue brings three elements to this discussion of democracy as a procedural ethic. First, there is the importance of position; for dialogue to begin, parties need to know their respective positions and articulate them clearly. Second, the positions need to be open to testing and modification. And finally, a respect for persons needs to accompany any testing or disagreement. Combining a democratic and dialogic orientation into what I am calling dialogic influence requires the protection of three basic components: public, agreed upon procedure for decision making; opportunities for positions to be taken and tested; and consistent respect for persons.

Founders of our democratic nation, such as Thomas Jefferson, made it clear that the power of a democracy depends on representative participation in the ongoing decision making of a community. As campuses become more pluralistic, there will be greater need for such participation on campus committees and in decision making. With this, we need to continue reminding one another that we come together on a campus of higher learning to teach and to learn—everything else needs to facilitate such responsibilities.

The narrow ridge in this chapter necessitates a balance between two extremes: ignoring the importance of participation in decision making on campus and becoming so involved in campus politics that teaching and scholarship begin to take a back seat to efforts at campus influence. Dialogic influence is simply a way of increasing the quality of education on a campus. We need to give clear messages that such participation is needed, while encouraging one another to be wary of becoming intoxicated with political life on campus.

Max Wise suggests that the shift from authoritative and religious domination on some campuses to more professional and scholarly faculty will necessitate more, not less, faculty participation in the life of the campus. Wise's statement is hardest on presidential leadership and administrations of undergraduate colleges where faculty input is not routinely sought.

> This study has confirmed the common observation that collegiate government is in a state of disarray and is ineffective in several important regards. However, causes for ineffective college government do not lie—as some would argue—in the presence of obstreperous students and uninterested faculty on the campus but rather in the failure of the private college to adapt to modern conditions of society and the scholarly world.[4]

Democratic participation offers an opportunity for core leaders of an institution to introduce new people to the unique contributions of the university. Participation in decision making has philosophical and educational value as campuses mature and develop more professional connections to academic disciplines and the scholarly world.

The following quotation offers a view of what this democratic atmosphere of decision making provides on campus.

Democratic education supplies the foundations upon which a democratic society can secure the civil and political freedoms of the adult citizens without placing their welfare or its very survival at great risk. In the absence of democratic education, risks—perhaps even great risks—will still be worth taking for the sake of respecting the actual preferences of citizens, but the case for civic and political freedom and against paternalism is weaker in a society whose citizens have been deprived of an adequate education (although not as weak as Mill suggested). Democracy thus depends on democratic education for its full moral strength.[5]

Learning the process of influence permits faculty and students to use official campus committees as laboratories for dialogic education. Dialogic education is based on the assumption that civil participation in decision making can increase the quality of the educational environment.

Dialogic influence rests on the assumption that respecting others is important. Efforts to win at any cost or attempts to alter perception by personality assassination may work as some pursue election to a government office, but these methods violate the relational nature of dialogic education. In addition, dialogic influence assumes that democratic procedure is only one avenue for discussion. If and when political interests of a campus become so dominant that the primary common center, conversation about ideas and between persons, is drowned out by political fighting, then the core of dialogic education is put at risk. A faculty member interested in dialogic education needs to be wary of shortcuts that lessen the personhood of another or that center professional identity more around politics than inquiry. A campus will have politics, but it is not another house of representatives; rather it is a home of inquiry and concern for helping the next generation of leaders and scholars.

De Tocqueville's View—Ideals in Tension

Alexis de Tocqueville's comments on democracy in America remind us how unique the democratic experiment was and is. The 1989 student demonstrations in China revealed, once again, the novelty and importance of democratic rights that we can too easily take for granted. As I talked to students from China who had relatives struggling for democratic rights, I was repeatedly struck by how I take this procedural ethic for granted. A number of

Chinese intellectuals interested in democratic reforms for their country paid the ultimate price for advocating their dream.

De Tocqueville contended that the American Dream was composed of two competing factors: first, individual success; and second, commitment to a place and a group of people, which this book has called an academic home. The ability to feel individually successful is dependent on hard work, education, and good fortune. But without commitment to community, we are left with the possibility of excess resulting from individual achievement. Commitment to others keeps the emphasis on individual achievement under control. Individual achievement keeps a community from becoming too smug and complacent, thinking that all that is needed has already been found in the community.

The twofold vision of the American Dream detailed by de Tocqueville, when applied to dialogic education, calls on a faculty member to be committed to the profession (one significant measure of individual achievement) as well as to relationships within the university (commitment to a community). Dialogic education assumes the importance of a faculty member having one leg in one's discipline and the other in commitment and service to one's home college or university. The competing commitments of individual achievement and community building need to be held in creative tension with one another, both working to moderate and limit the excesses of the other.

The American Dream requires us to have a commitment to others through participation in collective efforts at persuasion and open discussion with students. Practical efforts at persuasion on the campus and democratic decision making within a dialogic spirit are an important part of an American effort to "overcome that separation of the American intellect from practical affairs."[6]

However, as I emphasize throughout this chapter, without a dialogic concern for relational well-being of one another on a campus, the chance for dialogic influence will be bypassed for excessive political pressure and maneuvering. Perhaps we could surmise that de Tocqueville would have wanted a university of ambition and concern for others in the home institution, where opposing tensions are pulled together in a creative fashion and, I would add, in an environment respectful of persons.

Thomas R. Nilsen states that "how we make up our minds" in a democracy is as important as what we decide. He suggests that time be made available to discuss issues, persuade one another, and to invite choice making whenever possible.[7] Dialogic influence involves democratic efforts at persuasion, reminding us, as Lincoln did in his Gettysburg address, of the importance of the people and ideals.[8] Persuasion grounded in dialogue takes the personhood of others seriously, working to contribute to conversation about ideas on the campus and attempting to minimize the proliferation of ideologically narrow political pressure groups.

Keeping the Conversation Going

Efforts at persuasion keep the conversation going on a university campus with a system known and understood by the participants. Richard Fenno, in his study of congressional committees, began with the assumption that committees matter.[9] Such a straightforward way of examining congressional committees is more insightful than it may at first appear. Any participatory decision making structure needs to be taken seriously; one needs to attach importance to corporate decision making in order for such group activity to be effective. If we believe in what we do, the quality of collective decisions will be enhanced.

Loyalty to an organization can be enhanced and productivity assisted when people know the formal channels of persuasion and how to use them. Participatory decision making that follows a predictable public process of input, debate, and recommendation can strengthen academic management and faculty leadership.

The following is a reminder of the potential vitality that can come from the diffusion of power within multiple levels at the university. University governance on many campuses is more vibrant than some outside the university setting would understand or perhaps admit.

> Academic institutions tend to diffuse power. Many managerial decisions are made at the department, school, or college level. In the spirit of collegiality, or shared governance, most significant institutional decisions are made in conjunction with faculty. Indeed, based on the precedent established by the U. S. Supreme Court in *National Labor Relations Board v. Yeshiva University* (1980), the NLRB has determined that faculty at several independent colleges are more akin to manager than employees and thus not eligible to bargain collectively. Trustees wary of collegiality might be reassured somewhat by observing the currency now attached in the corporate sector to participatory, or Japanese management style.[10]

Participation in persuasion and decision making is not only good for education and loyalty to a campus, but also has the potential of increasing commitment and the quality of campus contribution.

It is clear that not all colleges or universities are willing to take the step into participatory decision making. Decisions at some schools are lodged in the hands of just a few leaders, resulting in the disempowerment of many people in the community.[11] In some cases, the erosion of faculty participation and morale has occurred.

> Faculty involvement in all decision-making has declined. Faculty participation in governance structures has declined over recent years, and faculty governance structures spend their time on matters of less than critical importance. This decline in the level of participation has affected morale. Even in time of difficult decisions, morale will be bolstered by faculty involvement.
>
> . . . to offset the negative effects on faculty perception of their autonomy and job satisfaction requires addressing the necessary issues of accountability . . . [involving] faculty directly in the study of and promulgation of regulations for professional conduct. The more faculty participate in the decisions, the more likely they will accept them.[12]

Dialogic education needs to encourage faculty and administration to offer an environment that is person-sensitive and inquiry-centered.

The above discussion reminds us that the old way of doing things, involving faculty participation, being respectful to one's colleagues, and recognizing the unique role of the university as a place of learning may not be anachronistic after all. Such awareness may be a new trend in business management, but an old idea on the university campus. John J. Corson, in an early statement on governance, makes it clear that authoritarian models do not work well on the college campus and a leader needs to recognize the difference between a business environment motivated by profit and a college concerned about educating young people for leadership.[13]

The dialogic influence model is essentially a collegial model where faculty and administration are committed to a common task, offering the finest education possible within given limits of a campus. It seems that we are moving farther from this objective, and toward a business model, further delineating the difference between faculty and administration. As Freire suggested, dialogue will not work in an environment where images of oppressor and oppressed dominate.[14] For many, the only hope of dialogic influence is within the department or with a small cadre of learners. I lament this solidifying of ideological supporters, which I believe has negative impact on morale and productivity on campuses. It is possible to have participatory decision making in polarized environments between faculty and administration. But the temptation is for members of each group to lose respect for the other, objectifying persons into preconceived views of their roles.

The difficult decisions that must be made by leaders of our institutions of higher learning are more likely to succeed when all parties on a campus work toward some collective task and commitment to an institution. The university is in a time of change, facing strained budgets, large numbers of retiring faculty, and basic questions about the curriculum.

> There are perhaps 700 colleges and universities, nearly one fourth of the total, where faculty, administrative, and constituency leadership recognizes that the characteristics of the nation's culture in the next ten to twenty years will affect the character and activities of institutions of higher education. They will see that changes in society necessitate changes on campus, that colleges for a new culture cannot be stagnant.[15]

Bringing people together on campus for conversation and debate and understanding the procedure in which decisions are made is necessary for institutional planning and policy as we enter unchartered territory. Again, as we offer opportunity for persuasion and a chance for ideas to be considered, the importance of personhood and common center of inquiry need to be upheld. We must be cautious that we do not limit awareness of new positions and turn the campus into a political home of ideological propaganda campaigns.

The views of faculty, administration, staff, and students will not always be in agreement. Governance does not ensure agreement, but simply offers a procedure for persuasion. Our task is to search for the common good, as outlined by the American Association of University Professors in 1940. "Institutions of higher education are conducted for the common good and not to further the interest of either the individual teacher or the institution as a whole."[16] We must do our best as professionals to facilitate the common good of a campus and higher education in general, being wary of efforts that coincide too closely with the vested interest of individual ideology. Perhaps a commonsense rule of thumb might be to ask whether or not our action has contributed to quality education for the campus and the larger commitment to higher education, or has our work been motivated solely by personal gain?

All of us on a campus need to be reminded that the notion of the common good is generally larger than our individual concerns. Many decisions on a campus reflect concerns that will not be of direct interest or benefit to us. But the common good does include both oneself and others. If we can work to assist the quality of a department, campus, and higher education in general, we will benefit as faculty. Such a view of benefit has a long-term character. Dialogic educators attempt to take into account not only those present, but the tradition present before we came to a campus and possibilities needed for the next generation. Our responsibility is not just for now, but for shaping of the future. Decisions carry a concern not just for us, but for those that will follow and for the community of memory generated by those who laid intellectual grounding on the campus years earlier.

Governance Caution

Values, relationships, and participatory decision making on a campus are very important. Each university has a culture—some focus primarily on research, others on students, and yet others on participatory decision making and faculty input. Dialogic education is less probable when excess concentration on anything other than conversation about ideas and between persons becomes dominant. Perhaps a rule of thumb for evaluating when such an orientation has gotten out of hand would involve three questions: Is status achieved on the campus by being a teacher/scholar or a member of committees? Is committee work viewed as a professional service, an act of a campus citizen, or as the most enjoyable part of one's job? And is committee work done primarily to help a campus or department home or to protect turf and lessen the influence of others? When the pursuit of helping the common good and respecting of colleagues gives way to political posturing and manipulation, the chance for dialogic influence diminishes.

Generally, each good idea is a double-edged sword. The positive attributes of participatory decision making involve the importance of involvement and persuasion in idea generation and policy making, modeling participation in a democratic society—the message of John Dewey. In addition, as de Tocqueville stated, participation can offer a feeling of importance, of being a part of a community, or a home campus.[17] With the positive characteristics

in mind, however, there are four potential concerns about participatory decision making.

Sociocultural Role Violation

This phrase suggests that it is possible for us to forget what
we were hired to do. Most undergraduate campuses evaluate
teaching, scholarship, and service in that order of importance.
Each of the three elements is of significant importance to the life
of a campus. It is dangerous for future generations of students
when faculty take too much time from teaching and scholarship
and become more concerned about campus service. From a dialogic
perspective, participatory governance is a means to facilitate
teaching and scholarship, not a goal in itself.

As we take persuasion and opinions on a campus seriously,
we should keep in mind that not all campus decisions can or should
be decided by majority vote. Sometimes those in decision-making
and accountability roles need to forge ahead with a course of
action, leaving the debate still unresolved. One of the basic myths
about communication is that we will always be able to come to
agreement if we just take enough time to talk out our differences.
A similar myth was dispelled by a group of human conflict scholars, who concluded that the term *conflict management* more accurately reflected human experience than *conflict resolution*. In
short, communication cannot resolve all differences and some differences will be no more than manageable.

Participation in decision making involves multiple constitu-
encies who offer input, but not necessarily final decision-making
power. Dialogic education seeks input from a variety of contributors on campus, encouraging an active decision-making process.
But there needs to be a willingness to permit decision makers to
make a final decision. One faculty member did not get his way on
a computer decision; seven years later he is just as angry and
unwilling to permit anyone in an appropriately designated role to
make a decision without invoking his ire. Even if the decision was
not the best decision, seven years is a long time to remain angry.
In that time another line of computers had been introduced. As I
have discussed with my daughter about softball, the umpire may
not always be right, but without someone calling balls and strikes
we are left playing a form of sandlot softball, where everyone is a
rule maker. Martin Buber and Carl Rogers discussed the importance of roles, with Buber emphasizing the importance of recognizing the different demands of various sociocultural role obliga-

tions.[18] Buber called for a democratic understanding of roles based on expertise and flow of information. He was opposed to roles based on aristocratic birthright and connections. Rejecting an aristocratic understanding of roles should not lead us to the conclusion that a functional view of roles should be ignored in a large organizational structure. Roles defined by function suggest that information flow makes one a designated decision maker in certain settings.

Permitting input does not eliminate the need for different functional roles on a campus. The way a functional view of role is played out on a campus requires faculty or committee input and general acceptance of a decision by the person or committee in the functional decision-making role. We need to follow decisions made by persons in functional decision-making roles, unless the decision is so far off from our professional and ethical beliefs that we cannot possibly permit such a position to direct us. We need to discourage one another from becoming people who hold anger over a professional decision for seven years, unable to permit an organization to move on and for one's own life to be stimulated by new and perhaps even more important ventures.[19]

Too Much Governance

A teacher/scholar model can be pushed aside when concentration is given to the community in which one lives. A sectarian flavor, where the world of significance seems to stop at the end of the campus map, can become dominant. Even though I consider an academic home very significant, it is possible to expect the home institution to provide more support and reward than it can offer. When faculty are grouped together, one must realize an important and humbling fact—being the best on one campus may not be such a major accomplishment compared to the number of professionals regionally and nationally.

Not all undergraduate institutions committed to teaching actually believe that great teaching provides status on the campus. When scholarship is not a major expectation beyond teaching, status is often equated with the committee service. When rewards for involvement in the committee structure are very significant, committee work ceases to be a service to the community and begins to enhance individual status—competing with and even, at times, outmaneuvering teaching and scholarship as primary missions of a campus.

One colleague, considered a great teacher, was demoralized

each year during campus elections. His name never seemed to reach the final ballot in major committee elections. Perhaps lack of political skills keeps him out of the running and the campus ethos of committee participation. My comment to him was that when most of the committees are forgotten and work completed, his students will remember and be influenced by his time and effort.

Perhaps a campus centered on conversation about ideas is healthy when the faculty model participation in committee decision making out of professional service, but with reluctance— being cautious about giving up time as a teacher/scholar. It is possible to be too willing and too eager to give up teacher/scholar time to join a committee. Like any good act in life, we need to seek a balance between too little and too much. Either extreme can harm a campus environment.

Ignoring the Academic "Home"

Not only can we misuse participatory decision making, we must also reject the other extreme: refusing to be involved in any campus decision making. A campus that encourages persuasion and debate works with the assumption that involvement in social leadership and decision making is a major key to the success and strength of the campus.[20] There is an awareness that faculty often reap what they sow. If faculty and administrators do not watch over the curriculum the campus can too easily become a business sensitive to customers and forgetful of the first and primary mission: education of students for leadership in professions and communities.

Philip Slater warned of the dangers of the "do your own thing" movement. While some were out "doing their own thing," those in charge of the board rooms made the decisions and marched the country forward.[21] Faculty must not give up their right to input, particularly in today's competitive marketplace of higher education, where there is a temptation to take steps to market programs that may, in the long run, decrease the quality of education on a campus. In essence, without some involvement in decision making, faculty give up the right to shape and to critique the development of a campus.

Too Much Management

The administration may want to lessen faculty decision making, as some colleges move to a corporate/managerial model. A managerial model attempts to increase the productive life of the campus by augmenting the visible results of the work of a faculty, which may be permissible until the increased emphasis on output results in a lessening of input from various faculty committees. Dialogic education transpires not only in the classroom; it also takes place in the committees where we work and discuss the direction of a campus.

A campus environment can offer decision making concerned not just with results, but with the correspondence between the mission and actions of a campus. Warren Bennis says that a "manager" is concerned about results, but a "leader" sets the tone and the pace for excellence.[22] Academic leaders work to establish an environment where excellence is pursued. Concern for the environment of excellence permits the leader to see value, not just in results, but to foster enthusiasm for campus life and commitment to life as a teacher/scholar.

Therefore, four different problems need to be watched in a quality faculty decision-making environment: rejecting the need for functional decision making roles, viewing faculty status as more closely tied to committee work than that of a competent teacher/scholar, underestimating the importance of persuasion in determining the direction of a campus, and recent administrative fascination with business management over educational leadership. The above concerns reflect a need to balance the extremes of excess (too much emphasis on faculty interest in decision making) and deficiency (too little regard for the viewpoint of faculty by the administration). With the above cautions in mind, it is possible to offer a view of faculty decision making that rests between those extremes.

Participatory Decision Making and Dialogue on the Campus

As the influence of perceived legitimate authorities on some of our campuses has lessened, the importance of a democratic spirit of participation has increased. William James, known for his commitment to both tough-minded science and tender-minded human issues, offers a synthesis of an attitude that might assist in combining participation in decision making and dialogue on a campus. We need to be tough in following known rules on a campus, while keeping in mind that the objective is to encourage an environment of inquiry.

James developed a "strenuous alternative to both pessimism and optimism, the genuine mediation he called 'meliorism.'" To James, "the world stands really malleable, waiting to receive its final touches at our hands. Like the kingdom of heaven, it suffers human violence willingly, Man *engenders* truth upon it." The obstacles to shaping the world beneficently, to engendering humanly valuable truth on it, are formidable, of course. Not the least of these obstacles are human beings themselves. But all in all for James, the call to transform the world—to help save it—is both a noble vocation and a personally healthy and invigorating adventure.[23]

Participation in decision making and input needs to keep in mind the difficulty of change and the importance of a rhetorical vision that supports conversation about ideas and the importance of persons as its primary charter.

This conversational view of decision making with a dialogic base has a threefold purpose: to get tasks and jobs completed, to model participation in the democratic decision-making process, and to socialize people to the values of an institution. If an administrator believes in the educational value of participatory democracy, he or she has two major tasks—putting forth ideas and responding to requests through known channels of conversation, and being willing to lose on an issue or an idea in order to keep the channels of debate open and clear. The best ideas change, but the importance of searching for such ideas remains a key in dialogic education. In addition, and perhaps most importantly, an administrator interested in dialogic education cannot ask for participation and then not take input seriously. Such pseudoparticipation can generate cynicism.

Participation of faculty and students working on committees and through known channels of debate can remind us of the importance of listening, generating a clear and organized case, and knowing the procedures through which decisions are made in a democratic culture. Each major decision-making task accomplished through known structures offers an opportunity to be reminded of the mission of the college or university and to model the means of decision making by those committed to conversation about ideas.

Good ideas that involve a major policy shift are less likely to survive when members of a faculty are not provided opportunities for consultation and debate. Practically speaking, concealing information is likely to be met with resistance, if not outright hostility. Such action forfeits the opportunity for an administration to test an idea.

Thomas I. Emerson, a major scholar on the First Amendment, provides us with helpful insight into the need to remind one another of the importance of freedom of expression and inquiry. "Further, as already observed, the theory of freedom of expression is a sophisticated and even complex one. It does not come naturally to the ordinary citizen but needs to be learned. It must be restated and reiterated not only for each generation but for each new situation."[24]

Democracy with a dialogic attitude creates a decision-making structure that Clark Kerr called a "conservative institution with a dynamic environment."[25] The conservative nature of democratic governance involves conserving the importance of discussion and debate while being willing to change ideas and actions if persuaded.

An effective faculty manual should clarify the roles of faculty, chairs, deans, vice-president of academic affairs, and president, as well as departments and committees, in hiring, promotion, tenure, curriculum, and decision making in general. The dynamic nature of a campus needs to be nourished. The conservative contribution is the decision-making structure, which attempts to conserve an environment hospitable for debate and interaction.

When change occurs on a university or college campus, it is most likely to succeed when a decision-making structure is already in place, assuring input though faculty, chairs, committees, and deans. Such an environment limits the possibility of power misuse or idea implementation without faculty consideration. Knowing how to gain access to input through existing decision-making structures permits the dynamic process of testing new ideas.

A Dialogic Environment for Decision Making

A dialogic environment for influence and decision making requires three basic elements: a habit of inquiry; a commitment to the social dimension of education; and a willingness to place a high priority on relationships, as well as intellectual positions.

The Habit of Inquiry

The habituation of inquiry involves a democratic environment that encourages conversation about ideas, and fosters an atmosphere of discussion. Karl Wallace, known for his work in democratic issues of free speech and persuasion, detailed the characteristics necessary for keeping conversation going in a democratic environment. First, there needs to be a "habit of search" that encourages people to explore multiple sides of an issue. Second, people should be expected to present information fairly and justly, modeling a "habit of justice." Third, it is important to discuss biases and information sources honestly, displaying a "habit of preferring public to private motivations." Open discussion of motives lessens the possibility of hidden agendas that can lessen trust. Finally, Wallace suggests a need to respect diversity and difference of opinion, forming a "habit of respect for dissent."[26]

One additional habit that I would add to Wallace's contribution is outlined in chapter 2: civility. The work of Harold Barrett, *Rhetoric and Civility: Human Development, Narcissism, and the Good Audience*, offers further insight on the notion of civility. He suggests the importance of rhetorical detachment that does not confuse decision making with one's own self-worth. In the case of participatory decision making a campus can pursue a direction contrary to one's own vote and wishes without demeaning one's own self. "The civil person recognizes that situations outside the self and the demands of self are distinct and separable. Common patterns of civil behavior are acts of 'persuading, soliciting, consulting, advising, bargaining, compromising, coalition building, and so on'—as opposed to 'such forms of behavior as coercing, confronting, deceiving, manipulating,' etc."[27]

Barrett outlines eight characteristics to assist in keeping participatory decision making civil: "awareness" of self and other, the "will" to play a part in shaping the environment, "respect" for self and others, "courage" to act, "ability" to do the job that is needed, being capable of acting "independently" when needed, willingness to foster an atmosphere of "freedom," and "responsibility" to do one's part.[28]

A university should explore multiple sides of an issue with fairness, public/private congruence, respect for dissent, and a commitment to civility. Dialogic influence rejects short-term strategies of direct or indirect personality assassination. The quality of an educational environment is won as much by a culture of support as it is by its innovation and change. A university needs to be a place where ideas can still win the day, without bashing an opponent. In a world that is increasingly interested in interpersonal style and intimidation, we need places where ideas can still have a major impact.

Just as any good taken too far can become a wrong, civility

taken to the extreme of insincere charm will be destructive to a campus. A decision-making structure needs to minimize the emphasis on personality and maximize a focus on information. The postscript to Bennis' book *Why Leaders Cannot Lead* makes this point well. "Now we believe that success is based in our personality alone. If we can please other people, we will succeed. Instead of working at work, we work on our personalities. Instead of being good at what we do, we opt for charm.[29] Respect for ideas and persons needs to be the foundation of decision making to uphold the ideal of dialogic education. But our commitment to both inquiry and people needs to be genuine, or we bring to a campus superficial idea examination, where style and charm are expected to reign over substance and hard work.

Decision making that involves the collective wisdom of the faculty may help us steer clear of some of the pitfalls pointed to by Andrei D. Sakharov.

> Nothing threatens freedom of the personality and the meaning of life like war, poverty, terror. . . . [But educationally such important societal goods can be lost by] excessive standardization, extending to the teaching process itself, to the curriculum, especially in literature, history, civics, geography, and the system of examinations.
>
> One cannot but see a danger in excessive reference to authority and in the limitation of discussion and intellectual boldness at an age when personal convictions are beginning to be formed. In the old China, the systems of examinations for official positions led to mental stagnation and to the canonizing of the reactionary aspects of Confucianism. It is highly undesirable to have anything like that in a modern society.[30]

The above statement from Sakharov is an important reminder that persuasion is needed, particularly as education faces the era of increased accountability, assessment, management by objectives, and evaluation of goals.

The Social Dimension of Education

Being together is an unofficial part of the governance structure, in that committees tend to be a social outlet. The committee structure bonds people interpersonally to each other and to the mission of a campus. Democratic decision making is not just a way to make decisions; it is part of the social fabric of an institution of higher learning. Perhaps no one has stressed the importance of the social, participatory nature of problem solving in higher education more than John Dewey.[31]

Dewey's classic work, *Democracy and Education*, offers an outline for connecting democracy and participatory decision making, providing a base for checking campus commitment to such a value.

> To say that education is a social function, securing direction and development in the immature through their participation in the life of the group to which they belong, is to say in effect that education will vary with the quality of life which prevails in a group. Particularly is it true that a society which not only changes but which has the ideal of such change as will improve it, will have different standards and methods of education from one which aims simply at the perpetuation of its own customs.[32]

Dewey details some basic connections between education and a democratic environment helpful for a campus interested in dialogic education. First, he described the importance of "human association," which translates well into the participatory impulse of "shared decision making" among administration, faculty, students, and staff, which brings people together from different perspectives. Such a structure offers opportunity for intellectual and emotional exchange between persons of different academic rank and function on a campus.

Second, Dewey upheld the democratic ideals, permitting people of different classes or functional positions in an institution to come together for collective decision making. Third, Dewey affirmed the worth of individuals and their ideas. Knowledge of the structure of democratic decision making and an ability to work within it provides a practical way for people and their ideas to be affirmed.

Fourth, Dewey invited the social arrangements that make it possible for persons to share insight and ideas. Democratic governance offers opportunity for input in a public process. A democratic governance system takes social life seriously, affirming a person's worth, ideas, and ability to make a difference.

The social aspect of decision making reminds us of the importance of doing business with a long-range plan as a guide, recognizing that the people we work with and the students we teach are influenced by our behavior and we by their actions. Dialogic educators recognize the necessity of politics on any campus, but realize something more is needed to guide the interaction of an institution of higher learning. Karl Jaspers describes the drive beyond politics as the glue that holds a community together.

> One of the driving forces in politics is something above politics.
> This is why purely political thinking . . . supposedly realistic, is a smoke screen in which the human self is forgotten—just as the illusions of some other ways of thinking would have us forget the realities of human nature. Something above politics must guide political institutions, legislation, designs—if they are to endure. This is the font of the spirit that must pervade their reality in concrete situations, if they are to be trusted.[33]

Dialogic education contends that recognition of the importance of ideas and persons must guide the political life of a campus. An educational environment that goes beyond style and narrow ideology offers a set of general guidelines within which persuasion, influence, and the political life of a campus can attempt to function and prosper.

Dialogic Persuasion

A form of persuasion sensitive to people is an essential part of a healthy decision-making system. The final test is whether or not people actually use the known committee structures when engaging one another in persuasion and change. Carl Rogers' description of a quality interpersonal exchange assists in understanding this problem. Rogers states that we need to have empathy, unconditional positive regard, and congruence, but if the other does not perceive these values as authentic, they will not work in facilitating the relationship.[34]

The same is true of a dialogic effort at decision making. If the faculty and staff do not use the structure that is set before them, it is unlikely they will respond positively to its existence. Also, if people are consistently abused as they enter debate, a chilling effect will occur. For any decision-making system to work, the participants must be willing to use it within agreed upon guidelines.

In essence, dialogic decision making and efforts at influence might be tested by the following questions: Does the campus place a higher priority on the quality of ideas than on who one knows?; Do people have some collective ownership in the future of the university?; Do the faculty, staff, and students know the decision-making structure and how to use it?; Do the members of the campus recognize that the quality of life on a campus cannot be determined by politics alone? Our commitment to higher learning and the manner of interacting and caring for one another will determine the quality of a campus as much as, if not even more than, the policies we agree to follow.

Finally, one may ask, Does democratic participation on this campus make a difference? On a campus committed to dialogic education, one individual can make a difference and the content of one's argument can still win the day and carry the action. A campus with such an idea and person-centered political life might offer a model of the good life to our students, who must learn not only a vocation, but how to contribute as citizens of communities and become productive contributors to their professional organizations.

Such a hope is ideal, but perhaps a campus can still be a place where lofty goals guide our daily interaction and our concern for the future.

9

Athenian Leadership

The Athenian ideal—

To be an Athenian . . . is to organize your life around a set of values. An Athenian is an idea. . . .

To be an Athenian is to hold knowledge and, especially, the quest for knowledge in high esteem. To contemplate, to reason, to experiment, to question—these are, to an Athenian, the most exalted activities a person can perform. . . .

To be an Athenian is to cherish language because you believe it to be humankind's most precious gift. . . .

To be an Athenian is to understand that the thread which holds civilized society together is thin and vulnerable; therefore, Athenians place great value on tradition, social restraint, and continuity. . . .

To be an Athenian is to take an interest in public affairs and the improvement of public behavior. . . .

And, finally, to be an Athenian is to esteem the discipline, skill, and taste that are required to produce enduring art. . . .

The purpose of your having been at this university was to give you a glimpse of the Athenian way, to interest you in the Athenian way.

> Neil Postman,
> *Conscientious Objections:*
> *Stirring Up Trouble About*
> *Language, Technology, and Education*

Lincoln's leadership—

To be sure, the values in the vision [Lincoln's] were so high and the code of conduct implied by it required such perfection that the practices of the community sustained by it were continually falling short of achieving them. Lincoln's vision was an impossible dream and such a vision is always dangerous, for disillusionment can

159

destroy the community that shares it. However, the restorative theme can save the high and noble ideals and discharge the guilt of falling short of their achievement at the same time that it gives to the vision a new vitality.

Ernest Bormann,
The Force of Fantasy:
Restoring the American Dream

Dialogic educators are wary of ideological managers. The possibility of dialogue is lessened by inflexible ideological positions that make it difficult to listen to others. The intention of this chapter is not to glorify some form of classical ideology. The Athenian experiment was marred by its slave structure and treatment of women. But Postman does draw our attention to important ideals of the Athenian culture worthy of conversation and emulation. Dialogic education seeks an alternative to ideological closure, while looking for ways to encourage ideals that can guide us. Bormann's quotation on Lincoln suggests a similar hope: ideals without closure of a rigid ideology.

In an essay on what an Athenian was, written as a commencement speech, Neil Postman outlines an "educated Athenian" that calls for questioning, love of language, involvement in public affairs, discipline, and the development of intellectual skill. Postman suggests the need for an Athenian perspective in education, which I believe reveals a form of leadership compatible with dialogic education.

Dialogic leadership in education protects and supports an Athenian concern for reason, democratic process, and education of the whole person. The value of dialogic education is that the entire environment contributes to the education. Education emerges not just from one faculty member or one department, but from the gestalt of a campus or department.

The issues Postman associates with an Athenian philosophy are clearly tied to ideas I have described as fundamental to dialogic education. Postman's concerns are congruent with suggestions offered by Aristotle, who wrote for his polis, the city-state of Athens. Aristotle spoke both for and to a people whose identity was firmly tied to a home setting. Due to the manageable size of many universities or departments, such organizations can be viewed as a polis establishing its own rules and regulations.

The formal and informal leadership in the polis set the tone for an Athenian ideal of participation, involvement, and questioning. Athens, as the birthplace of democracy, gave us insight into the importance and the value of having a home that survives by the necessity of protecting conversation about ideas. The remainder of this chapter outlines an Athenian leadership style consistent with a dialogic attitude.

The Limits of Interpersonal Style

Before outlining more fully the Athenian perspective in dialogic education and how it might affect leadership on a campus, it is helpful to provide the context for why such a model is needed today. An Athenian model for leadership is a direct response to the limits of interpersonal style. It is not that interpersonal style is wrong or unhelpful, but there is a limit on how much emphasis we can productively put on interpersonal style. This chapter contends that the myth of the importance of conversation about ideas, competence, and work is more worthy of a college campus than myth centered on "who one knows" and interpersonal style.

An Athenian view of leadership affirms values of work, dedication, and knowledge over personality and interpersonal linkings and cliques. An Athenian environment keeps strong and secure the assumption that knowledge and discussion of various opinions are at the heart of a life of learning. We need to be reminded of this simple but fundamental viewpoint stated by Warren Bennis: "Once we believed that success was achieved through hard work, frugality, industry, diligence, prudence, and honesty, not just our personalities and our charm."[1] It may seem idyllic to propose a leadership model based on reason, hard work, and competence as we near the next century. This model is an alternative to a focus on getting along, an organizational demand predicted by William Whyte in the 1950s.[2] Bennis' comments suggest that Whyte was not far from the mark. Bennis cautions us about the limitations of leadership by charm. It is not enough to get along with those in the organization; we need to encourage people to actually learn and use their intelligence for their own good and that of the public.

I was asked to consult with a small college interested in student retention. This school had just instituted mandatory seminars on caring for students. As my earlier comments have indicated, I was distressed by their use of the term *caring*. I suggested that all people be expected to do their job well, which includes knowing one's subject, being able to assist others in learning, and treating persons with dignity. I would call such actions part of the necessary work and expectations of doing a job well. Once the word *caring* was a focus, some on the campus interpreted their task as keeping students comfortable and happy, tying caring to the placating of the customer. My advice to the college administration was to have the courage to market excellence and try to measure up to their own pronouncements. Beware of marketing charm. Our task is not to simply find customers, but to shape the future with ideas. There are limits to interpersonal style. Ask anyone who has bought goods or services because of the personality of the salesperson, only to discover the inferior quality of the purchase.

The Athenian model of leadership is based on classical values, such as work, virtue, conversation, and the public good. While this view of leadership may not reflect what is most saleable today, the task of higher education is not just to respond to a market. We are, in addition, charged with creating a market and shaping the direction of the future. An Athenian perspective works to create a climate where work, dedication, and virtue are held in high esteem and modeled by leaders in the administration and faculty. If we cannot model such behavior in our own lives, we should not expect students to carry forth such values in their professions or in graduate school.

Dialogic education is both person- and information-centered. When one of these two main tasks is forgotten and the other is overemphasized, we miss the mark. I am very interested in and committed to the value of interpersonal interaction. Style is part of any communicative act. But when the content of what one says and the authenticity of what one believes becomes less important than the effort to appear contemplative and authentic, danger emerges. Buber makes this distinction as he distinguishes between "being and seeming."[3] More recently, Neil Postman in *Amusing Ourselves to Death: Public Discourse in the Age of Show Business* describes a similar concern.[4] Postman states that style is used to get our attention and to entertain. But perhaps we have gone too far in emphasizing style, to the point of forgetting that learning is hard work. Undue emphasis on interpersonal style that seeks to charm and entertain is a temptation that dialogic education needs to reject, particularly as we are faced with pressures to bring in increasing numbers of students and larger amounts of fiscal support. Students and the financial support for the university must depend first and foremost on the competency of the faculty and administration, not on leaders that are socially able to convey a suave smoothness, giving the impression that friendship has begun before people even know one another. A university must first work to sell its academic content programs, only then offering interpersonal attention.

Friendship needs to be secondary to the more fundamental issue of being competent, qualified teachers and scholars. But this does not occur in all cases. I received a phone call from a colleague whose husband was denied a job offer because the university he applied to did not believe he would fit the interpersonal style of the organization. My friend and her husband were looking for teaching positions at universities that were within commuting distance, thus rejection for one meant no job for the other. I was sympathetic to their plight, but was even more anguished by the potential employer's comments on interpersonal style. If a candidate is incompetent or less competent than another applicant, it is understandable that the job will not be offered. But when a decision is primarily made on the grounds of likability, an organization is putting its level of content excellence at risk. Each applicant needs to be judged on what professional qualifications will be brought to the position, not whether he or she would be a good social buddy in the organization.

One college president put this issue in a light that reveals the importance of conversation about ideas. When asked if the dean was "his" dean, the president of a college uttered an unequivocal, no. True, the dean worked under the president at the institution, but he had never been simply an arm of the president.[5] It is sometimes necessary to inform people that any leader on the campus need not be a buddy or friend. Any college leader's role goes beyond representing a given constituency to include representation of quality higher education.

An Athenian Environment

A dialogic leader in education offers support and encouragement for the discerning of ideas, or the practical testing of ideas in conversation—the key to an Athenian perspective. Alasdair MacIntyre offers a clear philosophical picture of ideas important to Athenian life, revealing some significant implications for dialogic education.

MacIntyre stresses two major points. First, in Athenian life the drama was not just the person or the individual, but the life of the entire city. Keeping the conversation going was not done so much to enliven the person, but to help the community or polis remain strong with knowledge and insight. The implications for dialogic education are significant. A primary task of dialogic education is to keep a university intellectually strong and vibrant. Relationships between people support such an intellectual environment.

Second, MacIntyre critiques the notion of the *emotivist self* guided primarily by personal preference, as contrary to an Athenian environment.[6] Instead, Athens was more rooted in what MacIntyre terms the *heroic self*, dependent more on sociocultural role than on personal preference. A faculty member working from such an orientation places trust in the importance of the roles of teacher, student, and administrator. The roles call a person to a more responsible set of actions than personal preference might encourage. The heroic self of Athens was willing to sacrifice for the good of the community when role responsibility called for such action. Fulfillment comes not just from what one does, but from passing on the values and health of a community or institution to the next generation.[7]

The above two ideas, polis and the heroic self, contribute to the Athenian ideals of commitment and participation. It was more important to keep the process of conversation going than to have one's own idea accepted—again requiring a heroic self, rather than the emotivist self. Dialogic education is based on the assumption that both oneself and the other are vital to the communicative and informational encounter. What the Athenian perspective adds is the importance of various and needed roles in an educational environment.

Dialogic education requires a campus leader to be willing to assume the sociocultural role of patron or supporter of conversation about ideas through questioning, love of language, involvement in public affairs, discipline, and the development of skills, as faculty and students attempt to work within the demands and responsibilities of their respective roles. I asked a department leader why he had organized a function honoring a retiring faculty member. Paraphrased, his answer was that as a chair he did not lead by personal wishes, but by what would be best for the department, the college, and the discipline. He stated that his colleague and all the people he had touched deserve this honor. In addition, those attending will contribute to a student research scholarship. The role of chair called him to be fair to colleagues and students while continuing to build the department; the celebration permitted him to accomplish both objectives.

The goals of Martin Luther King, Jr. were not based merely on personal preference, but on roles calling for a change in the society. Personal preference would have resulted in King turning his back many times from the risks and dangers of such a campaign, but the role of a leader in a civil rights movement called for a much different response.

> Although Martin Luther King, Jr. was acutely aware that the Beloved Community is "not yet," but in the future, perhaps even the distant future, he believed that it would be actualized within history, and he saw approximations of it already. Thus he worked unceasingly for the realization of his dream, and he never lost hope that "there will be a great camp meeting in the promised land." His hope was rooted in his faith in the power of God to achieve his purpose among humankind within history.[8]

King's hope was not only grounded in a future, but in a role that was bigger than simply personal preference. Dialogic education ceases when our personal position becomes oblivious to the needs of the polis and our professional role.

Athenian leadership reminds us of a task bigger than ourselves—ushering in the next generation of leaders. The role of teacher goes beyond the question of whether or not one likes a student, asking something much more fundamental. How can I assist a given student, regardless of how I feel toward him or her? The role of teacher, of educator, needs to guide actions and do whatever it takes to offer insight and discussion of ideas to students.

In recognizing the sociocultural implications of the role, the committed teacher must remember not to personalize the struggle and conflict that is inevitable. Some difficulties just come with the job. Life in ancient Athens was not always quiet and conflict free, just as the task of a teacher is at times full of struggle and disagreement. As Charles Cooley has stated, " 'Conflict, of some sort, is the life of society, and progress emerges from a struggle in which individual, class, or institution seeks to realize its own idea of good.' "[9] The Athenian call to assume a role for the betterment of the common good is still of value today. The teacher who takes all student comments as personal attacks might be reluctant to do what is necessary to offer a fine education for a given student. The role of teacher requires that we do what is needed, even when our actions are not appreciated, at least in the short-run. The criteria for determining what a student needs requires balancing the demands of a professional role, the needs of a student at a given time, one's own personal strengths, and an overall concern for the polis. In short, no decision should reflect blind adherence to institutional rules or simply the personal preference of teacher or student.

For instance, a professor gave a student an *F*, later changing the grade to an incomplete. She was convinced, after much discussion, that the student had misunderstood and therefore failed an assignment. Her objective was to help the student learn the discipline. She altered the grade, even as the registrar cautioned her that the change was professionally risky. On the other hand, this same professor had failed another student who had plagiarized. She believed that this student had no respect for the limits and rules in higher education and required a stern message.

Such a teaching style requires judgment on many issues. An Athenian leader is willing to be stretched by the responsibilities of a given role and to make tough decisions that will contribute to a quality education. There is no guarantee that our actions will always be right, but our role calls us to make the best judgments possible.

Empowered by Myth

An Athenian environment that upholds the importance of conversation about ideas is indeed a myth, even in classical Athens. There is much debate on the nature of the Athenian experiment. Such a learning environment was pursued at the expense of resident aliens, women, and slaves. But as we knowingly admit the flawed reality, we can still be inspired by a goal that was pointed to in early Athens. At its best, Athens was a place where conversation about ideas was nourished and the responsibilities of a given sociocultural role were taken seriously.[10] Our task is to applaud what went right in their experiment, opening the door for the formerly excluded to participate and lead.

As we acknowledge the limits of the Athenian experiment, we can still be guided by the myth that inquiry and responsibility of role accountability are important to a campus. Dialogic education lives by the myth that information, relationship sensitivity, and concern for value discussion can together make a difference in the quality of the human community. A myth is not necessarily untrue when it is only partially followed; it is a story that points to behavior appropriate for a person and a community. Telling and retelling ourselves the story of education based in a professional role commitment to inquiry and students is perhaps a myth worth keeping alive and vibrant on any campus.

Living by myth is not the same as living by the unreal. Myth points us to the stories that guide how we should live. According to Bettelheim, myth is central to mental health. A myth can describe how life should be lived. We cannot always live up to a given myth, but myths still set guidelines for action and can call us to a higher form of behavior.[11] Myths in organizations require us to live up to certain standards that may not even be the actual norm in a community, but are necessary for excellence and quality performance.

A myth in an organization points to how people live, reflecting the organizational culture.[12] For instance, at one college there is an ongoing commitment to teaching. A story that has taken mythic form is that of one professor so dedicated to teaching that he taught with a heart condition and died while giving a final exam. The professor was told by his physician to stay at home in bed. Against doctor's orders, he showed up for the final exam. He passed out the exam, wished his class well, ordered someone to collect the exams when all were completed, and walked calmly out into the hallway where he died of a heart attack. Over the years this tragic event has taken on a mythical dimension, revealing the value that the institution places on teaching.

Joseph Campbell further reminds us that society does indeed need to live by important myths.[13] He, too, was interested in the Greek emphasis on the heroic myth of making a difference. Similarly, dialogic education needs to live by the myth of the Athenian perspective that calls us to strive for a home where intellectual conversation and debate about ideas is not only welcomed, but respected. We can then offer a model of leadership that takes role responsibility seriously and works daily to support inquiry and people on the campus.

Some believe the Athenian myth was present in the life of the Kennedy administration. Like Athens, flaws in the reality of policy and character were present, yet the myth was powerful for many. In the first chapter of his *Profiles in Courage*, John F. Kennedy offers a vision that seems appropriate for higher education and is consistent with the demands of role and inquiry that an Athenian perspective requires.

> Our political life is becoming so expensive, so mechanized and so dominated by professional politicians and public relations men that the idealist who dreams of independent statesmanship is rudely awakened by the necessities of election and accomplishment. . . . only the very courageous will be able to make the hard and unpopular decisions necessary for our survival in the struggle. . . .

We shall need compromises in the days ahead, to be sure. But these will be, or should be, compromises of issues, not of principles. . . . We can resolve the clash of interest without conceding our ideals. And even the necessity for the right kind of compromise does not eliminate the need for those idealists and reformers.[14]

Kennedy's words on political life are echoed by Ernest Boyer. He quotes a recent college graduate calling for Athenian leadership based on knowledge, participation, and service. "She asks, 'What kind of nation will we be if we cannot even commit ourselves to other people, much less to a set of abstract values?'. . . [Boyer continues] The goal is not to indoctrinate students, but to set them free in the world of ideas and provide a climate in which ethical and moral choices can be thoughtfully examined, and convictions formed."[15] The stakes for us as educators are great as well; we need to be reminded that we assume a role bigger than ourselves in the Athenian myth. This role calls for responsibility toward ideas and people that might make a difference in the quality of human life.

The Athenian myth may seem demanding and unrealistic. But such a goal is, at least to a degree, within reach of colleges and universities in a country founded by the pragmatic dreamers who penned the Declaration of Independence and later the Bill of Rights. These documents support philosophically and practically the myth of the importance of persons and principles to guide a life well lived.[16] It seems that some myths are not only worth keeping, they are sometimes worth building institutions and even countries around. The best of an Athenian culture still needs to be nourished in conversation with our students and one another as we work to respect both ideas and persons.

Christopher Matthews, in *Hardball: How Politics Is Played Told by One Who Knows the Game*, describes the use of power through image, positioning, and style in an effort to gather influence in a media age.[17] While his views may not be wrong, they are contrary to an Athenian effort to live up to role expectations, keeping free inquiry possible in a democratic environment. Matthews' perspective emerges out of a view of power motivated more by personal gain than education of the next generation of leaders.

A college must be committed to rewarding competence and productivity over acceptance into an organizational culture. Having devoted much of my life to the study of interpersonal relationships, I am a believer in the importance of quality communication in organizations. But it is possible to go too far in stressing interpersonal style. Leadership today must encourage acquisition information and application, not just how well those persons will fit into the ongoing organizational style. As Steven Cahn reminds us, a college campus must equate excellence with merit.[18] Educators interested in Athenian leadership need to uphold the myth that one's merit is less dependent on who one knows and how well one has packaged one's personality than on one's competence with ideas and application.

As this section questions the overuse of interpersonal style, I want to reemphasize the importance of civility in interaction. It is possible to be content-wise and civil without trying to use style to compensate for lack of preparation, hard work, and idea direction. Dialogic education takes the bold step of trying to elevate the myth of the pursuit of truth in an Athenian environment. This type of leadership provides the best education a college or university can offer and is sensitive to the importance of inquiry, learning, and competence, while valuing students as human beings.

Athenian Wisdom

Athenian leadership in dialogic education depends on the assumption that wisdom is not just based on information. Dialogic education fuses information and values in the construction of the learning environment. Dialogic education encourages a life of virtue in which long-term character is more important than personality. I was consulting with a college interested in increasing their commitment to teaching. They asked me to discuss the presentation of self as teacher. I emphasized the notion of self as a by-product of what we do and as the virtue that guides a life. A teacher may be so committed to the story of an academic discipline that he or she would do almost anything professionally appropriate to help another understand and appreciate the material.

By emphasizing the story of one's discipline and virtues, character emerges as the long-range result of living out a worthy story, guided by a set of virtues. Personality is the outward presentation of the self. Character development takes consistent work over a lifetime. The notion of character grounds Athenian wisdom in knowledge of and commitment to a virtue system sympathetic both to the polis and the heroic self.

The value dimension of dialogic education is not centered on prescription. Leaders must be willing to recognize inquiry as a fundamental part of the task of learning; they should not forget the personhood of students, and they should be guided by the Athenian virtues. A campus committed to dialogic exchange assumes the importance of virtue tied to choice and free-will commitment, rather than reliance on compulsion. Leadership propelled by an Athenian view of virtue and within the dialogic spirit outlined in this book conceptualizes acts of virtue as voluntary, not forced. One can be forced to engage in helpful action, but virtuous motivation for the action would involve concern for the common good.[19] Virtue can be invited, but not demanded.

Reluctance to totally demand adherence to any one set of virtues suggests that there will always be some students, faculty, and administrators who behave in a fashion incongruent with the spirit and aims of a university or college. If no one has the opportunity to act differently than a clear set of guidelines dictates, Aristotle's view of voluntary leadership of virtue is violated and an institution simply becomes a place of rules, rule followers, and rule enforcers. The Athenian view of virtue is conscious and voluntary. To be good and not know why or to be unable to conceive of a contrary action is not a life of virtue, but simply the blind action of a rule follower. Dialogic education encourages people of vision, not followers of blind obedience.

The significance of this idea is important for institutions based on learning and wary of propaganda. We need to question efforts that pursue shortcuts to virtuous leadership. A rigid moral structure that permits little decision making may not be virtuous at all. Niebuhr reminds us that the beginning of an ethical life is choice.[20] Any college can have a general consensus that caring about students is important. That same college may be in trouble if all members of the community define what it means to care in an identical fashion. When leaders are expected to follow a script, unable to offer a genuine response dependent on their expertise, their relationships with others, and their own personality structure, the opportunity for virtue driven leadership ceases.

Sissela Bok, known for her work in ethics, cautions about the danger of a moralistic environment that ignores the importance of choice. She makes it clear that moral language can be used to oppress, exploit, and justify behavior that requires debate and conversation.[21] In short, beware of calls to virtue that give no choice, only dictating how to carry out the virtuous action.

In addition to misusing virtue language through imposition, the absence of virtue guidelines may signal a campus in significant transition. A university in a major structural shift of responsibilities or spending an inordinate amount of time working on policy statements may be attempting to make up for a lack of leadership. A virtue structure that is held too tightly can discourage inquiry on a campus, but disagreement on virtue guidelines can place the mission of a school up for perennial debate, causing considerable confusion and lack of focus.

A virtue structure that has flexible and clear guidelines nourishes dialogic education. To be in dialogue with another presumes knowing one's own position and then listening to those of others, recognizing the limits placed upon both parties by time, the environment, and the mission of a school. Dialogue assumes a willingness to agree on a set of constraints that will limit behavior and action. Such internally accepted limits make it possible for people to interact on various issues without a need for official policy-making on every issue.

Every modern organization, of course, needs policy guidelines. However, it is a barometer of the changing virtues of an organization when there is a consistent call for more and more policy to curtail behavior that at one time was limited by each person. Setting the internal constraints in an organization needs to be initiated by the leader. When leaders are in disagreement about the virtues that guide a campus, it is a certainty that the faculty and students will soon follow with a call for more and more formal policy-making in order to clarify the direction.

The above concern does not imply that structural changes and policy statements are unimportant. But we may want to be cautious as we observe an organization attempting to rely increasingly on the technique of structure, without a strong sense of virtue that sets the implicit guidelines for behavior. Structures and policies are the guidelines by which the ball game is to be played. But how well the ball is hit is still dependent on the quality of the formal and the informal leaders involved in the game.

In short, one hopes that dialogic education will invite some wisdom, within a life of virtue and choice. "Some people are wise in general, not wise in some [restricted] area. . . . Wisdom is understanding plus scientific knowledge of the most honorable things."[22] A general wisdom that guides dialogic education is an awareness of the danger of extremes—a rigid institutional value system or an organization without clear limits to guide daily interaction with one another. Both extremes can detract from inquiry and quality time with students; the rigid system keeps the focus on following rules and the lack of value clarity consumes too much time in debate about who and what we should be.

Athenian Virtues

In writing for the polis of Athens, Aristotle offers a list of virtues central to leadership that might invite an Athenian perspective on campuses today. Although Aristotle did not provide a "how to" guide of the virtues, he did offer a clear framework for what the cultured Greek citizen should hold as important values. The following discussion of virtues relates appropriately to leadership within a dialogic framework. The virtues are discussed with a description of Aristotle's well-known "golden mean" situated between the extremes of deficiency and excess.

1. *Bravery* requires one to stand firm for what is fine, or what the excellent person would uphold in spite of pain. The excess of bravery is recklessness or rashness and the deficiency is cowardliness.

2. *Temperance* is the mean between life without passion and indulgence in the extreme pursuit of pleasure. Intemperance is more blameworthy than cowardice, because it is the voluntary pursuit of pleasure. The deficient extreme is represented by not enjoying pleasure at all. Temperance is the base of Athenian virtues, generally acknowledging more wisdom in moderation than in extremes.

3. *Generosity* implies that one that will "give to the right people, the right amounts, at the right time."[23] The excess of wastefulness is more easily cured than the deficiency of ungenerosity.

4. *Magnificence* involves a person of wealth spending large amounts of money in the right fashion. This is contrasted with the deficiency of begrudging and stingy behavior and the excess of spending with poor taste and vulgarity.

5. *Magnanimity* seemingly exaggerates claims about one's ability, but the person can match each claim. The person of magnanimity brings together all the virtues. He or she is willing to face danger for large causes, but not for small ones. This person would rather give than receive and has the right view of honors and dishonors. This person is honored only by true honors worthy of receiving. The deficiency of magnanimity is pusillanimity, requiring us to deprive ourselves of appropriate awards, and the excess is vanity.

6. *Mildness* results in being angered only by the right things. The excess is irascibility, being angered too often, and the other extreme is not being angered by the right things.

7. *Friendliness* is contrasted with the excess of the flatterer, relying on style and charm and the deficiency of the cantankerous person.

8. *Truthfulness* is the mean between the excess of the boaster telling falsehoods and the deficiency of self-depreciation.

9. *Wit* is the alternative between the excess of the vulgar buffoon and the deficiency of the boor.

10. *Shame* is the recognition of wrong after the fact, which is more appropriate for children. The virtuous person will not feel the disgrace of shame; instead, he or she will act on guilt that calls one back to active participation with a given virtue that has been momentarily ignored or misused. In fact, Aristotle did not consider the experience of shame a virtue at all. Virtues call for action; shame calls for intense self-reflection. "If someone is in a state that would make him feel disgrace if he were to do a disgraceful action, and because of this thing he is decent, that is absurd. For shame is concerned with what is voluntary, and the decent person will never willingly do base actions. . . . it . . . does not follow that to do such actions and then to feel disgrace at them is decent."[24]

An overview of these virtues leads to a trinity of bravery, honor, and justice, giving the right amounts to the right people at the right time. Such a life calls one to live with a feeling of responsibility that guides one's actions toward others and the use of one's own life.

One of the major obstacles for implementing an Athenian set of virtues is that many of us in a modern age are moved more by the introspection of shame than by the call to action that a virtue structure offers. Harold Barrett, in *Rhetoric and Civility*, states that a narcissistic culture will increasingly be motivated by shame, placing self-reflection and concern for image on a higher practical level of use than action that calls for a virtuous change in behavior.

Barrett quotes the work of Heinz Kohut, who calls our current era the time of the "tragic man." Kohut suggests that we have moved from a sense of guilt that informs us when we have transgressed a virtue, to a feeling of shame about defects that are a detriment to our own self-image. Self-criticism becomes the motivating factor in such an environment.[25] The sobering implications of this work are that an Athenian environment of virtue sensitivity, which has infrequently been the norm in organizations, is even more difficult to invite in our current world.

Dialogic education, however, does not rest on the preoccupation with the tragic, but focuses on the hope that education that is centered on projects, a common center of conversation about inquiry and concern for persons, can make a significant difference in the quality of life on a campus and in organizations in general.

Such a hope is an example of trying to shape the future, not just capitulate to the present. Athenian leadership is based on the premise that leadership of virtue sets the pace for an organization, realizing that a life of virtue based more on action than self-reflection is becoming more difficult to invite.

Translating the above virtues into a model for leadership that invites an Athenian environment supportive of conversation about ideas might involve three general virtues that I consider representative of the Athenian value structure: bravery, honor, and justice. Athenian leadership in a dialogic context of education might operationalize these three virtues. First, in order to keep academic freedom alive and well on a campus, one needs bravery. There are many subtle ways that one can be discouraged from taking a particular viewpoint seriously. One must be brave enough to speak what seems true, and examine what seems appropriate and relevant without undue fear of the social consequences that might result. Rather than concur with intellectual positions that one finds faulty or limited in order to get along with others, bravery requires walking into the midst of disagreement and relational discomfort. However, for bravery to fit within a dialogic context it still needs to be grounded in what has been called civility throughout this book.

Second, honor is evident when we recognize excellence in students and others. Honor requires that we look straight at our own weaknesses and willingly acknowledge the strengths of others. Such a view of bravery and honor might be practically displayed on a campus home as one attempts to hire those with the best potential, even if they may be better than oneself. This position is summarized by the following paraphrased remarks of mine in the role of chief academic officer.

An administrator, faculty member, or a parent need not be the best. But we must have a sense of honor that calls us to recognize the best and admit our shortcomings, not all of which we can alter. A leader need not be the best to lead, but he or she must have enough honor to look honestly at the truth and act accordingly, even when the necessary action may not fit his or her own personal hopes and aspirations. The final act of honor for any campus is the genuine effort to hire those more skilled as teachers and as scholars than oneself.

Honor is present in the daily routine of life, just as it is in major world decisions. Honor is evident when we attempt to be the college that we say we are, encouraging the best from each other, not being intimidated by another's excellence, and finding value in the work done in service for others.

The final key virtue for an Athenian leadership style is justice. One way justice is revealed on a campus is by how leaders treat extremes, such as the weakest and the strongest faculty. How are personnel cases handled that involve weak faculty who have been accused of some questionable action? A willingness to follow correct procedure and to give a person the benefit of the doubt is necessary, not just for the rights of that person, but for assuring an atmosphere of justice on the campus.

One campus took three years to process a case of faculty incompetence. The faculty member was given more than ample opportunity to present his position. When asked why so much time was spent with one faculty member who had engaged in an infraction, the president offered a statement similar to the following. Confidence in the administration and in the university environment is tested more by our willingness to protect academic freedom and due process when a case involves a faculty member of questionable competence than by gracious responses to our star faculty on campus. The quality of justice on a campus is exemplified more by how the leadership supports the weak than its praise of the gifted. We do, however, need to work to be fair to our strongest faculty as well. As an administrator, I was surprised to discover low student evaluations of one well-published professor. I quickly found out through key students in the department that other faculty, who, incidently, were not publishing, were telling students jaded stories about this person, either not true or highly colored with subjective interpretation.

I confronted the faculty comments by direct conversation. The weakest and the strongest faculty should be given a just environment in which to work. We must honestly evaluate what another does, lessening the influence of jealous colleagues' efforts at personality assassination.

A former president at Antioch College states that being good is not enough to lead.[26] There is no guarantee that virtue alone will make one a leader. There is, however, a fundamental assumption that accompanies dialogic education. If the leadership does not try to be virtuous, the chance of inviting an Athenian environment on a campus is unlikely.

In summary, the task for leaders interested in dialogic education is complex, offering more than information, while rejecting the impulse toward propaganda and holding one another accountable. Robert Bellah, in *The Broken Covenant: American Civil Religion in Time of Trial*, offers a reminder of the importance of a lofty and complex mission statement that calls us to accountability, requiring us to be propelled not only by the present, but by what we might be.

> The Declaration of Independence, the Bill of Rights, and the Four-teenth Amendment to the Constitution have never been fully imple-mented. Certainly the words "with liberty and justice for all" in the Pledge of Allegiance are not factually descriptive. But while I can understand the feeling of a Garrison that such hypocritically em-ployed documents should be rejected, I would follow the course of . . . [those insisting] that they be fulfilled. . . . In a period like our own, when we have lost our sense of direction, when we do not know where our goal is, when our myths have lost their meaning and comprehensive reason has been eclipsed by calculating technical reason, there is need for a rebirth of imaginative vision. In the face of such a situation imagination can sometimes fuse myth and ecstatic reason to tender a new vision, a new sense of direction and goal. Such a new vision is never unrelated to older vision—that is why tradition is so important; but neither is it identical with them.[27]

Some might say that lofty goals of bravery, honor, and justice in education are seldom realized. But flawed application of ideals should not have us toss them aside, but rather remind us of how much further we need to travel.

Practicing Leadership

The list of virtues may not change as much as the way in which we carry out acts that can assist the common good. Dialogic education will not automatically empower a leader with bravery, honor, or justice. How we interpret such acts will influence the campus culture and our own sensitivity and wisdom. But the general guideline is that such virtues are still important and need to be considered as we make concrete decisions at a given time. In addition, no virtue orientation is innate or comes neatly packaged as a birthright; it is learned through practice.

According to Aristotle, virtue is learned through education and practiced through habituation, the act of continual practice. No one learns to play the piano without many hours of practice, and no one exhibits the Athenian virtues without practice. "For we learn a craft by producing the same product that we must produce when we have learned, becoming builders, e.g., by building and harpists by playing the harp; so also, then, we become just by doing just action, temperate by doing temperate actions, brave by doing brave actions."[28] There is no magic formula for being virtuous. Like any task worth striving to achieve, it takes time, practice, and commitment.

When addressing a health and welfare organization, I was asked what leadership lacks today. I offered three basic qualities: patience, endurance, and prudence. Patience is a learned skill for those pulled by a teleology or project that one envisions as possible. Endurance is learned by those who move from being sprinters to long-distance runners. Leaders of organizations that offer a home environment often possess the endurance of long-distance runners. Prudence is an old-fashioned word reminding us to do what is needed at the right time in the right amounts, no sooner and no more. Asked how one can acquire such traits, I reiterated Aristotle's simple, yet demanding answer: practice.

The notions of virtue and practice lead us to find ways to encourage leadership to develop the habit of interacting in a way that encourages asking questions about what is virtuous for the common good. Martin Buber also discussed the importance of education for character. He made it clear that information-based education alone is not enough. We need to invite a blending of the acquisition of information and values.[29] It is this lesson that Buber as a Jewish theologian and philosopher learned all too well from the results of the educational "excellence" and moral deprivation of the Third Reich.

The virtues of bravery, honor, and justice need to be present in committee structures, in decisions about insurance and benefits, in relationships with staff, and in relationships among faculty and between faculty and students. The character of an institution is revealed more readily in how leadership relates in everyday operations than in public rhetoric broadcasted to a general audience.

Dialogic education coincides with an Athenian environment encouraging and supporting virtues for leaders to follow and the institution to be identified with in everyday life on the campus. It is only in the practice of virtue that we can hope to bring to fruition a model of dialogic education as part of daily operations by faculty, students, and staff. In Postman's commencement essay, part of which opened this chapter, he closed with this: "You are young and it is not given to us to see your future. But, I will tell you this, with which I will close: I can wish for you no higher compliment than that in the future it will be reported that among your graduating class the Athenian mightily outnumbered [all the others]."[30] Only the knowledge and practice of virtues in everyday acts will allow Athenians to grow in number.

The Athenian emphasis, while frequently not the norm, is still valuable for encouraging students to examine one example of a virtue system, applying what they know about the limits of the original experiment and the limits of the life we now live. But even as we admit the flaws of Athens and our own shortcomings, and work for a more inclusive world based on competence, not birthright, or ethnic and religious orientation, the virtues of bravery, honor, and justice are helpful guides in a complex and demanding leadership era.

An Athenian Intellectual

Dialogic education encourages intellectuals interested in Athenian virtues to work at their profession with a commitment to inquiry and humane relationships. The notion of an intellectual has not always fared well in pragmatic settings.[31]

> What we often find is that the intellectuals, the educated classes, are the most indoctrinated, most ignorant, most stupid part of the population, and there are very good reasons for that. Basically two reasons. First of all, as the literate part of the population, they are subjected to the mass of propaganda. There is a second, more important and more subtle reason. Namely, they are the ideological managers. Therefore, they must internalize the propaganda and believe it. And part of the propaganda they have developed is that they are the natural leaders of the masses.[32]

Such a negative assessment of intellectuals is not totally uncommon in the United States. What is assumed in this critique of the intellectual is an individual attached to ideology and so committed to particular causes that persons are forgotten. The hope of dialogic education is to encourage a human intellectual wary of narrow ideology and aware of the importance of persons.

Intellectuals built this country as framers of the Declaration of Independence. Intellectuals are usually the first people the government seeks to control in a moment of crisis. Witness the oppressive actions of Lenin and of Chinese leaders in the countercultural revolution and student uprising in 1989. Intellectuals have the power to lead through ideas. The response of totalitarian governments wanting to control the discussion agenda is to limit the intellectual's ability to reach through ideas.

Perhaps some implications of the term *intellectual* can be reclaimed when connected with Athens and dialogue. A leader on an Athenian campus needs to hold conversation about ideas as a virtue.

> An intellectual is, in the first sense, a devotee of ideas, knowledge, values. "Intellect," Richard Hofstadter wrote, "is the critical, creative, and contemplative side of mind. Whereas intelligence seeks to grasp, manipulate, re-order, adjust, intellect examines, ponders, wonders, theorizes, criticizes, imagines." An intellectual is something more; a person concerned critically with values, purposes, ends that transcend immediate practical needs. By this definition the person who deals with analytical ideas and data alone is a theorist; the one who works only with normative ideas is a moralist; the person who deals with both and unites them through disciplined imagination is an intellectual. Some scholars regard value as corrupting the critical sense; they argue for moral detachment. But moral detachment is itself at best a modal value and one hostile to the concern of the free mind.[33]

A significant issue I have discussed with incoming students is the importance of taking the role of the intellectual seriously— the bringing together of ideas and values, asking what the practical consequences of actions will be for a given community or organization. The student who feels embarrassed when encountering discussion about ideas needs to be informed that the primary purpose for coming to a college is learning about ideas, no matter what one's major or vocational aspiration.

The emphasis on the importance of breadth in scholarship, conversation about ideas, public participation in persuasion, and people points to an intellectual orientation congruent with an Athenian perspective. Remembering the personhood of the learner and questioning ideological narrowness places an intellectual in a dialogic perspective.

The Last Intellectuals: An American Critique of the Age of Academe by Russell Jacoby can be read as an appreciation of dialogic education. Jacoby critiques an overspecialization of inquiry, which dialogic education attempts to avoid for practical and philosophical reasons. The intellectual that Jacoby describes is a person willing to learn and discuss ideas, even when there is no direct connection to career success. Jacoby warns us of the dangers of losing the importance of *why* we come together—to learn and discuss, not just to further a professional career.[34]

Charles J. Sykes, in his major critique of higher education *Prof Scam: Professors and the Demise of Higher Education* (examined closely in chapter 10), contends that some colleges still provide an intellectual environment that is clearly worth the cost and where conversation between teacher and student is encouraged. "The professors, among whose number are those few hardy souls who have kept the spirit of genuine intellectual commitment alive . . . [are] committed not only to teaching but also to the traditions of taste, reason, and a common intellectual discourse that were once taken for granted."[35] Perhaps dialogic education can be supported in places where ideas and people are as important as professional career development.

Putting the terms *intellectual* and *Athenian leader* together implies that ideas can influence people on a campus. MacGregor states that an intellectual leader, by nature of such a commitment that seeks to envision multiple sides of issues, will be internally conflict-ridden. One will struggle with the knowledge of danger in the areas of excess and deficiency, struggling to find the right proportions, the "pure and the applied, the negative and the affirmative, the analytical and the prophetic, the relativist and the absolutist, the classical and the rationalist—what has been called the quarrel of the ancients and the moderns."[36]

The leader within a dialogic education context takes an Athenian perspective *that protects the process through which conversation about ideas can take place, and upholds the virtues of bravery, honor, and justice.* Such a blending of the useful, the virtuous, and a commitment to higher knowledge was the aim of a classical education and is central to the orientation of dialogic education.[37] At its best, dialogic education encourages putting ideas into action in such a fashion that a department or college environment is affected. Education may take place in the classroom, in the dorm, during an internship, during extracurricular activities, and even while completing a work-study job in a campus office or on maintenance. Such leadership sets a tone where virtue of character permits the conversational process to direct the culture of a campus, both inside and outside the classroom.

Suzanne W. Morse states in "Leadership for an Uncertain Future" that we are at a crossroads in our national life. She argues that much happening in the nation, from budget deficits to crime, reveals us at a dysfunctional time in our history. In spite of, or perhaps due to the toughness of the historical moment, we seem to want to feel and look good, ignoring the need for genuine change.[38] Athenian leadership might assist us in this difficult moment in our history. Could we now benefit from Athenian leadership that seeks to be virtuous, keeps inquiry alive, and recognizes the interdependence and importance of people? Such a leadership style will not provide all the answers, but might offer a foundation for reminding us that hard work, knowledge, and commitment to the human community provides a more solid framework in leadership than style, charm, appearance, and a willingness to simply tell us what we want to hear.

PART 5

The Public Dialogue

10

Marketing:
The Public Dialogue

Professional ethics—

After a period of rapid growth in knowledge, power, wealth, and institutional influence, the professions currently face difficulties. Many of them are oversupplied with personnel; lay people have contested their authority, public scandal has shaken assumptions about rectitude in professional life; their power and wealth are often resented; their services are unevenly distributed; their guilds have shown an inability to keep their own house in order; increasingly, they are held responsible for the failures and defects of those huge institutions which they serve, advise, and oftentimes control; and even their successes, their very considerable technical successes, have generated moral quandaries which professional training does not address.

> William F. May,
> "Professional Ethics:
> Setting, Terrain, and Teacher"

Half truth—

Images of the world involving truths which are obvious to all do not become ideologies. It is the half truth, or at least the insincere truth which appeals to some but not to others, which is the best candidate to set up an ideology. . . . The danger of ideology is that it suppresses the learning process. If a man has an ideology which explains everything that happens to him, it relieves him of the necessity for learning. He knows everything already!

> Kenneth Boulding,
> *The Meaning of the Twentieth Century:*
> *The Great Transition*

185

Some people in the general population are skeptical about what takes place in the hallowed halls of higher education today. Lofty words, phrases, and motives that many of us associate with higher education do not coincide with the perceived reality; questions about what is actually going on in higher education are prevalent in public dialogue. From the way research funds are being used, to questions about what should be taught, to how professors spend their time, the public is becoming more aware of higher education's potential troubles.[1] Some observers are concerned that higher education has become a place of too many marketing lies. Peck's book, *The People of the Lie: The Hope for Healing Human Evil*, provides us with a provocative title that seems to fit the lay analysis of higher education marketing. Peck reminds us that groups, not just individuals, sometimes offer lies, exaggerating competency beyond what can actually be delivered.[2] Peck's work is not directly related to higher education, but his ideas and Sissela Bok's *On Lying* both point to the fact that the public is concerned about declining acts of honesty. It is little wonder that such questions would be directed to the major public influence of higher education. In short, the pervasive influence of higher education on society today makes it vulnerable to general societal questions and concerns.

Let me emphasize two significant points before continuing. First, higher education is still capable of offering an enormous service to the common good and generally does. Second, I do consider marketing a legitimate activity; it is what some schools are marketing that is my concern. When we claim to be what we are not or to give more than we can deliver, we begin to live a lie. Dialogic education assumes a commitment to inquiry and the pursuit of truth.

I open this question about higher education and marketing by referring to a controversial work, Sykes' *ProfScam*. Sykes calls for an examination of group narcissism in higher education. As concern for self-protection increases on campuses and in departments, any group can begin to protect its own interests by hiding behind self-protective lies.

A student met with a colleague of mine that I consider a fair and honest person. My colleague was surprised to hear from the student that one department was advising students not to take courses from a related department. The rationale was that job marketability would not be as good in the related department. The current data, however, reflects just the opposite. The department calling for students to be wary of non-marketable degrees has had a more difficult time placing its graduates in jobs. The discrepancy between the rhetoric and fact was so obvious that the advice sounded like a marketing lie to the students, or at least an uninformed exaggeration motivated by a desperate need to keep majors.

The question for higher education that I believe summarizes Sykes' work is, When does campus or departmental self-protection begin to cloud our ability to be candid with a questioning public? The answer is when self-protection becomes more important than teaching and scholarship. At such junctures we begin to violate the calling of higher education, engaging in inquiry with the next generation.

It is not that the above concerns of self-protection are unimportant. We all want institutions to survive and departments and individual careers to blossom. Trouble emerges, in terms of Peck's notion of the lie, when we engage in an action for one set of reasons, justifying that behavior with a different rationale. For example, a corporate lie can emerge when the public call to teaching and scholarship becomes subordinated to other agendas, such as sports, governance, or ideological propaganda, yet our public claim continues to be the importance of teaching and scholarship.

In this chapter I examine the scam or lie that some in the public sector believe is alive in too many campus decisions. We, as educators, may not like or agree with the assessment that higher education may be experiencing a chasm between its stated goals and the realities of a given campus, but as professional educators we owe an answer to our critics. This chapter describes the importance of straightforward dialogue with the public at large, announcing what we want to do and offering evidence that such goals are being pursued.

Sykes' Critique of Higher Education

Sykes' complaints about higher education may seem totally off the mark for many institutions of higher learning and for most faculty. However, he outlines a critique of higher education growing in intensity among the general public. Articles in *The Chronicle of Higher Education* frequently question the use of grant money and administrative privileges. Criticisms ranging from the political orientation of higher education and lack of commitment to teaching, to what should constitute the core of a undergraduate general education, to tuition increases that significantly outrace the rate of inflation, are but a few of the issues raised. Those of us interested in dialogic education can learn as we listen and respond to our public critics, inviting a constructive public dialogue. The following summarizes the list of concerns about higher education offered by Sykes. Each point reveals troubling issues that educators need to address, even if the charges are unfair for most faculty and colleges.

1. Faculty are overpaid.
2. Teaching is not taken seriously.
3. The better-known faculty are concerned about their own interests, leaving teaching to a lesser-trained and a lesser-paid underclass of employees, such as graduate students, nontenure-track faculty, and part-time instructors.
4. University curricula too often promote the professional interest of faculty members, not the student's best educational experience.
5. Teaching excellence may go unnoticed or may even be penalized.
6. Knowledge of questionable social and practical value is being studied with increasing intensity.
7. Too much research is unreadable or seemingly worthless to the educated public at large.
8. Academic freedom has become a guise for protecting teachers from accountability in their jobs.
9. Much of the research and teaching has become trendy.
10. Academic fraud has become too commonplace for an institution dependent on reputation and respect for authority.
11. Mediocrity in teaching has been encouraged by reward structures that often weigh other activities more heavily than teaching.
12. Efforts at higher education reform have been rejected, and "the professors' relentless drive for advancement . . . has turned American universities into vast factories of junkthink."[3]

The question for educators interested in dialogic education is, How can we avoid such pitfalls that might turn interest away from the development of the character of our students and conversation about ideas? We might find an answer as we examine these negative public perceptions of higher education more fully.

Warnings and Implications

If we address Sykes' specific accusations as a general set of warnings, we might be able to benefit from discussion of his assertions. Sykes' message revolves around three themes: the dangers of excess careerism; the need to rediscover the importance of teaching; and the need for honesty in advertising, recognizing what makes a college special. Any campus interested in dialogic education must consider the impact of prevailing public perceptions about higher education, learning from a public that depends on us for future leaders.

Concern for Career

Sykes points to a potential danger of faculty becoming overly career conscious to the extent that off-campus career concerns begin to take precedent over contribution to knowledge and the importance of teaching.

> The modern university—insatiable, opportunistic, and implacably anti-intellectual—is created in the image of the *Professorus Americanus*. Today, the professor is the university.
>
> The modern professorate bears little resemblance to the rumpled, forgetful, impractical academics of popular imagination. In the years since World War II, the profession has changed radically. The modern academic is mobile, self-interested, and without loyalty to institutions or the values of liberal education. The rogue professors of today are not merely obscurantists. They are politicians and entrepreneurs who fiercely protect their turf and shrewdly hustle research cash while they peddle their talents to rival universities, businesses, foundations, or government.[4]

A reader could interpret the above quotation as suggesting that the problem of public confidence in higher education is primarily due to the psychological disposition of the professor. But this would miss a significant opportunity to examine a common trend throughout American culture today. We are a people motivated by career advancement, and higher education is not immune to such an emphasis. Faculty, like many in the American work force, see shortages of good academic positions, and have attempted to find ways to protect themselves as cynicism and lack of trust in administration and management have become more prevalent. When studies show that 43 percent of the American work force believes that selfishness and fakery are at the heart of most social interaction,[5] we should not be surprised to find faculty members protecting employment through an increased concern for their careers.

For the last twenty years faculty have been competing in an educational environment with a surplus of faculty seeking positions, in spite of predictions of faculty shortages. Fair or not, the perception that a career focus has overtaken the campus is unlikely to dissipate in intensity in the near future. If Sykes' argument is taken seriously, then it is not surprising that the value system of many of our students is highly oriented toward careerism.[6]

Before going further with this critique, it is important to call attention to the positive components of careerism. A person with nothing to risk in an organization can be dangerous. One dean stated that she sought career-ambitious faculty, who wanted their colleagues to succeed in order to bring more recognition to the school and all the faculty associated with the institution. She was also wary of faculty without career commitments who functioned like unthinking zealots with nothing to lose, not needing to live with the results of their chaos making.

The lack of confidence in higher education that fuels careerism comes from both faculty and students.[7] In a difficult job market it is little wonder that many of our students have become careerists; they endure classes and view education as a means to an end, without learning to love the acquisition of knowledge. When faculty are pushed to publish, gain a national reputation, and acquire tenure and advancement, the door to careerism is opened for them as well.

When faculty feel undue pressure to conform to particular expectations in order to survive, scholarship and, at some institutions, teaching may be done, not out of commitment, but out of necessity. Scholarship can become a mechanical task and teaching a way to ensure student numbers in classes. Teaching and scholarship then become a necessary and burdensome regiment for advancing a career in higher education, instead of developing a fine career as a by-product of a commitment to high quality teaching and scholarship. The notion of career being the macro-result of many daily micro-efforts of teaching and scholarship suggests that a career is built on projects and the quality teaching relationships we experience each day. It is a slow result of consistent commitment. But if a faculty member ignores long-term commitments to academic excellence and concentrates on survival in the marketplace, short-run political action can dominate his or her time.

Careerism thrives as institutions of higher learning begin to view themselves as simply another industry that must fight to survive. My contention is that higher education is not just another industry; it is the heart of an educated populace and the foundation of a democracy. Excessive careerism may suggest more concern for the appearance of a great career than the development of a foundation of teaching and scholarship excellence that can invite a quality career to emerge over a number of years. Careerism wrongly encourages putting the cart before the horse, asking for a macro-judgment of a career, when much of the micro-work in teaching and scholarship is yet to be done. On the other hand, dialogic education encourages faculty to develop the type of reputation that can guide a career through hard work, a quality knowledge base, and concerned interaction with the next generation of leaders, both inside and outside the classroom. Such a career is a by-product of long hours in inquiry with students; the overall assessment of a career will rest in the hands of others.

The Preeminence of Teaching

Sykes contends that higher education may be in danger of losing sight of the primary function of a faculty member committed to undergraduate instruction: teaching the student. Sykes' remarks are consistent with those of Kenneth Eble, known for his commitment to college teaching. The following remarks by Eble are certainly not typical of all faculty, but unfortunately apply to some.

> Early in my academic career, I observed that faculties have a marked capacity to live with and even cherish their own deficiencies. That tendency may spring from a belief carried over from an earlier day that, having forsworn worldly ambitions, college professors have a right to be easy on themselves. The academic profession provided a haven for certain types, curious by nature and permitted by private means or institutional support to indulge their whims. College profession has moved well away from the traditions of gentility, yet an attraction to privilege, a liking for setting one's own terms, still characterizes the profession. As it affects teaching, the jealousy with which professors guard the prime hours for their own work is nearly a universal mark of self-indulgence.[8]

Eble's remarks indicate that it is not just critics like Sykes that believe that some professors have lost sight of what is important in higher education. Some colleagues are calling for reexamination of our commitments—not to the exclusion of scholarship, but as a necessary extension through scholarship in dialogue with our students both inside and outside the classroom. Dialogic education requires us not only to learn more, but to be willing to make relational contacts with our students as we engage in conversation about ideas together.

If we are to provide an alternative to this negative assessment, dialogic education might begin by reclaiming the importance of the word *teacher*. The term *teacher* dialogically suggests ushering in the next generation of leaders through conversation about ideas and relational concern. Dialogic education is compatible with a high level of quality teaching; teaching lays the ground where conversation about ideas and concern for relationships can be concretely given birth.

An implicit assumption about the term *teaching* is both a modest and a demanding one; faculty should know the historical and contemporary arguments and positions in their respective areas, informing students and permitting questions. In addition, they should find satisfaction in talking about ideas with students that are both inside and outside their own discipline. Accepting the importance of scholarship in dialogic education also requires a teacher to be committed to bringing those ideas to life for students. One must want to give information to others, as well as offer students a model of commitment to inquiry that a nonexpert can understand and follow.

One of my colleagues asked, "What if you are asked to teach out of your specialty area? Then should such teaching be viewed as a scholarly delay?" Earlier I discussed the importance of breadth in dialogic education. A person unable or unwilling to develop scholarly competency in a required course outside his or her major research area will have some difficulty selling scholarly breadth to students. A teacher who believes in breadth does not teach only a narrow area of his or her own expertise. Students are required to take courses they might not freely choose. Faculty need to continue to learn as well; class preparation can assist in broadening one's expertise.

Dialogic education has the potential to work when a faculty member loves both students and inquiry; this combination invites the student into exchange about ideas before having a similar scholarly base to the faculty member from which to draw insight and detail. "It [teaching] also involves developing as part of one's self, and encouraging in others, a vision of a shared life. Awareness of a future that is organized around an image of self-fulfillment or what one will do as an isolated individual is not as enlarging as a sense of future that includes relationships with others."[9] From the philosophical perspective of dialogic education, to be a great teacher requires a broad-based scholarly orientation and concern for relationships with students. From such a perspective, teaching can be envisioned as a natural extension of scholarship and commitment to relationships with others.

Honesty in Advertising a College

The beginning of an ethical life, according to Niebuhr, requires us to know our own limitations.[10] For both ethical and pragmatic reasons, a college or university should not oversell what it is and what it can do. A campus that claims teaching as its primary task cannot have students taught primarily by teaching assistants. A campus that claims to be church-related cannot ignore the importance of faith on the campus. A university that states the importance of scholarship cannot fail to reward research. In short, what we say we are as a university or college is what we should attempt to be.

Sykes' criticism once again calls us to accountability. "Schools that brag about the quality of their faculty should be required—by trustees and state legislators—to make those faculty members available to students by insisting that university administrators openly disclose the workloads of their faculty and spell out on a course by course basis in the school's catalog, the degree of the professor's reliance on teaching assistants."[11] Sykes offers a clear and simple reminder: we need to advertise not just what we hope we are, but to outline honestly who and what we are at a given time in the history of an institution.

As dialogic education is communicated to the public, I want to caution against overstressing three major issues: community, care, and answers. Though each of these is an important part of this teaching philosophy, each pushed to excess can become a negative in the education of students for lifelong learning.

Community. Dialogic education encourages building a community and an identity, an academic home for the students and faculty. Not all college and university campuses are cold and impersonal. More interest and personal attention might be given to students by teaching assistants than older faculty can provide. Like any social good, however, an emphasis on community can be oversold.[12] In the past year, I have witnessed four different colleges each selling a community theme, each having trouble retaining students. Perhaps the notion of community, when sold at an unrealistic level, invites disappointed students who leave when their hopes for great personal closeness do not quickly emerge.

Though I am deeply committed to community, I reject marketing of community that cannot be guaranteed. Such marketing sets students up for disappointment, because community only happens through invitation and good fortune. Formal community is a contradiction in terms; it is the tyranny of intimacy, a form of interpersonal manipulation. Dietrich Bonhoeffer warned us to beware of those wanting to join a community in order to satisfy every psychological need.[13] A college or university is not set up to satisfy all the psychological needs of students.

Instead of the word *community*, perhaps a better term is *involvement*. We cannot guarantee a student will feel a sense of community. But we can guarantee opportunities for involvement in extracurricular activities, governance, the arts, sports, and faith issues, in accordance with talent and available time. Community is a by-product of people involved in work or activities together. Those interested in dialogic education cannot demand that a community develop, nor can its emergence be assured. But we can invite a community to emerge as we make places of involvement and public conversation available and known to all on the campus.

Care. Dialogic education assumes that no one type of university or college campus has sole possession of the capacity to care. Like the term *community*, caring needs to be articulated with caution. Caring is a virtue that should be a part of any educational experience. The question is: Should a college or university market virtues? My answer is a definite no. Caring should not be marketed. It is too easy to translate caring into keeping the customer happy. Such action can be in opposition to the task of assisting students in short- and long-term growth as a learner.

Faculty and administrators interested in dialogic education should be wary of overselling a caring, relational environment. The human relations movement in business collapsed when perceived by workers as corporate self-interest, not genuine care for the employee. Anyone who discovers that efforts at caring are attempts at placating and manipulation is likely to be angered by the lack of genuine caring motivated by revenue needs at a college or university. Any campus needs to be careful when communicating what it can deliver in interpersonal relations or it faces the real possibility of being found out as phony and generating cynicism in students.

Perhaps a better phrase might be "availability outside the classroom." Campus residents in search of dialogue are interested in ideas and in people, willing to discuss both inside and outside the classroom setting. Faculty that maintain office hours and are excited about ideas and students encourage dialogue through their availability. In such an environment, we can communicate the opportunity to meet with faculty outside the classroom, without overstating what we can deliver.

Out of such an atmosphere, we may even invite the possibility of friendship that calls people to labor for the worthy cause of education. But this occasional friendship needs to be genuine, emerge on its own terms, and cannot be marketed. "The excellent person labors for his friends and for his native country, and will die for them if he must; he will sacrifice money, honors and contested goods in general, in achieving what is fine."[14] This classical understanding of friendship calls one to do good, not just feel good and to judge the good by standards of what is fine or excellent.

Friendship between persons that emerges from availability outside the classroom calls us to go to extra lengths, even to the extent of losing a paying customer, in order to assist that person's future education. The task of education does not always make a student happy; at times we need to ask him or her to do what is not considered fun or enjoyable.

A student stated in his parents' presence that he hoped to convince the dean to let him back in school after being academically disqualified. The dean and the student had become friends in conversation about baseball and many other issues. The student begged for another chance and was then asked by the dean, "If you were me, what would you do? Would you be lenient? How would you help this student to be more prepared for the long-term demands of life?" The student paused and looked at his friend in the role of final arbitrator and then looked at his parents. Finally he said, "You have asked me to stay out of school for one year. I will use that time to prove to you and to myself that I am ready for the responsibility of college." Such a confrontation between two people was not easy, but a necessary part of a dialogic environment.

Friendship implies upholding good action for another as more important than making that person feel good. Such caring has a sense of tough-minded ethics, permitting friendships where challenge and long-term concern for a student's welfare, not placating the customer, guides the interaction.

Answers. The major ingredients necessary for a quality higher education within a dialogic context can be viewed as a whole or gestalt composed of multiple interrelated parts. Caution is the key as we fight the temptation to offer answers too quickly, regarding how life is to be lived based upon the insight of one theory. Dialogic education encourages discussion of value-laden issues, but is wary of moving too quickly to any single paradigmatic presentation of information or values. A teacher can state where he or she stands on a given issue. Danger emerges, however, when the student is not informed of the reality of multiple perspectives. A one-sided message moves education into propaganda, often offering answers to complex issues that are too simple and tidy.

I have heard a significant emphasis on the word *complexity* in higher education. But it is possible to offer a description about complexity as an answer to questions and issues better discussed as difficult. *Complexity* is a quality, condition, or structure that is intricate.[15] *Difficulty* is a condition requiring hard work and much effort.[16] In conversation with the public we need to be careful to not claim complexity as an excuse for not completing a job that is manageable through hard work and better referred to as difficult. It is difficult, but not necessarily complex to encourage three major support systems for the academic life of a campus: clear commitment to teaching and scholarship; a quality study and work environment for students, faculty, and staff; and fiscal responsibility at every level of the institution.

However, too often complexity does arise when we overextend claims about the quality of our faculty, student environment, or the financial base of a school. Complexity is often the operational result of overextending our claims beyond what can be delivered, giving the appearance of excellence, yet being unable to back up the claims. We then offer answers to the public about questions of our quality that move us from a difficult job to a complex task of trying to figure out intricate maneuvers to keep the public from finding out the limited extent of what we can deliver for our students.

A Customer Mentality

Sykes believes that universities have lost sight of the student and that the student has become a customer. There is a temptation for schools in need of students and financial resources to encourage a customer mentality. Administrators may use an industrial vocabulary that reveals both a philosophical and operational shift on college campuses. In such an environment, maintaining the academic discipline and the quality of faculty and student learning must now compete with notions such as "the higher education industry," a "customer mentality," and the importance of "student perception of faculty." Such concerns have perhaps an even more immediate impact on campuses where survival is based on "enrollment maintenance" in a shrinking college population pool.

In 1969, Postman and Weingartner published *Teaching as Subversive Activity*, encouraging faculty to challenge conventional and status quo norms within society and in education itself.[17] Without arguing for or against the merits of an era known for its excesses, the 1960s and early 1970s encouraged academic freedom and educational experimentation, and were motivated by an optimism about the potential of higher education.

Today, an appropriate sequel to *Teaching as Subversive Activity*, might be "Teaching as Subservient Activity"—subservient to a customer mentality, and concerned more about retention than education. The current atmosphere on some campuses is one of faculty questioning the preparation of the average student for college work, the motivation of students who view education as a necessary rite of passage into employment and good money, and the lack of wisdom of students trying to avoid general education courses not directly related to future careers and employment.[18] In this negative light, faculty may feel called to keep students enrolled and happy. For many faculty and institutions, a customer mentality does not prevail. But for those campuses and departments in the midst of declining enrollment, a plea to please the customer is not an unheard cry from the administration.

Of course, the above comments do not reflect the attitudes and actions of all faculty and students. But some faculty do believe that the power of evaluation has shifted too far into student hands and away from the judgment of competent faculty, particularly on campuses where customer satisfaction and retention are directly tied to institutional survival. It is possible to care and be nice for less than noble reasons, such as keeping enough students in a course or increasing the revenue base for the college.

Bruce Wilshire, in *The Moral Collapse of the University: Professionalism, Purity, and Alienation* calls the university community to task, faculty and administration alike. One of his issues of concern is the support of a customer mentality on campus.

> I thought more about the ideology of consumerism as a reason for their [students'] numbness and detachment. After spending their lives barraged by images equating buying with goodness, they seemed deeply to believe (if they believed anything deeply) that anything good can be bought, and without ever looking closely at the images on the money. A college education meant a degree, and

this is a commodity which can be bought by paying fees and serving time. The possibility that knowledge could only be earned through diligent and at times drudging effort to come up to standards native to the enterprise of knowing itself, had apparently never entered most of their minds.[19]

It is the calling of a university to shape its constituency, not just respond to customer demands and offer a dedicated environment rich in a commitment to hard work and learning.

An institutional demand to care for students that is motivated by concern for the customer is much different than a philosophical belief in the importance of empowering students, as was the case during the 1960s. The shift to a customer mentality has been propelled more out of concern for survival or institutional narcissism than out of philosophical commitment to students.

The shift from a philosophical commitment to the intellectual growth of a student to customer satisfaction is understandable in light of the dramatic changes in the higher education environment. The experimental spirit of the 1960s was nourished by abundant resources in education, competition with the Soviet Union, and baby boom expansion in education at all levels. At that time, faculty could relocate relatively easily and graduating students did not fear unemployment. Many faculty and students sought not just any job, but a place of employment worthy of their talents.

Today we have a much different social environment in higher education—one that places pressure on faculty to satisfy customer demands. For example, let's briefly examine three related issues: grade inflation, student evaluations, and homogeneity of the faculty. Steven Cahn, Provost and Academic Vice President of the Graduate School of the City University of New York, considered these issues deviations from the task of teaching and scholarship. When faculty focus on pleasing students more than educating them and on continuing to broaden a knowledge base that will permit assisting the next generation of learners, we need to be called back to our original obligation of teaching and scholarship. Anything that takes too much time and energy from our original charge of teaching and scholarship should be suspect. "In addition to teaching, professors conduct research. . . . faculty members able to contribute should heed the injunction of an ancient Hebrew sage: 'It is not your duty to complete the task, but you are not free to desist from it.' "[20] The tasks are teaching, scholarship, and assisting the next generation of leaders, not customer appeal.

Grade inflation can take us from our task when it is more a sign of fear on the part of colleagues wanting a happy customer than a philosophical commitment to egalitarian grading. What is the mean grade given in summer courses when student enrollment is low? What happens when a faculty member gives no grade lower than $B+$ in the two years prior to being considered for tenure? Are some faculty tempted to give grades as political weapons to secure support from students? Are some tempted to protect themselves and their careers by appeasing the customer when the notion of a customer mentality is encouraged by an administration?

Student evaluations take on more significance in an environment where pleasing the student is important. It is appropriate for students to have input into the quality of classroom instruction. Danger emerges, however, when student evaluations begin to result in a similar teaching style among the faculty, generating an homogeneous environment. If faculty feel compelled to conform to a teaching standard in order to survive, we place diversity and nonconventional instruction at risk.

A customer mentality that indirectly encourages even some teaching conformity may limit exposure to new ideas and characters who do not fit our prior expectations. Without diversity of persons, ideas, and modes of instruction on a campus, we have no modern university. At best, we have a corporate mentality that determines if people fit. In the 1950s, Riesman and Fromm discussed the dangers of the marketing personality;[21] a customer mentality seems little different. The customer is encouraged to be proactive and the college or university a respondent to the demands of the market.

Many schools run summer orientation programs for students. Such programs vary in emphasis from an introduction to academic life, to an introduction to the multifaceted activities available on a campus, and may even include what Warren Bryan Martin describes as the opposition to a *College of Character*, "Welcome to fun and games, and a little learning, too!"[22] Martin's warning rings true, as exemplified by one freshman crying in a colleague's office saying, "No one told me I would have to study. I did so little in high school." Perhaps such a surprise about the demands of college is somewhat due to the impression of good times and comfort that may have been portrayed when the student was recruited. The student had to bear the burden of a misleading picture of the ease of learning.

Both profit and nonprofit organizational structures must be

fiscally responsible. However, a profit-making organization's goal is to create capital, to generate revenue. On the other hand, a nonprofit agency has a responsibility to protect the public good. A college or university is charged with assisting the public good of a community, nation, and even the world with the information it imparts within its own financial capability.

When revenue beyond projected needs for annual budgets and endowments becomes more important than educating the next generation of leaders, a college has slipped outside the domain of a nonprofit agency and begins to function as a for-profit institution. The key to keeping a nonprofit commitment requires keeping in mind first and foremost the public good, while working within fiscal responsibility of that charter. Using business-for-profit language to describe a college may erode the unique mission of a nonprofit institution. A university may do well to resist certain business language, such as calling the faculty "employees"; faculty need to be reminded of their special status and responsibilities, as do students.

Businesses have valuable lessons to teach colleges about fiscal responsibility. However, when revenue becomes an end, rather than a means to generate a quality education, a school can lose its mission and uniqueness.[23] As I worked as a consultant to a college, one faculty member indicated this in saying: "We have lost our way trying to survive; in fact, we have lost our soul, the depth of who we once were." The result of a customer mentality may be cynicism about whether or not colleges and universities have forgotten their special nonprofit status in our society.

Conceptualizing the institution's task as shaping the future may permit a campus to take a position from which a public dialogue can begin, rejecting temptations to shift from one curriculum to another, depending on what is marketable in the short-run. By so doing, the institution may lose its identity in the long-term process of repeated market adjustments. Again, a major key to dialogic educators, in relation to the public, is to invite conversation from a clear position or stance that can be defended, while being open to other possibilities that might emerge as new information becomes known. Our dialogue with the public can be guided by conversation that reminds ourselves and others that an institution of higher education has a primary purpose—to shape the future as a nonprofit organization committed to education for the public good within the fiscal limits available.

Beginning a Public Dialogue

The following is a list of some major points that a university or college might describe to the public, while staying within the confines of dialogic education:

1. The importance of blending discussion of multiple perspectives on information and values in education that takes place both inside and outside the classroom.
2. Breadth of scholarship for both students and faculty.
3. The practical connection between leadership and opportunities to be in conversation with faculty on the campus.
4. The priority of conversation about ideas with fellow students, faculty, and administrators as a major foundation for dialogic education.

My hope is that campuses interested in dialogic education might begin a conversation with the public that works at informing and persuading a "What's in it for me now?" society about the importance of education that offers a foundation for long-term leadership, conversation about ideas, values, and the importance of persons in whatever vocation they eventually enter.

Advertising is a new field for many professionals, such as physicians, lawyers, and educators. As we make information available to the public sector about who we are as professionals and openly advertise what we have to offer, we need to be wary that we do not oversell ourselves. Michael D. Bayles suggests the following concerns be addressed by professions interested in the use of advertising efforts. First, we need to be careful about tearing down one another in order to reveal our own strengths. Professionals should gain recognition for what they do, not for what others fail to do. A department, college, or university needs to inform the public about what is being and can be accomplished, rejecting the impulse to list the inadequacies of competitors. Second, no person should be talked into a professional service who cannot genuinely benefit from the service. When departments have too few majors, the temptation might be to suggest marketing possibilities that are beyond the probable reach of the average student. Selling success stories rather than clear data on all majors can lead to misinterpretations. And third, one should not exaggerate claims about what professional services will actually be provided.[24] This statement is consistent with my 80 percent suggestion; only market what is 80 percent certain, not the occasional and the sometimes.

The translation of the above suggestions for the university or college requires a public dialogue to begin with what we can do well, bypassing the temptation to discuss the inadequacies of other institutions or to exaggerate claims for our own. Second, we should avoid the temptation of talking a student into joining a campus to which they are not suited. We need to be clear and honest about the nature of our campus environment. And finally, we need to be careful that we articulate the limits of what we can offer when we recruit faculty and students; we should not advertise a professional service or academic environment that is not present on the campus.

Dialogic educators should advertise a campus with a clear mission and attempt to live up to it while working at broad-based scholarship for faculty and students, instilling values that embody concern for excellence. Perhaps such advertising may assist in restoring public confidence in higher education. Instead of careerism, former reputation, and hype, it is wise to market a commitment to corporate honesty that prevents us from overselling what a college or university has to offer.

Restoring a Broken Covenant

Borrowing a phrase from Robert Bellah, we in higher education need to restore the "broken covenant" between the public and higher education.[25] The covenant of dialogic educators with the public requires a commitment to educate leaders for the future, rejecting the temptation to view ourselves as a business concerned only about our own future. In addition, our covenant cannot be with our institutions first, even those places we call home. First and foremost, a commitment to higher education needs to guide us. A commitment to quality higher education will, in the long run, be the surest foundation for our institutions.

When universities communicate what they can actually deliver they do their best to keep an honest covenant with the public. Such schools need to lead the way as role models. Just as Aristotle stated that one must find a "good person" in order to find a standard worthy of pursuing,[26] one must attempt to locate the "good university" that adheres to its basic covenant of marketing what it can deliver.

The following suggestions further clarify the keys to dialogic education, as we attempt to restore a "broken covenant." First, we need a continuing commitment to excellence—quality faculty and students are the standard-bearers of a campus. Students and faculty who go beyond the norm of performance on a campus deserve some form of recognition. Dialogue not only affirms persons, but recognizes the important role of great characters. If a campus does not permit great characters to thrive, then the pursuit of excellence will be limited. Homogeneous faculty, encouraged to be clones of one another, limit the likelihood that the creative nonconformist or the potential great character will find a good academic home in a restrictive environment. Second, if we want students to maintain and enhance an image of academic excellence, this standard must be modeled by the administration and faculty.

Third, campuses interested in dialogic education can work to reward love of inquiry both inside and outside one's discipline. The study of music, foreign languages, and academic areas related to one's own training need to be supported, modeling the importance of lifelong learning central to dialogue between persons of different expertise and training.

Fourth, we should hold the line on quality admission and graduation standards. When we do admit students with low scores or grades, close supervision of study skills and remedial work may be necessary. Dialogue suggests affirming persons; if we admit such students we have an obligation to assist them in becoming successful students. Fifth, we can hold firm on the importance of a quality liberal arts education that can support more vocationally specific academic majors. Again, dialogue implies an education of breadth, capable of initiating conversation with others of diverse backgrounds.

Sixth, clear messages need to guide the values of the institution; we need to know who we are and what our limits must be. Finally, I still have the conviction that, in the long run, quality does attract a market; dialogic educators might be able to pursue students willing to be consumers of excellence, not soft standards. There is risk in such an administrative effort, but Bloom, Hirsch, and numerous reports on higher education are calling faculty and administrators to care more for education than the short-run success of our own institutions.[27]

The spirit of dialogue requires taking a position, defending it, and listening to opposition. With that in mind, a colleague asked me to make my position on Bloom and Hirsch public. First, I am convinced that Bloom and Hirsch are correct in their call for content education. The theme of this book, conversation about ideas, is grounded in a content emphasis. Second, I am not as confident as Bloom and Hirsch about what the content should be. I would suggest that dialogic education needs to be sensitive to tradition while being open to learning from persons and new perspectives, rejecting claims that are totally exclusive of other positions. I rest within the paradoxical tension of tradition and change. Third, the tone of these authors, particularly that of Bloom, is too cynical. I am concerned about any educational effort on the political left or right that gains credibility by bashing the shortcomings of other perspectives. As one of my colleagues stated, "You are a hopeless humanist." Perhaps I am. I believe it is more helpful for a society to have scholars known for their own work, rather than for discussion of the shortcomings of rival perspectives. Argument is possible within a humanistic paradigm of concern for others, as long as the other's ideas and personhood are taken seriously. Cynicism lessens how seriously we take the opposition. Jeffrey C. Goldfarb, in *The Cynical Society*, suggests that two forms of cynicism surround Bloom's book: a cynicism toward ideas that are contrary or different and a cynicism that refuses to take the opposition seriously.[28] But in spite of these differences, Bloom and Hirsch point to the importance of a public dialogue centered on educational content. They suggest greater commitment to content education, reflected in college policy and in the distribution of revenue.

We may even discover that the consumer is attracted to excellence that seeks to combine conversation about ideas and values without indoctrination of more than we might initially speculate. The success of higher education in the United States must eventually be judged, not only by numbers and quantity, but by commitment to providing the next generation of leaders with the information, vision, values, and wisdom necessary to make difficult decisions and contributions based on thoughtful, well-rounded knowledge.

Robert Bellah offers the wisdom that some covenants are so important that they are worth trying to repair and follow, even after they have been broken.[29] Even though the covenant on what higher education should be has not always been upheld, we can get closer to the covenant that takes seriously phrases like "the best ideas rise to the surface of debate" and "values without indoctrination." Dialogic education is based upon a public dialogue that can honestly be delivered. Then the covenant with the public will have two major supporting pillars in place, honesty and integrity, not only in advertising, but in knowing who and what we can deliver within the particular missions and charters of our institutions.

There are many ways to honestly communicate the mission of a particular college or university. But there is no shortcut to a student being knowledgeable, and there is no quick method of cultivating academic excellence. Dialogic education is grounded in the day-by-day hard work of reminding one another why we gather together at a university or college—to teach what we know and are learning, and to pass on an important value that life is meant to be lived in interaction with others. In small ways, dialogic education offers a model of the humane intellectual. Knowledge in dialogic education is not just for the learner, but should be shared as we learn from one another. An environment interested in dialogic education that strives to live up to such a covenant without false guarantees and displays just might find consumers interested in answering the call to become students and enter into conversation about ideas and between persons.

11

Dialogic Teaching: A Vocation

The vocation of a teacher—

A recent article in *The Chronicle of Higher Education* (October 23, 1985) claims that 40 percent of all teachers in higher education are considering, or have considered, leaving the profession, because they are so dissatisfied with their present position. My crystal ball—or should I say my computer modem?—does not reveal what the "job market" will be in five, ten, or fifteen years. But, I do know that too many wonderfully promising teachers have been driven elsewhere by our current practices. . . . I must say "almost," because "callings," vocations, are chancy; by their nature they can simply evaporate without a trace, boiled away by the fires of adverse circumstance. I must not hide the fact that at least two of my former graduate students now say that they regret their years of preparing to teach English. And that wonderful freshman English teacher of mine later confessed that he rather wished he had become—an anthropologist.

> Wayne C. Booth,
> *The Vocation of a Teacher:*
> *Rhetorical Occasions, 1967–1988*

Teacher as mentor: practice—

In the case of virtue, the practice of actions will obviously be more complex. Virtuous action, as we have said, will combine a judgement of circumstances, reactive emotions, and some level of decision about how to act. Here too the learner will follow the examples of emulated models, and may have in mind general precepts and rules of thumb. Becoming sensitive to the circumstances in which action is called for as well as flexible in one's conception of the require-

206

ments of a precept is all part of practising virtuous action. . . .
We learn how to play the lyre . . . by practising not merely with
persistence, but with an eye toward how the expert plays and with
attention to how our performance measures against that model.
Without the instructions and monitoring of a reliable teacher, a
student can just as easily become a bad lyre player as a good one.

Nancy Sherman,
The Fabric of Character:
Aristotle's Theory of Virtue

A college dean taught each semester, even though her schedule was already demanding. She stated that the job of an administrator is to make the teaching environment better for students
and faculty. An administrator teaches to remind himself or herself
of what a dean must protect—the learning exchange between
faculty and student. He or she must remember that teaching is
the primary vocation of a college or university community.

Dialogic education places a high value on teaching, both
inside and outside the classroom. Dialogic education is fundamentally motivated by a desire to have conversation about ideas, while
taking relationships between people seriously. Such an interac-
tional and conversational style of working with students makes
teaching a natural act in dialogic education. One college teacher
said that being a professor could be a great life if the students
would stay home and quit disrupting time needed for research
projects. I was unimpressed by the thought of a studentless campus; dialogue requires communicative partners. Dialogic educators put a premium on interaction with students, bringing together scholarship and relationships. Dialogic education is
centered not only on the passing on of information, values, and
cognitive tools, but on conversation about information, values,
and relationships. Dialogue is a constitutive act involving both
student and teacher. Teaching dialogically requires one to give
and to get, offering and gaining information and insight. The tone
for this type of education is described by Parker Palmer.

The minds we have used to divide and conquer were given to us
for another purpose: to raise to awareness the communal nature of
reality, to overcome separateness and alienation by a knowing that
is loving, to reach out with intelligence to acknowledge and renew
the bonds of life. . . . This love is not a soft and sentimental virtue,
not a fuzzy feeling of romance. . . . "Love in action," said Dostoevski,

"is a harsh and dreadful thing," and so it can be. A knowledge that springs from love may require us to change, even sacrifice, for the sake of what we know. It is easy to be curious and controlling. It is difficult to love. But [necessary] if we want a knowledge that will rebind our broken world . . .[1]

Dialogic teachers are hopeful that concern for information and relationships can provide an education that offers a foundation for knowledge and later wisdom in leadership.

This emphasis on the relational nature of teaching is not a new idea. Dewey recognized the importance of the educational system addressing the relational components of young people. Dewey was inclined to use the term *social individual* to emphasize the importance of the relational nature of education. He felt that when the social and relational elements of a person's education are ignored, we are left with an education that ignores the person.[2]

Aristotle also provided classical support for a relational focus in education. He showed that virtues and a noble life are learned and tested more in interaction with one another than in study alone.[3] The relational emphasis of dialogic education is central to this approach, but should not be confused with a therapeutic environment. A therapeutic culture has been described by a number of recent authors. I will focus on two: Robert Bellah and Christopher Lasch.

Bellah discusses a therapeutic culture as one where questions of right and wrong are substituted for questions about how our experience affects the self. No one is viewed as right or wrong, but as merely presenting a position. Collectively, instead of seeking to contribute to the common good, we look for ways in which the community can contribute to our individual good.

> What is not questioned is the institutional context. One's growth is a purely private matter. It may involve maneuvering within the structure of bureaucratic rules and roles, changing jobs, maybe even changing spouses if necessary. But what is missing is any collective context in which one might act as a participant to change the institutional structures that frustrate and limit. . . . This therapeutic view not only refuses to take a moral stand, it actively distrusts "morality" and sees therapeutic contractualism as a more adequate framework for viewing human action.[4]

The therapeutic culture is tied first to the individual good, second to an effort to minimize winners or losers, and third to a promotion of the self. Lasch, in *The Minimal Self*, states that self-development is not enough. We need to play a part in the construction of stories or narratives worthy of participation and that contribute to the common good.[5]

Dialogic education offers conversation about ideas as central to education, not self-development. The student is invited to learn about ideas that can contribute to the common good, which involves both others and oneself. Conversation links us to ideas and to others, making learning a project with the teleological objective to assist the common good, not just ourselves.

The interplay of relationship and content in a teaching life means that one will never be able to give oneself completely to books and experimentation. Conversation about learning with others takes time and effort. The life of scholarship becomes one that naturally accompanies and supports teaching. Jacoby, in *The Last Intellectuals*, makes the case that scholars need to make contact with the public.[6] The first public for a teacher is the student audience that she or he meets on campus. An interested scholar is more likely to excite students with information, engaging in conversation that uses examples from their lives, decision-making choices of leaders, or even discussion about the importance of memorization as a foundation for later synthesis of ideas in a competitive world.

Before outlining the teaching style of a dialogic educator, let me caution against the unthinking use of any one teaching style and orientation, including the dialogic one advocated in this book. One of my friends asked, "Should we all teach using dialogic methods?" My answer was a definite no. What can assist dialogic education is the offering of information and the shaping of persons through relationship. I am convinced of the value of such an education because it was given to me. But we need to affirm the unique role of a university, keeping diversity of scholarship and teaching styles available and supported. Academic tenure assures, at least theoretically, that such diversity will be possible. It is difficult to imagine an effective teacher adhering to a form of teaching that he or she does not believe.

The danger of imitation is in conceptualizing that there is only one way to accomplish a task. Wayne Booth offers a good way to avoid *monism*, the belief in one perspective. He suggests that we use an orientation as long as it works, with full knowledge that other perspectives exist that can and will reap different and interesting results.[7] Dialogic teaching, of course, is not a panacea for the ills of higher education or of an individual student. It is but one way to improve education today by reaching out to others, and being willing to envision the teaching task as involving information and conversation among people.

Dialogic Teaching—A Corporate Act

Philosophically, dialogic teaching is the antithesis of a solitary act as one enters the classroom. Such teaching involves conversation with material and great ideas we encounter in reading, experiments we do, and students we meet. One way to describe the corporate nature of dialogic teaching is to use the following notion from Camus: "We are." Camus, like Kenneth Burke, uses "we" to indicate the corporate nature of one's thought. Our ideas and views do not emerge out of a vacuum, but are part of a corporate position pointed to by numerous other thinkers and articulated by a particular author.[8]

Camus discusses how an individual act can be more than an action of individualism. He suggests that each individual bears responsibility for maintaining the dignity of all people—a corporate act. "We are" more than our own individual actions. Such a philosophical orientation results in the actions of each person calling us to accountability, reminding us of the potential of a given vocation, such as teaching.

According to Wayne Booth's notion of teaching as vocation through the conceptual eyes of Camus' "we are" philosophy, each professor is a symbolic representative of a group of people called teachers. Only as each individual becomes deeply engaged in the vocation of teaching does the whole of the profession pursue excellence. No profession pursues excellence on its own in the abstract. The individual members, each with a commitment to excellence that is lived out in the ongoing action of the community, can begin to build a corporate understanding of excellence.

> The "We are" paradoxically defines a new form of individualism. "We are" in terms of history, and history must reckon with this "We are," which must in its turn keep its place in history. I have need of others who have need of me and of each other. Every collective action, every form of society, supposes a discipline, is only a stranger, bowed down under the weight of an inimical collectivity. But society and discipline lose their direction if they deny the dignity that I cannot allow either myself or others to debase. This individualism is in no sense pleasure; it is perpetual struggle, and, sometimes, unparalleled joy when it reaches the heights of proud compassion.[9]

The "we are" philosophy of Camus implies that each one of us assumes the vocation of a teacher as she or he walks into a classroom or onto a university campus. From that point onward, our actions reflect more than just ourselves. An individual faculty member known for teaching excellence assumes a significance and influence beyond the classroom through the continuing memories and actions of those intellectually and relationally touched by teaching interaction.

Each time a teacher upholds the importance of learning, the collective enterprise of education is supported. Each time one of us fails to contribute constructively in the classroom we do harm, not just to ourselves and our own students, but to those that depend on a thoughtful and well-educated population from which to elect future leaders.

Camus' notion of "we are" emphasizes the corporate nature of life and the natural importance of what Bellah has called a "community of memory." We live not just for ourselves, but for others as well. As a community discusses stories about great teachers over and over again in conversation, the symbol of one person begins to assume a larger importance for the whole campus. Bellah's "community of memory" encourages us to tell important individual stories that have collective implications.[10]

In short, when we view teaching as a vocation within a dialogic context, we need to recognize that each time we walk into the classroom, meet a student outside of class, or engage in scholarship, we are symbolizing an importance beyond ourselves. Christa McAuliffe was right when she said that teachers have a great task and opportunity: We touch the future through the students we teach.[11] Her statement points to the importance of carrying on a dialogue between generations. Teachers are more than individual workers; we are the carriers of conversation and value discussion between generations. We touch the future not only for our students, but for fellow teachers as well. Our task is to pass the baton of conversation about ideas, not just information and value positions that have worked for us.

Dual Demands

When teaching is viewed as a corporate act of representing the profession of educator, the question is, What type of teaching will we model for students and fellow teachers? Using Camus' notion of "we are," the teacher symbolically sets the agenda of excellence in two major areas: content and relationship. For a teacher to be excellent, he or she must know the information and have the ability to make relational contact with students who may not want to learn the material with the same vigor as the teacher.

We can shed additional light on the content/relationship demands of a teacher interested in dialogic education by examining a definition of *communication* that recognizes the information or content, as well as the relationship dimensions of any communicative interaction. "Every communication has a content [information] and relationship aspect such that the latter classifies the former."[12]

For example, the relationship one has with a professor can affect what one learns and how one interprets that information. Unless a student is extremely sure of what profession to pursue, the selection of an academic major is often based on a relationship with an instructor. On a personal note, I chose a graduate program as much on the power of the relationship I had with one of my undergraduate professors as I did because of the academic subject matter itself. I was impressed by the teacher, the person who brought the content to life in the classroom, inspiring me to learn more. In my case, the professor was content-wise and relationally sensitive; content supported by relationship is the foundation of dialogic education.

The dual demands on the dialogic educator are to first work on competency and the ability to present that information, and then to invite quality relationships with students both inside and outside the classroom. The next three parts of this section emphasize the importance of content, the danger of too much relational focus in any relationship, and the person-to-person commitment of dialogic education with knowledge of the dangers of an excessive relational focus.

In Search of Content

First and foremost, the teacher must have something to offer students. A dialogic teacher loves the content or subject matter being taught and does whatever is necessary to make that information understandable to others. It is not enough to want to teach; one must have knowledge of content, both historical and contemporary in nature, to be prepared for the role of teacher. As an article in *The Chronicle of Higher Education* has emphasized, we need teachers who pass on a love of their academic discipline, who take teaching seriously, and are content-wise, expecting their students to know the material well.[13]

Some surveys indicate that contemporary students lack an information base necessary in the modern world. For instance, a National Geographic study found that young people in the United States are not performing as well as they did in years past in their knowledge of basic information about the global community. In identifying countries on the map, 18–24 year olds in the United States scored below youth in Sweden, West Germany, Japan, Soviet Union, Canada, Italy, France, United Kingdom, and Mexico.[14] This and other findings suggest that content in education requires more attention.[15] There is growing agreement among diverse groups of intellectuals and the public at large that students graduating from our high schools and colleges are content-shy in too many academic areas.

At a conference of college deans, a discussion centered on the question of what students will need to know in the latter part of this decade. There was general agreement that more content and a general education background that assists in interpretation of our culture and the global community must become a necessary and standard complement to any professional or technical degree. The conversation continued by discussing student themes of prior decades. The sixties were defined by our students asking the question, Who am I? The seventies were centered around students asking the question, Am I being self-actualized or self-fulfilled? The eighties were a time of students asking the question, How can my organization help me?

Then I suggested that future students will be required to answer the question, What do you know? Perhaps this will be the first time in generations that American students are not in the position of generating the questions. They will need to be prepared to answer questions with content and formulate questions from information that can be referenced, in order to get a hearing in an increasingly competitive world economy. I contend that we are entering a paradigm shift in higher education—a movement from concentration on questions to a recognition that more content is needed as we enter conversations in the international marketplace, guided by a knowledgeable position open to challenge and modification.

It is possible to underscore the importance of content in education, while admitting that we must struggle to discern what that content will be. I am a proponent of multicultural education fueled by content. Can the student understand the international market? What are the competing impacts of the various religions of the world? What are the differences and similarities between

Western and Eastern cultures? What is the role of education and public policy in an increasingly diverse culture? My call for diverse content may differ from Bloom or Hirsch, but their call to know more needs to be heeded.

I met with a group of students who suggested that all people should become more aware of other cultures. They then discussed at length the narrowness of the average United States citizen. When they asked what I thought, I agreed that we need to be more aware of other cultures. Then I asked "What can you and I do to model such a life commitment? How many are fluent in one or more foreign languages? How many have lived in another country? How many are members of or participants in events sponsored by minority culture organizations on campus?" Less that 25 percent answered affirmatively to the questions. My point was to suggest that it is not enough to simply talk about multicultural education; we need to find concrete ways to learn content about different persons and cultures. Diversity on campus is supported by relational sensitivity and content that we can learn from others and take into future conversations.

This emphasis on content is consistent with the North Central Association (NCA) Commission on Higher Education requirement on assessment of content learning in the area of student achievement. The NCA accreditation review teams are requiring universities to assess programs, revealing quality and success of student achievement. "An institution should consider a broad range of institutional outcomes, but it must have and describe a program by which it documents student academic achievement."[16] The NCA does not dictate content; they want universities to prove that they are accomplishing what they market and advertise as significant and unique about their programs. This requirement is an effort to assist with honesty in the public dialogue between what the university says and what actually is accomplished.

If we accept the assumption that the fundamental reason for being a teacher is to pass on knowledge, and if we are convinced that students need even more information in an increasingly competitive international environment, then we have a unique challenge in higher education. We have a chance to emphasize conversation about ideas and still be practical and competitive. Being multilingual and multicultural are not just acts of being compassionate. Such learning is essential for a culturally diverse and competitive global economy. We need to reward teachers who are content-rich and able to stretch and engage students.

Again, we may debate the exact content to be taught, but I

support the assertion that increased content is necessary in the future if our students are to understand a changing and competitive global environment. As Hirsch has stated:

> Those who might consider our specific recommendations to be defective are being challenged to improve upon them, but not to perpetuate the illusion that we can continue, in honesty, to avoid a discussion of the specific contents of the extensive curriculum.
> I hope that in our future debates about the extensive curriculum, the participants will keep clearly in view the high stakes involved in their deliberations: breaking the cycle of illiteracy for deprived children; raising the living standard of families who have been illiterate; making our country more competitive in international markets; achieving greater social justice; enabling all citizens to participate in the political process; bringing us closer to the Ciceronian ideal of universal public discourse—in short, achieving fundamental goals of the Founders at the birth of the republic.[17]

In short, dialogic education puts content first. Only after making such a commitment is the relational concern for the students an educational asset. Conversation about ideas is based on the premise that content is the common center of conversation with another and is supported by relational concern.

The Danger of Relational Overload

It is possible for a dialogic educator to have an excessive focus on relationship. One young faculty member came to my office anguished over a student evaluation that suggested that she did not pay enough relational attention to the students. My colleague had more than adequate office hours, met each class on time, held midterm and final exam study sessions, and had the class to her house for a meal. I then asked, "Do you offer relational support to assist learning or do you offer it to get positive feedback from students?" I have asked myself that same question when I am surprised by similar comments coming from someone that I did spend a lot of relational time with, both inside and outside the classroom.

Dialogically, my first commitment is to the common center of content discourse and then to relationship development. When I get the sequence mixed, I am tempted to move to the role of companion and out of the role of teacher and presenter of information. My colleague, with relational concerns like my own, suggested that we ask one another each semester, "Do you offer relational support to assist learning or do you offer it to get positive feedback from students?" It is possible to take an apparent legitimate relational concern and turn it into a self-centered manipulation, using students to fill a social vacuum in one's own life.

The notion that a great teacher must sometimes forego the hope of being liked, at least in the short-run, is borne out in an examination of communication that is excessively centered on relationship. I have sometimes met teachers who have given up their right to judge and to offer necessary critical insight in order to keep a comfortable relational style in the classroom. For some instructors, maintaining a friendship psychologically based on good feelings is more important than a classical view of friendship based in accountability.

One of the ironies of life is that we can focus so much on a good action that it is difficult to understand when the good turns against us. Concern about relationship is needed in dialogic education, but a good thing can be overdone to the point of being counterproductive. As I work with students in the midst of relationship struggles, I find it interesting that different optimum levels of relationship discussion need to be found for different communicative partners. But some people can begin to build a relationship around discussion of the relationship. Take away talk about the relationship and there is little left to keep the conversation going. Being relational is important in dialogic education; discussion of the relationship is necessary at times, but excess moves us away from content discussion.

As stated earlier, danger can result from marketing the relational focus of dialogic education. This message of a relational good taken to an extreme is summarized by Paul Watzlawick, Beavin, and Jackson. "It seems that the more spontaneous and 'healthy' a relationship, the more the relationship aspect of communication recedes into the background. Conversely, 'sick' relationships are characterized by a constant struggle about the nature of the relationship, with the content aspect of communication becoming less and less important."[18] Too much focus on relationships can have a smothering effect on a child, spouse, student, or community.[19] Bruno Bettelheim, in *Love is Not Enough*, suggests that relationships need to emerge naturally, not artificially out of a mechanical need or desire to make them happen.[20] Studying with one another can often bring students closer together than talk about relationship building. As Philip Slater suggests, it is possible to have "too much of a good thing."[21] Perhaps an even worse scenario is giving the impression that quality relationships are possible for all when in fact they only materialize for a limited few. Closeness cannot be guaranteed; no quality relationship can be assured. When demand, not invitation, begins to steer relationships, we head down a road that will end in cynicism for many.

Too much focus on the other person places a relationship in a limited sphere. Common sense suggests that any relationship needs outside stimulation in order to grow and mature. Too much focus on the relationship itself can smother both parties, limit opportunities for each person to learn, and decrease the potential for depth in the relationship. In short, quality relationships are built as much out of what we do together as how we feel about one another.

Alexander Solzhenitsyn, in *One Day in the Life of Ivan Denisovich*, parallels the importance of relationship as a by-product of working together. The relational bonds of the people are enhanced as a by-product of hard work together. One subtheme of the novel is that the tasks of life can make life worth living, even in the midst of an adverse environment. Solzhenitsyn's description of Shukhov and his companions building a brick wall in a Soviet prison camp reveals life as meaningful through coordinated accomplishment of a task. The prisoners became so absorbed in the building task that fear of the guards became less powerful than the drive to do the task well. After the building job was over, Shukhov went back to admire the accomplishment, to look over his work and that of his comrades, much to the displeasure of the guards.

With a feeling of pride for a job well done, the scene ended with Shukhov taking one last look at the brick and mortar job they had just completed—seeing not just the work of a newly built structure, but the result of coordinated work in the midst of human struggle.[22] The job had been done well together, permitting the men to forget for a moment the dire state of their own lives. Shukhov and his comrades escaped the bondage of prison for a few hours through their collective absorption in work at hand, and, as a by-product, they enhanced the relational bonds between them.

It is interesting to witness relationships nurtured in a college peace studies program and an accounting department at the same school. I was surprised to find so much student commitment in such diverse programs. Then I examined the common link: conversation about tasks that needed to be done. Both programs are centered on a task outside the building of relationships of the members. In both programs, the students and the faculty talk about content issues of their studies, not only in the classroom, but outside the classroom setting. Ongoing conversation and work together allow relationships to develop naturally. The relationships are a strong by-product of interaction with one another. Friedman, in *Hidden Human Image*, purports that most important relationships are developed as a by-product of engaging in an activity that is mutually important to one another, not just as a result of discussing the nature of the relationship.[23]

In essence, dialogic education tries to offer a sense of realism and caution about a relational teaching style. We offer a student a realistic understanding of a teacher/student relationship, not based just on good cheer, but grounded in long-term accountability. We need to assume that a relationship based on hard work will in the long run offer more assistance to a student than short-term efforts at personality and charm. Bettelheim, in his discussion of fairy tales, made the point that youth need more than models of artificial good endings. They need to see the difficulties of life and witness how others are able to survive in spite of such circumstances.

> Today children no longer grow up within the security of an extended family, or of a well-integrated community. Therefore, even more than at the times fairy tales were invented, it is important to provide the modern child with images of heroes who have to go out into the world all by themselves and who, although originally ignorant of the ultimate thereins, find secure places in the world by following their right way with deep inner confidence.[24]

A teacher interested in dialogue with students can offer a relationship that has the goal of long-term assistance, which may at times not satisfy immediate emotional needs. Thus, as a teacher invites a relationship with a student, he or she should not give an impression of more short-term emotive concern than can be delivered. Realistic relationships need to have beginnings, endings, and calls of accountability between the two parties. A student needs to know that most relationships with a faculty member and other students in the class will not survive the duration of the class, the year, or long after graduation. When approached realistically, however, such relationships can assist the learning environment.

When a classroom experience is over, a teacher cannot expect most of the students to express appreciation. Most of our relationships are acts of utility, lacking long-term reciprocal goodwill. But if both teacher and student recognize that the primary reason for coming together in a classroom is to learn about information, the short-term nature of most relationships can be turned into realistic learning about a mobile society. Again, my caution is against extremes. Somewhere between the faculty member offering more than can be delivered and the person unwilling to talk to students outside the classroom is a realistic and appropriate relational style for dialogic education.

With this relational caution it is important to outline how constructive concern for persons is a key to dialogic teaching. I have based concern on two major notions: conversation about ideas and a conviction of hope that human beings can make a difference as relationships are taken seriously in human community. Conversation about ideas relies first and foremost on content. One learns that a conviction of hope for relationships is more often a by-product of working together. The athlete learns a sport and, frequently, the importance of human relationships from his or her coach, just as the teacher has the opportunity to offer content and relationships to students.

Person to Person

With the above cautions in mind, we can turn to the importance of relationships in dialogic teaching.

> The key point is that there is no substitute for human relationship and presence, for listening, for sharing silence and wonderment, and for caring. There is no expert knowledge of the human self which can be claimed by any particular academic field. There are merely insights here and there which must be tested through experience to see if they contribute to a more sane and vital life, or to a more empty, insane, and boring one.[25]

In discussing this book with a friend and colleague, I was asked: "Don't you really see content and relationship as interdependent?" My answer was yes but that they should not receive equal emphasis on a campus. Students need content first, along with a supportive relationship that facilitates learning. I confessed to my colleague that I may be overreacting to some teachers who try to be buddies with students; such an approach is as far away from dialogic education as the cynicism of Bloom. In my view of dialogic education, content and relationship are interdependent and copresent, with the greater emphasis on content.

The title of this section comes from a book by Carl Rogers and Barry Stevens entitled *Person to Person: The Problem of Being*

Human—A New Trend in Psychology. While Rogers' view of education is not the center or theme of my book, his emphasis on interpersonal relationships is illustrative of a part of education central to dialogic teaching. Rogers points out that the quality of the relationship between therapist and client has much to do with the eventual health of any relationship. Dialogic teaching relies on the quality of relational life together on a campus as one important way in which education occurs outside the classroom.

> In a variety of clients—normal, maladjusted, and psychotic—with many different counselors and therapists, and studying the relationship from the vantage point of the client, the therapist, or the uninvolved observer, certain qualities in the relationship are quite uniformly found to be associated with personal growth and change.
> These elements are not constituted of technical knowledge or ideological sophistication. They are personal human qualities—something the counselor *experiences*, not something he *knows*. Constructive personal growth is associated with the counselor's realness, with his genuine and unconditional liking for his client, with his sensitive understanding of his client's private world, and with his ability to communicate these qualities in himself to his client.[26]

Rogers discusses four elements of a constructive interpersonal relationship appropriate for the classroom: positive regard, congruence, empathy, and the other's perception of this interpersonal attitude.[27] In dialogic teaching, these four elements work together to facilitate the teaching environment. First, it is important to have positive regard for students and help them discover the character potential necessary for becoming persons knowledgeable of the maxims and norms and capable of violating those rules in order to meet the needs of the concrete moment. Such an attitude suggests that, to a large degree, a teacher finds what he or she envisions are the possibilities with a given student or group of students.[28]

Second, congruence asks a person to have agreement between what one says and what one believes. It is important to bring together internal positions and stated viewpoints (when socially and interpersonally appropriate) if trust is to be maintained in a teaching environment. Trust is violated when one finds a hidden agenda emerging later in the relationship. Third is the importance of empathy. A good teacher needs to feel the struggle of a student who does not understand the material, is unsure of his or her potential, or wishes to change majors.

Rogers' final reminder is that a person needs to recognize the above traits of positive regard, congruence, and empathy in order for those traits to facilitate a relationship. Not all students will see concern for personhood or even want such a relationship. Dialogic teaching needs to make information available to all, but the depth of the relationship will be dependent not only on the teacher, but the student. On a practical level, it is helpful to have teachers with different styles in order to give students choices, not only in what information they learn, but in the types of people that might have an influence on their lives outside the classroom.

The relational focus of a dialogic teacher is a complement to the "teacher as stranger" emphasis from chapter four. The stranger teaches with a content-rich vision open to discovery and insights. A "person to person" focus suggests that a major reason for the accumulation of information is to contribute to our personal lives, professions, and communities, and to be of service to others personally and professionally.

Time and timing are crucial as we approach one another. Dialogic education requires that time be made available to students, to let relationships naturally grow without undue pressure for interpersonal friendship. In addition, we need to be aware of the art of timing as we work with others. It takes sensitivity to know when and how much to say. For dialogic teaching to take place, a teacher and a student require both structured and unstructured time to reflect, meeting one another in conversation outside the classroom.

In emphasizing the relational nature of dialogic teaching, the accompanying term to *stranger* is *friend*, which Aristotle defines as "reciprocated goodwill."[29] Friendship or reciprocated goodwill lessens the need for excessive reliance on rules, regulations, and rigid policy. An example might be a colleague who teaches in such a way that friendship is invited between herself and the students. Such friendship carries the assumption that she is concerned about the person's education and the long-term well-being of that person. She still maintains contact with some graduates, discussing what they are learning in their profession and life in general. She keeps ties with her students long after graduation.

In examining the role of friendship in teaching, we can turn to Aristotle's discussion of three different types of friendship: utility, pleasure, and complete friendship. Friendship for utility suggests that useful results undergird friendship and after those results are obtained, the friendship ceases. This utility formula grounds much of the interaction in the classroom where the teacher and students are each necessary and important to one another. Friendship for pleasure is likely to be of limited duration, lasting only as long as people are feeling enjoyment. This "sunshine" friendship stops short of complete friendship, which requires expressing goodwill in attitude and action, even in the midst of adversity. It is important for a teacher and student to understand that while friendship of utility can be guaranteed, complete friendship can only be invited and earned. Em Griffin's book on friendship states that the friendship mandate involves both content and relationship—the ability to get things done, while keeping in perspective the importance of human beings. Griffin states that in the first draft of the Declaration of Independence, Thomas Jefferson used the term *friendship*. He conceptualized democracy as a way of getting things done without ignoring relationships between people. The interplay of content and relationship is evident in Griffin's reference to C. S. Lewis. "As C. S. Lewis notes, friends sit side by side, their gaze on a common goal. Lovers sit face to face with eyes fixed on each other."[30] The common goal in dialogic education within a context of friendship is the nurturing of a life of learning together, both in the present and long after the classroom work has been completed.

Jaksa and Pritchard, in *Communication Ethics: Methods of Analysis*, state that the types of relationships we have with others will ultimately determine the quality of our own lives.[31] The quality of one's life is significantly determined by one's relationships with others. Perhaps the best way to describe what needs to happen in dialogic teaching is a "mutual entanglement of students and teachers."[32] The teacher must become involved in the learning of the students and in their lives.

Bruce Wilshire, in *The Moral Collapse of the University: Professionalism, Purity, and Alienation*, makes the case that we, in higher education, generally underestimate the importance of the individual person in the classroom at all types of educational institutions. We forget how important the task of an individual professor is for the development of a student as a thinker, leader, and as a person. We teach as much by our personal example as we do by the expertise we bring to the classroom.

> [There is a] special authority . . . [that] the professor carries, the special responsibility to exemplify personally what every investigator presupposes: the nature and value of meaning and truth. The ultimate educating force is who I am. Since it is the humanities professor who is especially obliged to teach what being human

involves, it is especially this person who must exemplify *in person* what self-knowledge and goodness are.[33]

It is the person, armed with information and values, that can make a difference in a human life. This book began with Ellul's concern that human beings do not feel as if they can make a difference in the latter part of the twentieth century. Wilshire comments that it is up to the teacher more than anyone else to make such a difference. The teacher is the person that can change the life direction of a student as the common center of conversation about ideas brings them together. It is not money, laboratories, or the library that are primary—it is the personhood of the individual teacher that makes the biggest difference in the life of a student as they engage in inquiry together.

One can find a relational emphasis in teaching on any type of campus, whether at a regional state university, national research university, or a small liberal arts campus. I have encountered dialogic educators on a large state university campus who shaped the lives of students with quality advice and care outside the classroom setting. I have also seen faculty on small liberal arts campuses ignore student concerns because of the disruption to their reading, recreational, and political activity. Dialogic teaching can be invited by a teacher on any type of campus. The determining factor is not so much the campus, but the person with the responsibility of teacher, willing to bring inquiry and concern for personhood together.

Dialogic teaching works on a premise that education involves time with students outside the classroom, talking about ideas, professional objectives, and personal adjustments. Relationships are most often built discussing issues other than relationship.

> Happiness! It is useless to seek it elsewhere than in this warmth of human relations. Our sordid interests imprison us within their walls. Only a comrade can grasp us by the hand and haul us free. . . .
>
> No man can draw a free breath who does not share with other men a common and disinterested ideal. Life has taught us that love does not consist in gazing at each other, but in looking outward together in the same direction. There is no comradeship except through union in the same high effort.[34]

Relational happiness most often comes from work accomplished together on a task worthy of being done.

Dialogic Teaching as Vocation

After this lengthy discussion on dialogic teaching, there is one obvious yet significant question that needs to be answered. Why spend time attempting to exemplify dialogic teaching after being warned against monistic approaches, the dangers of excessive reliance on relationship, and the need to increase skilled and theoretical information as we prepare to enter the twenty-first century? My answer to this question is threefold. First, dialogic teaching is not a narrow technique that can be copied. It is a perspective that reminds us of the importance of information and persons in the educational task. Second, dialogue cannot occur without a person standing his or her own ground, taking a position which requires us to know something before speaking; this orientation is dependent on a rich information base. Third, teachers that made a difference in many of our lives took the dual responsibilities of information and relationship seriously. The great teachers I have known had a passion and a love for both ideas and people.

The rationale for dialogic teaching and dialogic education agrees with Ellul's critique of Western culture as being in love with technique.[35] Dialogic education is not technique-centered, but grounded in conversation, ideas and concern for the personhood of our students. If education is to make a difference in the lives of people, it will need to offer the best information available, while attempting to meet with students in conversation and humane interaction.

Dialogic education is not just a task or a job; it is a form of secular calling. It is an opportunity to shape, not just the future of ideas and application, but the character of the world in which we live. This shaping should not be in our own image, but needs to nurture the uniqueness of the next generation of students through thoughtful conversation with them.

To be a great teacher involves being excited about what and who one is teaching. Using yellowed notes and old texts will not invite excellence in a student or a professor. Granted, any teacher needs to cover the basic information in a given area, but in most disciplines, there are debates about what basic core of essential information is needed. Dialogic teaching encourages exposing students to such debates. A classroom can be enlivened by sharing not only what we understand, but by being honest about what we are uncertain of and why. Undergraduates can be exposed to the ongoing debates in a given field. A professor should know what those debates are and work along with students attempting to understand them. Taking a stand in dialogic teaching requires honesty in sharing the limits of our knowledge, as well as what we do know.

As Wayne Booth stated in the beginning quotation of this chapter, finding a vocation is not always easy. In fact, we cannot always be sure that we have discovered the best without actually trying out a chosen vocation. Testing the vocation of teaching requires beginning conversation with students and carrying on the best from past teachers, always seeking to learn more and to question past assumptions.

Gandhi offered good advice on how to find truth that might assist in determining the fit of a vocational selection.

> But how is one to realize this Truth. . . . By single-minded devotion (*abbyasa*) and indifference to every other interest in life (*vairagya*)—replied the Bhagvada Gita. In spite, however, of such devotion, what may appear as truth to one person will often appear as untruth to another person. But this need not worry the seeker. . . . there is nothing wrong in everyone following Truth according to one's lights. Indeed it is one's duty to do so. Then if there is a mistake on the part of any one so following Truth, it will automatically be set right . . . [if] one takes to the wrong path one stumbles, and is then redirected to the right path.[36]

At times there is no better way to decide the best path leading to a vocation than to experience it. One of the paths is simply beginning the conversation.

I began this book with a quotation from a great teacher, mentor, and friend of mine that talked about the nobility and the challenge of teaching. This book is offered as one way of interpreting what some have done so well and others continue to do in a profession charged with keeping the conversation of inquiry alive. Dialogic teaching takes the importance of conversation about ideas with students as fundamental in education, not because it is a technique, but because it gets at the heart of what life offers to us: information and relationships. As Friedman suggests, a dialogic teacher seeks to shape without imposing— taking both information and persons seriously.

> The . . . educator may not legitimately impose . . . beliefs and values on his charges. What she does communicate must take place in a dialogical relationship founded on respect for the created uniqueness of each of her students. On the other hand, neither is she called

to a permissiveness or simple good-fellowship that turns the task of . . . education into a sharing on the part of equals. To act as teacher . . . one must avoid both the pitfalls of the sermonizer and of the discussion moderator.[37]

Dialogic education is based upon the premise that a humane intellectual shares information, while learning from others, opening up conversation with students that points to the importance of a life of knowledge, values, and relationships—reminding us all that both ideas and people count in all of life's realms, inside and outside the classroom.

NOTES

BIBLIOGRAPHY

INDEX

NOTES

1. Introduction: Dialogue and Education

1. Martin Buber, *The Knowledge of Man: A Philosophy of the Interhuman* (New York: Harper & Row, 1965), 75–78.

2. For a thoughtful examination of education and character with a dialogic sensitivity, see for example, Betty A. Sichel, *Moral Education: Character, Community, and Ideals* (Philadelphia: Temple University Press, 1988).

3. Howard B. Radest, *Can We Teach Ethics?* (New York: Prager, 1989), 121–45.

4. Gilbert C. Meilaender, *The Theory and Practice of Virtue* (Notre Dame, IN: University of Notre Dame Press, 1984), 165.

5. "The 1915 Declaration of Principles," in *Academic Freedom and Tenure: A Handbook of the American Association of University Professors,* ed. Louis Joughin (Madison: University of Wisconsin Press, 1969), 155–76.

6. John W. Gardner, quoted in Ernest L. Boyer, *College: The Undergraduate Experience in America* (New York: Harper & Row, 1987), 278.

7. Nietzsche, quoted in Viktor E. Frankl, *Man's Search for Meaning: An Introduction to Logotherapy* (New York: Pocket Books, 1974), 121.

8. Herman Hesse, *Siddhartha* (New York: New Directions, 1951).

9. William A. Darkey, ed., *Three Dialogues on Liberal Education* (Annapolis: St. John's College Press, 1979), 126.

2. Ideas, Persons, and Value Discussion

1. Ernest Simon, "Martin Buber, The Educator," in *The Philosophy of Martin Buber,* ed. Paul Arthur Schilpp and Maurice Friedman (La Salle, IL: Open Court Press, 1967), 557.

2. Aristotle, *Nicomachean Ethics,* Translated by Terence Irwin (Indianapolis: Hacket, 1985), 1099a23.

3. See for example, Richard L. Johannesen, "The Emerging Concept of Communication as Dialogue," *Quarterly Journal of Speech* 57 (1971): 373–82; Johannesen, *Ethics in Human Communication,* 3d ed.

(Prospect Heights, IL: Waveland, 1990); and John Stewart, "Foundations of Dialogic Communication," *The Quarterly Journal of Speech* 64 (1978): 183–201.

4. Rob Anderson, "Anonymity, Presence, and the Dialogic Self in a Technological Culture," (Paper presented at Central States Communication Association, Chicago, 11 Apr. 1991), 3–4.

5. W. F. R. Hardie, *Aristotle's Ethical Theory*, 2d ed. (Oxford: Clarendon, 1990), 31.

6. Buber, *The Knowledge of Man: A Philosophy of the Interhuman* 171–74.

7. Maurice Friedman, *Touchstones of Reality: Existential Trust and the Community of Peace* (New York: E.P. Dutton & Co., 1974), 154–55.

8. Carl R. Rogers and Barry Stevens, *On Becoming A Person* (Boston: Houghton Mifflin, 1961), 63.

9. Scott Heller, "Colleges Becoming Havens of 'Political Correctness,' Some Scholars Say," *The Chronicle of Higher Education*, 21 Nov. 1990, A1, A14–A15; Carolyn J. Mooney, "Academic Group Fighting the 'Politically Correct Left' Gains Momentum," *The Chronicle of Higher Education*, 12 Dec. 1990, A1, A13, and A16; and Jerry Adler et al., "Taking Offense," *Newsweek* 24 Dec. 1990, 48–54.

10. Dinesh D'Souza, *Illiberal Education: The Politics of Race and Sex on Campus* (New York: The Free Press, 1991).

11. See for example Molefi Kete Asante and Diane Ravitch, "Multiculturalism: An Exchange," *The American Scholar* 60 (1991): 267–76.

12. Allan Bloom, *The Closing of the American Mind* (New York: Simon & Schuster, 1987).

13. "Hate in the Ivory Tower: A Survey of Intolerance on College Campuses and Academia's Response," People for the American Way, (Dec. 1990); Ernest L. Boyer, "Foreword," *Campus Life: In Search of Community* (Princeton, NJ: The Carnegie Foundation for the Advancement of Teaching, 1990).

14. Boyer, xiii.

15. The phrase "a modest proposal" is an accurate reflection of what I feel this book is: a particular view of education, but not *the* view. This phrase has stuck in my mind since reading an article by one of my teachers, Paul Keller, as an honest appraisal of what most of our theoretical contributions actually are: modest proposals. See Charles T. Brown and Paul W. Keller, "A Modest Proposal for Listening Training," *The Quarterly Journal of Speech* 48 (1962): 395–99.

16. In conversation with Paul W. Keller, North Manchester, Indiana, coauthor of *Monologue to Dialogue: Exploration of Interpersonal Communication* (Englewood Cliffs, NJ: Prentice Hall, 1973).

17. Carl R. Rogers, "The Politics of Education," in *The Carl Rogers Reader,* ed. Howard Kirschenbaum and Valerie Land Henderson (Boston: Houghton Mifflin, 1989), 325.

18. John Dewey, *Democracy and Education* (New York: Free Press, 1966).

19. Boyer, *College*; Warren Bryan Martin, *College of Character* (San Francisco: Jossey-Bass, 1982); Parker J. Palmer, *To Know as We Are Known: A Spirituality of Education* (San Francisco: Harper & Row, 1983).

20. Stephan Toulmin, "The Recovery of Practical Philosophy," *The American Scholar* 57 (1988): 337–52.

21. Paulo Freire, *The Pedagogy of the Oppressed* (New York: Seabury, 1974), 75–118.

22. Richard J. Bernstein, *Beyond Objectivism and Relativism: Science, Hermeneutics and Praxis* (Philadelphia: University of Pennsylvania Press, 1983).

23. Calvin O. Schrag, *Communicative Praxis and the Space of Subjectivity* (Bloomington: Indiana University Press, 1986), 32–47.

24. Schrag, 214.

25. Richard Weaver, *Ideas Have Consequences* (Chicago: University of Chicago Press, 1948).

26. John Lyne, "Idealism as a Rhetorical Stance," in *Rhetoric and Philosophy*, ed. Richard Cherwitz (Hillsdale, NJ: L. Erlbaum Associates, 1990), 184.

27. Parker Palmer, *The Company of Strangers* (New York: Crossroad, 1989), 49–55.

28. "'Incivility' Threatens Colleges," *Chicago Tribune*, 30 Apr. 1990; Boyer, *Campus Life*.

29. *The New Webster Encyclopedic Dictionary of the English Language*, 1969, s.v. "civility."

30. Glenn Tinder, *Community: Reflections on a Tragic Ideal* (Baton Rouge: University of Louisiana Press, 1980).

31. See Ronald C. Arnett, *Communication and Community: Implications of Martin Buber's Dialogue* (Carbondale: Southern Illinois University Press, 1986).

32. Michael Polanyi, *Personal Knowledge: Towards a Post-Critical Philosophy* (New York: Harper & Row, 1964).

33. Wayne Booth, *Critical Understanding: The Powers and Limits of Pluralism* (Chicago: University of Chicago Press, 1979), 1–34.

34. Ronald Duncan, ed. *Gandhi: Selected Writings* (New York: Harper & Row, 1972), 276.

35. Tinder, 188.

36. Tinder, 199.

37. William Barrett, *The Irrational Man* (New York: Doubleday, 1962), 280.

38. Muzafer Sherif and Carolyn W. Sherif, referred to in Robert D. Nye, *Conflict Among Humans* (New York: Springer Publishing, 1973), 180.

39. Gary R. Orren, "Beyond Self-Interest," in *The Power of Public Ideas*, ed. Robert B. Reich (Cambridge, MA: Ballinger, 1988), 27.

40. David Gelman, "A Much Riskier Passage," *Newsweek*, special edition, (Summer/Fall 1990), 16.

41. Hermann Hesse, *Beneath the Wheel* (New York: Noon Day, 1968).

42. I. F. Stone, *The Trial of Socrates* (Boston: Little, Brown, & Co., 1988), 115.

43. Frederick J. Antczak, *Thought and Character: The Rhetoric of Democratic Education* (Ames: Iowa State University Press, 1985), 196.

44. Martin Buber, *The Way of Response* (New York: Schocken, 1966), 57.

45. David Augsburger, *When Enough is Enough: Discovering True Hope When All Hope Seems Lost* (Ventura, CA: Regal, 1984), 156.

46. William James quoted in Antczak, *Thought and Character*, 88.

47. Nikos Kazantzakis, *Zorba the Greek* (New York: Ballantine, 1952), 42.

3. An Academic "Home"

1. Christopher Lasch, *The True and Only Heaven: Progress and Its Critics* (New York: W. W. Norton, 1991), 358.

2. Lasch, *The True and Only Heaven*, 360.

3. Peter Berger, Brigette Berger, and Hansfried Kellner, *The Homeless Mind: Modernization and Consciousness* (New York: Random House, 1974), 82, 96.

4. Christopher Lasch, *The Culture of Narcissism: American Life in a Time of Diminishing Expectations* (New York: W. W. Norton, 1979), 42–43.

5. Rob Anderson, personal correspondence, 19 Jan. 1991.

6. Frankl, *Man's Search for Meaning*, 121.

7. Robert N. Bellah et al., *Habits of the Heart: Individualism and Commitment in American Life* (Berkeley: University of California Press, 1985), 290.

8. T. S. Haiman, "A Re-examination of the Ethics of Persuasion," *Central States Speech Journal* 3 (1952): 4–9.

9. Jacques Ellul, *In Season, Out of Season* (New York: Harper & Row, 1981), 172–200.

10. William Barrett, *The Illusion of Technique* (New York: Anchor Books, 1979), 1–29.

11. Buber, *The Knowledge of Man*, 82–85.

12. Aristotle, *Nicomachean Ethics*, 1125b.1–1125b.25

13. T. R. Nilsen, *Ethics of Speech Communication*, 2d ed. (Indianapolis: Bobbs-Merrill, 1974), 46.

14. Marjorie Hyer, "Rev. Curren Crusades for Academic Freedom," *The Fort Wayne Journal Gazette*, 24 Apr. 1988.

15. Marie Rohde, "Maguire Must Go, Some Say: But Marquette Resists Pressure to Fire Liberal Theologian for Abortion Stance," *The Milwaukee Journal*, 27 Oct. 1985.

16. John Winthrop, "A Model of Christian Charity," *The Norton*

Anthology of American Literature, comp. Ronald Gottesman (New York: W. W. Norton, 1979), 109–15.

17. Peninnah Schram, *Jewish Stories One Generation Tells Another* (London: Jason Aronson, 1987), xxi.

18. Thomas Merton, *No Man Is an Island* (New York: Doubleday, 1955), 107–28.

19. Bellah, et al., *Habits of the Heart*.

20. Bellah, et al., *Habits of the Heart*, 69.

21. Hans-Georg Gadamer, *Truth and Method* (New York: Seabury Press, 1975), 325.

22. Boyer, "Foreword," *Campus Life*.

23. Walter Brueggemann, *The Land: Place as Gift, Promise and Challenge in Biblical Faith* (Philadelphia: Fortress Press, 1977).

24. Maurice Friedman, *Martin Buber's Life and Work: The Early Years 1878–1923* (New York: E. P. Dutton, 1981), 133.

25. Bloom, 19–43.

26. Charles R. Joy, ed. *Albert Schweitzer: An Anthology* (Boston: Beacon, 1967), 240.

27. Erich Fromm, "A Theory of Love," in *Bridges Not Walls: A Book About Interpersonal Communication*, ed. John Stewart, 4th ed. (Reading, MA: Addison-Wesley, 1986), 309–23.

28. Michael J. Sandel, "The Political Theory of the Procedural Republic," in *The Power of Public Ideas*, ed. Robert B. Reich (Cambridge, MA: Ballinger, 1988), 114.

29. R. Eugene Rice, "Report on Institutional Case Studies—'High Morale and Satisfaction Among Faculty: Ten Exemplary Colleges'" in *Community, Commitment, and Congruence: A Different Kind of Excellence* (Washington, D. C.: Council of Independent Colleges, 1987), 20.

30. Rice, 4–5.

31. Berger, Berger, and Kellner, 96.

32. Robert B. Young, "The Small College Point of View: An Ideology of Student Affairs," *Journal of College Student Personnel* 27 (1986): 4–18.

33. *The World Book Encyclopedia Dictionary*, 1963, s.v. "colleague."

34. Dietrich Bonhoeffer, *The Cost of Discipleship* (New York: Macmillan, 1949), 102–3.

35. Aristotle, *Nicomachean Ethics*, 1157a–1160a.

36. Aristotle, *Nicomachean Ethics*, 1162a23.

37. Aristotle, *Nicomachean Ethics*, 1156b32–33.

38. Dietrich Bonhoeffer, *Life Together* (New York: Harper & Row, 1954), 28.

39. Abraham Maslow, *Motivation & Personality*, 2d ed. (New York: Harper & Row, 1970), 53.

40. Maurice Friedman, *Martin Buber: The Life of Dialogue* (Chicago: University of Chicago Press, 1976), 3.

41. Major point in Christopher Lasch, *Haven in a Heartless World* (New York: Basic Books, 1979).

4. Teaching with a Vision

1. *The New Webster Encyclopedic Dictionary of the English Language*, 1969, s.v. "vision."

2. Walter Fisher, *Human Communication As Narration: Toward A Philosophy of Reason, Value, and Action* (Columbia, SC: University of South Carolina Press, 1987), 78.

3. Stanley Hauerwas, *The Community of Character: Toward a Constructive Christian Social Ethic* (Notre Dame, IN: University of Notre Dame Press, 1981), 14.

4. *Public Papers of the Presidents of the United States—John F. Kennedy, January 20–December 31, 1961*, Vol. 1 (Washington, D. C.: U. S. Government Printing Office, 1962), 3.

5. Aristotle, *Nicomachean Ethics*, 1115a6–1117a5.

6. Catherine B. Burroughs, "Teaching and/or Scholarship," *Liberal Education* 76 (1990), 16.

7. Martin, xiii.

8. Fritz Machlup, "In Defense of Academic Freedom," Joughin, 338.

9. Christopher Lasch makes this point in his repeated comments on the dangers of non-binding relationships in *The True and Only Heaven*.

10. Personal conversation with Dr. Larry Underberg, Department of Communication Studies and debate coach, Manchester College, North Manchester, IN, April 1991.

11. Martin Buber, *Between Man and Man* (New York: Macmillan, 1972), 83–117.

12. Maxine Greene, *Teacher As Stranger: Educational Philosophy for the Modern Age* (Belmont, CA: Wadsworth, 1973).

13. Alfred Schutz writes, "To solve the problem, whether of a practical or theoretical nature, we have to enter into its horizons in order to explicate. . . [a possible answer]," in Greene, 132.

14. Geertz, quoted in Bernstein, 94–95.

15. Darkey, 53.

16. Erich Harth, "From Specialization Toward Integration: A Scientist's Perspective," *Contesting the Boundaries of Liberal and Professional Education: The Syracuse Experiment*, ed. Peter T. Marsh (Syracuse, NY: Syracuse University Press, 1988) 232.

17. Martin, 46.

18. Boyer, *College*, 279–80.

19. Boyer, *College*, 143.

20. Frankl, *Man's Search For Meaning*, 194.

21. Robert M. Pirsig, *Zen and the Art of Motorcycle Maintenance* (New York: Morrow, 1974).

22. Anna Otten, ed. *Hesse Companion* (Albuquerque: University of New Mexico Press, 1977), 249.

23. Alexis de Tocqueville, *Democracy in America* (New York: Modern Library, 1981), 603.

24. Karl R. Wallace, "An Ethical Basis of Communication," *The Speech Teacher* 4 (1955), 1–9.

25. Ronald C. Arnett, "The Status of Communication Ethics Scholarship in Speech Communication Journals for 1915–1985," *Conversations on Communication Ethics*, ed. Karen Joy Greenberg (Norwood NJ: Ablex, 1991), 58–60.

26. Dewey, 192.

27. Boyer, *College*, 279–80.

28. Sidney Hook, *Philosophy and Public Policy* (Carbondale: Southern Illinois University Press, 1980), 173–74.

29. B. F. Skinner, *Walden Two* (New York: Macmillan, 1948).

30. Walter R. Fisher, "Narration as a Human Communication Paradigm: The Case of Public Moral Argument," *Communication Monographs* 51 (Mar. 1984): 13.

31. Aristotle, *Nicomachean Ethics*, 1095a.

32. Paul Weiss, *The Making of Men* (Carbondale: Southern Illinois University Press, 1967), 152.

33. Weiss, 141–52.

34. Bellah, et al, *Habits of the Heart*, 3–51.

35. Weiss, 135.

36. Darkey, 35.

37. Jacques Ellul, *Perspectives On Our Age* (New York: Seabury, 1981), 44–47.

5. Conversation About Ideas

1. Thomas J. DeLoughry, "Study of Transcripts Finds Little Structure in the Liberal Arts," *Chronicle of Higher Education* 18 Jan. 1989, A1 and A32.

2. B. Robert Kreiser, ed., *AAUP: American Association of University Professors—Policy Documents and Reports* (Washington, D. C.: American Association of University Professors, 1990), 75–76.

3. Maurice Friedman, *Hidden Human Image* (New York: Dell, 1974), 286–314.

4. Dewey, 52–53.

5. Ron Beathard, "Colleges, Swimming Pools, and Teachers," *Fort Wayne News Sentinel* 12 Jan. 1989.

6. Kenneth E. Eble and Wilbert J. McKeachie, *Improving Undergraduate Education Through Faculty Development* (San Francisco: Jossey-Bass, 1985), 132.

7. Eble and McKeachie, 114–37.

8. Jacques Barzun, *Begin Here: The Forgotten Conditions of Teaching and Learning* (Chicago: University of Chicago Press, 1991), 176.

9. Richard Rorty, quoted in Janet Hook, "A Disconcerting Philoso-

pher Challenges the Pretensions of His Discipline," *Chronicle of Higher Education* 9 Dec. 1981, 25–26.

10. Russell Jacoby, *The Last Intellectuals: American Culture in the Age of Academe* (New York: Basic Books, 1987).

11. Ronald C. Arnett, "Teacher/Scholar: A Continuing Tradition," *Manchester College Bulletin* 81 (Jan. 1989): 1.

12. Martin Buber, *Meetings* (La Salle, IL: Open Court, 1973), 60–61.

13. Buber, *Meetings*, 60–61.

14. Susan Resneck Parr, "The Teaching of Ethics in Undergraduate Nonethics Courses," in *Ethics Teaching in Higher Education*, ed. Daniel Callahan and Sissela Bok (New York: Plenum, 1980), 233.

15. Dag Hammarskjöld, *Markings* (New York: Alfred Knopf, 1977), 131.

16. E. D. Hirsch, Jr., *Cultural Literacy: What Every American Needs to Know* (Boston: Houghton Mifflin, 1987), 9.

17. Buber, *Between Man and Man*, 19–22; Jacques Ellul, *In Season, Out of Season*, 172–200.

18. Erika Vora, Professor of Intercultural Communication, St. Cloud State University, St. Cloud, MN. Personal Conversation, Mar. 1991.

19. Patti McGill Peterson, "Small Independent Colleges: A Sector At Risk," *National Forum: Phi Kappa Phi Journal* 65 (1985): 9.

20. Robert M. Hutchins, *The University of Utopia* (Chicago: University of Chicago Press, 1953), 49–74.

21. Herant A. Katchadourian and John Boli, *Careerism and Intellectualism Among College Students* (San Francisco: Jossey-Bass, 1985), 83–117.

22. Frankl, *Man's Search For Meaning*, 176–83.

23. For instance, Allan Bloom, *The Closing of the American Mind*; Derek Bok, *Higher Learning* (Boston, MA: Harvard University Press, 1988); Ernest L. Boyer, *College: The Undergraduate Experience in America*; E. D. Hirsch, *Cultural Literacy: What Every American Needs to Know*.

6. The Two Sides of Caring: Hope and Disappointment

1. Mary Field Belenky, et al., *Women's Ways of Knowing: The Development of Self, Voice, and Mind* (New York: Basic Books, 1986), 227.

2. Sissela Bok, *A Strategy for Peace: Human Values and the Threat of War* (New York: Pantheon Books, 1989), 148.

3. Alva Myradal, quoted in Bok, *A Strategy for Peace*, 156.

4. Ashley Montagu, *On Being Human* (New York: Hawthorn Books, 1966), 106.

5. William Zinsser, "A Visit to Ed Roush," *The American Scholar* 58 (1989): 113–16.

6. George Will, "The Fuse that Lit the Fire," *Newsweek* 13 Apr. 1987, 88.

7. Richard Johannesen connects vision and teleology in "Virtue Ethics in Political Communication," *Proceedings of the First National Communication Ethics Conference* (1990), 219–56.

8. See for example, Toulmin, 337–52.

9. Johannesen, "Virtue Ethics in Political Communication," 233.

10. Alasdair MacIntyre, *After Virtue* (Notre Dame, IN: University of Notre Dame Press, 1984), 54.

11. See for example, Martin Buber, *Good and Evil* (New York: Charles Scribner's Sons, 1952), 139–43.

12. Henry H. Crimmel, "The Myth of the Teacher-Scholar," *Liberal Education* 70 (1984): 192.

13. Augsburger, 8.

14. Buber, *Between Man and Man*, 104–17.

15. Aristotle, *Nicomachean Ethics*, 1103a13–18.

16. Claude Brown, *Manchild in the Promised Land: A Modern Classic of the Black Experience* (New York: Signet Books, 1965).

17. See for example, the Hawthorne studies where subjective perception of attention given to students affected their performance. G. H. Bantock, "Educational Research: A Criticism," in *Philosophical Essays on Teaching*, ed. Bertram Bandman and Robert S. Guttchen (Philadelphia: J. B. Lippincott, 1969), 232.

18. Ivor Pritchard, *Moral Education and Character* (Washington, D. C.: U.S. Department of Education, 1988), 3–4.

19. Aristotle, *Nicomachean Ethics*, 1113a18–23.

20. Pritchard, 3–4.

21. Brian L. Porto, "The Small College Experience: Not for Students Only," *Liberal Education* 70 (1984): 229–30.

22. Lauro Martines, "Large and Little School Teaching," *The American Scholar* 54 (1985): 202.

23. Zelda F. Gamson, et al., *Liberating Education* (San Francisco: Jossey-Bass, 1984), 112.

24. Betty L. Siegel, "Knowledge with Commitment," *Vital Speeches of the Day* 50 (1984), 396.

25. Christina Hoff Sommers, "Ethics Without Virtue: Moral Education in America," *The American Scholar* 53 (1984): 388.

26. Sidney Hook, "Closing of the American Mind: An Intellectual Best-Seller Re-visited," *The American Scholar* 58 (1989): 128.

27. Eric Hoffer, *The True Believer* (New York: New American Library, 1951).

28. Donald L. Kanter and Philip H. Mirvis, *The Cynical Americans: Living in an Age of Discontent and Disillusionment* (San Francisco: Jossey-Bass, 1989), 88–90.

29. Lasch, *The True and Only Heaven*, 81.

30. Hauerwas, 127.

31. Em Griffin, *Making Friends and Making Them Count* (Downers Grove, IL: InterVarsity Press, 1987), 38.

32. Martin Luther King, Jr., "I Have a Dream," *A Testament of Hope: The Essential Writings of Martin Luther King, Jr.*, ed. James Melvin Washington, (San Francisco: Harper & Row, 1986), 220.

33. Martin Luther King, Jr., Address, Manchester College, North Manchester, IN, 1 Feb. 1968, audiotape.

34. Denton L. Watson, "Scholars' Focus on Martin Luther King Has Skewed Our Understanding of the Civil-Rights Struggle," *The Chronicle of Higher Education* 23 Jan. 1991, A44.

35. James C. Dobson, *Straight Talk to Men and Their Wives* (Waco, TX: Word Books, 1984), 31–32.

36. Rosemary Ashby, "The Public Image of a Small College," *New Directions for Higher Education: Management Techniques for Small and Specialized Institutions*, ed. Andrew J. Falender and John C. Merson (San Francisco: Jossey-Bass 1983), 46.

37. Steven M. Cahn, *Saints and Scamps: Ethics in Academia* (Totowa, NJ: Rowman & Littlefield), 1986, 40–41.

38. Toulmin, 337–52.

39. William James, *Pragmatism and Other Essays* (New York: Washington Square Press, 1963), 5.

40. Edward Shils, "Robert E. Park," *The American Scholar* 60 (1991): 122.

7. Between Persons

1. Buber, *Between Man and Man*, 104–17.

2. Kenneth E. Eble, *The Craft of Teaching: A Guide to Mastering the Professor's Art*, 2d ed. (San Francisco: Jossey-Bass, 1988), 104.

3. Katherine Jean Babbitt, "Instructional Leadership Behaviors of Principals and Teachers' Professional Zone of Acceptance," (Ph.D. diss. Marquette University, Milwaukee, WI, 1990), 111–12.

4. Ernest T. Pascarella, "College Environmental Influences on Students' Educational Aspirations," *Journal of Higher Education* 55 (1984): 767.

5. Jack Gibb, "Defensive Communication," in *Bridges Not Walls: A Book About Interpersonal Communication* ed. John Stewart (New York: Random House, 1986), 256.

6. See for example, Barbara Kantrowitz and Pat Wingert, "A Dismal Report Card," *Newsweek* 17 June 1991, 64–67.

7. Aristotle, *Nicomachean Ethics*, 1131a–1131b23.

8. Viktor E. Frankl, *Psychotherapy and Existentialism: Selected Papers on Logotherapy* (New York: Simon & Schuster, 1967), 37–52.

9. Hans-Georg Gadamer, *Truth and Method* (New York: Crossroad Publishing, 1986), 266, 325–26.

10. Erwin Boschmann, *Teaching Tools: Ten Secrets to Total Teaching Success* (Dubuque, IA: Kendall/Hunt Publishing, 1987), 20.

11. James R. C. Adams, *John Baldwin: 1922–1987* (North Manchester, IN: Manchester College, 1989).

12. Arnett, *Communication and Community*, 172–74.

13. Bonhoeffer, *Life Together*, 26–39.

14. Warren Bennis, *Why Leaders Can't Lead: The Unconscious Conspiracy Continues* (San Francisco, Jossey-Bass: 1989), 160.

15. Jeffrey T. Fouts and Loyde W. Hales, "A Controlled Environment: The Nature of Small, Liberal Arts, Christian Colleges," *Journal of College Student Personnel*, 26 (1985): 524–31.

16. John Stewart, "Interpersonal Communication: A Meeting Between Persons," Stewart, ed. *Bridges Not Walls*, 15–29.

17. Freire, 57–74.

18. Alan Richardson, *A Theological Word Book of the Bible* (New York: Macmillan: 1952), 175–76.

19. Jacques Ellul, *Violence* (New York: Seabury Press, 1969), 81–125.

20. James Lynch, quoted in Stewart, *Bridges Not Walls*, 7.

21. Norman Cousins, *The Healing Heart* (New York: W. W. Norton, 1983), 131–37.

22. Reinhold Niebuhr, *The Irony of American History* (New York: Charles Scribner's Sons, 1952), 154–55.

23. Buber quoted in Maurice Friedman, *The Hidden Human Image* (New York: Dell Publishing Co., 1974), 301.

24. Kathleen K. Reardon, *Interpersonal Communication: Where Minds Meet* (Belmont, CA: Wadsworth), 1987.

25. Ronald C. Arnett, "The Hurried Professor: What is Our Disciplinary Responsibility?" *The Speech Association of Minnesota Journal* 14 (1987): 1–11.

26. Bertrand Russell, *A History of Western Philosophy* (New York: Simon & Schuster, 1972), 47.

27. Paul Ricoeur, *Time and Narrative* (Chicago: University of Chicago Press, 1983), 20.

28. Bellah, et al, *Habits of the Heart*, 153.

29. MacIntyre, 23–35.

30. Bernstein, 155–56.

31. Jacoby, 30–31.

32. Ernest L. Boyer, "Buildings Reflect Our Priorities," *Educational Record* 70 (1989): 27.

33. Boyer, "Buildings Reflect Our Priorities," 27.

34. Edward T. Hall, *The Silent Language* (New York: Anchor Books, 1990), 140–61.

35. Buber, *The Knowledge of Man*, 59–71.

36. Robert M. Hutchins, "The Socratic Dialogue," *The Human Dialogue*, ed. Ashley Montagu and Floyd Matson, (New York: The Free Press, 1967), 328–29.

37. Edward Shils, "Robert Maynard Hutchins," *The American Scholar* 59 (1990): 220.

38. Audrey W. Remley, "Real Versus Ideal—A Response," *Journal of Student Personnel* 27 (1986): 17.

8. Dialogic Influence: Persuasion and Choice

1. Bok, *A Strategy For Peace*, 3–30.

2. See for example, Arthur Koestler, *Darkness at Noon* (New York: Bantam Books, 1941).

3. Arnett, "The Status of Communication Ethics Scholarship in Speech Communication Journals from 1915–1985," 58.

4. W. Max Wise, *The Politics of the Private College: An Inquiry Into the Processes of Collegiate Government* (New Haven, CT: Haven Foundation, 1968), 66.

5. Amy Gutmann, *Democratic Education* (Princeton, NJ: Princeton University Press, 1987), 289.

6. Merrill P. Peterson, *The Humanities and the American Promise: Report of the Colloquium on the Humanities and the American People* (Austin, TX: The Texas Council for the Humanities, 1987), 9.

7. Thomas R. Nilsen, "Free Speech, Persuasion, and the Democratic Process," *Quarterly Journal of Speech* 43 (1958): 235–43.

8. Joseph Villiers Denney, ed., *Washington, Webster, and Lincoln* (Chicago: Scott Foresman, 1920), 145.

9. Richard F. Fenno, Jr., *Congressmen in Committees* (Boston: Little, Brown & Co., 1973), xiii.

10. Richard P. Chait, et al., *Trustee Responsibility for Academic Affairs* (Washington, D. C.: Association of Governing Boards of Universities and Colleges, 1984), 8.

11. Gutmann, 115–21.

12. Steven G. Olswang and Barbara A. Lee, *Faculty Freedoms and Institutional Accountability: Interactions and Conflicts* (Washington, D. C.: Association for the Study of Higher Education, 1984), 56–57.

13. John J. Corson, *Governance of Colleges and Universities* (New York: McGraw-Hill, 1960), 182.

14. Freire, 27–58.

15. Martin, 192–93.

16. AAUP, quoted in Joughin, 9.

17. Morris Keeton, *Shared Authority on Campus* (Washington, D. C.: American Association for Higher Education, 1971), 152.

18. Buber, *The Knowledge of Man*, 171–74.

19. This inability to release anger and permit life to move ahead is discussed in a *Newsweek* article, which asks questions about what has happened to the American character. Ann Blackman, et al., "Crybabies: Eternal Victims," *Newsweek*, 12 Aug. 1991, 16–18.

20. Ernest I. Pascarella, Corinna A. Ethington, and John C. Smart,

"The Influence of College on Humanitarian/Civic Involvement Values," *Journal of Higher Education* 59 (1988): 430.

21. Philip Slater, *The Pursuit of Loneliness* (Boston: Beacon Press, 1976), 138.

22. Bennis, 17.

23. Antczak, 178.

24. Thomas I. Emerson, *The System of Freedom of Expression* (New York: Vintage Books, 1970), 12.

25. Clark Kerr, *The Uses of the University* (Cambridge, MA: Harvard University Press, 1963), 94–95.

26. Wallace, 1–9.

27. Harold Barrett, *Rhetoric and Civility: Human Development, Narcissism, and the Good Audience* (Albany: State University of New York Press, 1991), 147.

28. Harold Barrett, 148–50.

29. Bennis, 160.

30. Andrei D. Sakharov, *Progress, Coexistence, and Intellectual Freedom* (New York: W. W. Norton, 1968), 60.

31. C. A. Bowers, *Elements of a Post-Liberal Theory of Education* (New York: Columbia University Press, 1987), 138.

32. Dewey, 81.

33. Karl Jaspers, *The Future of Mankind* (Chicago: University of Chicago Press, 1967), 23.

34. Carl R. Rogers, *A Way of Being* (Boston: Houghton Mifflin, 1980), 113–36.

9. Athenian Leadership

1. Bennis, 160.

2. William Whyte, *The Organization Man* (Garden City: Doubleday, 1957).

3. Buber, *The Knowledge of Man*, 72–88.

4. Neil Postman, *Amusing Ourselves to Death: Public Discourse in the Age of Show Business* (New York: Viking, 1985), 142–54.

5. Francis H. Horn, "The Dean and the President," *Liberal Education* 50 (1964): 466.

6. MacIntyre, 19.

7. MacIntyre, 121–45.

8. Kenneth L. Smith and Ira G. Zepp, Jr., *Search for the Beloved Community: The Thinking of Martin Luther King, Jr.* (Valley Forge, PA: Judson Press, 1974), 140.

9. Charles Cooley quoted in Lewis Coser, *The Functions of Social Conflict* (New York: Free Press, 1969), 20.

10. Gutmann, 185–187.

11. Bruno Bettelheim, *The Uses of Enchantment: The Meaning and Importance of Fairy Tales* (New York: Vintage Books, 1977), 23–28.

12. Ernest G. Bormann, "Symbolic Convergence: Organizational

Communication and Culture," in *Communication and Organizations: An Interpretive Approach* ed. Linda Putnam and Michael Pacanowsky (Beverly Hills: Sage, 1983), 118.

13. Joseph Campbell, *The Hero With a Thousand Faces* (Princeton, NJ: Princeton University Press, 1973), 382–86.

14. John F. Kennedy, *Profiles in Courage* (New York: Harper & Row, 1964), 16–18.

15. Boyer, *College*, 284.

16. Peterson, *The Humanities and the American Promise*, 8.

17. Christopher Matthews, *Hardball: How Politics Is Played Told by One Who Knows the Game* (New York: Summit Books, 1988).

18. Cahn, 13–14.

19. Aristotle, *Nicomachean Ethics*, 1114b25–1115a5.

20. H. Richard Niebuhr, *The Responsible Self* (New York: Harper & Row, 1963).

21. Bok, *A Strategy for Peace*, 116–17.

22. Aristotle, *Nicomachean Ethics*, 1141a10–1141a19.

23. Aristotle, *Nicomachean Ethics*, 1120a28.

24. Aristotle, *Nicomachean Ethics*, 11128b27–1128b30.

25. Heinz Kohut, quoted in Barrett, *Rhetoric and Civility*, 8–11.

26. Douglas McGregor, *Leadership and Motivation* (Cambridge: MIT Press, 1966), 30–45.

27. Robert N. Bellah, *The Broken Covenant: American Civil Religion in Time of Trial* (New York: Seabury, 1975), 151, 153.

28. Aristotle, *Nicomachean Ethics*, 1103b.

29. Buber, *Between Man and Man*, 104–17.

30. Neil Postman, *Conscientious Objections: Stirring Up Trouble About Language, Technology, and Education* (New York: Alfred A. Knopf, 1988), 189.

31. See, for example, Andrew Ross, *No Respect: Intellectuals and Popular Culture* (London: Routledge, 1989).

32. Ross, 209.

33. James MacGregor Burns, *Leadership* (New York: Harper & Row, 1978), 141.

34. Jacoby, 221.

35. Charles J. Sykes, *Prof Scam: Professors and the Demise of Higher Education* (Washington, D. C.: Regnery Gateway, 1988), 264.

36. Burns, 143.

37. Earl F. Cheit, *The Useful Arts and the Liberal Tradition* (New York: McGraw-Hill, 1975), 3.

38. Suzanne W. Morse, "Leadership for an Uncertain Future," *National Forum: The Phi Kappa Phi Journal* 71 (1991): 2.

10. Marketing: The Public Dialogue

1. See for example, Colleen Cordes, "Universities Charging High Overhead Rates Could Be at Disadvantage Under NIH Plan," *The Chroni-*

cle of Higher Education 14 Aug. 1991, A, A19; Karen Grassmuck, "Stanford's Kennedy to Step Down in Effort to End the Controversy on Overhead Costs," *The Chronicle of Higher Education* 7 Aug. 1991, A1, A10; Mary Crystal Cage, "States Questioning How Much Time Professors Spend Working With Undergraduate Students," *The Chronicle of Higher Education* 7 Aug. 1991, A1, A20.

2. M. Scott Peck, *People of the Lie: The Hope for Healing Human Evil* (New York: Simon & Schuster, 1983), 223–26.

3. Sykes, 7.

4. Sykes, 7.

5. Kanter and Mirvis, 1.

6. Charles S. Green III and Richard G. Salem, "Assessing the Prospects for Liberal Learning and Careers," in *College Teaching and Learning: Preparing for New Commitments*, ed. Robert E. Young and Kenneth E. Eble (San Francisco: Jossey-Bass, 1988), 5.

7. Carolyn J. Mooney, "Professors are Upbeat About Profession But Uneasy About Students, Standards," *The Chronicle of Higher Education*, 8 Nov. 1989, A1, A18.

8. Eble, *The Craft of Teaching*, 226.

9. Bowers, 172.

10. Niebuhr, *The Irony of American History*, 170.

11. Sykes, 259–60.

12. See for example, an earlier book of mine, *Communication and Community: Implications of Martin Buber's Dialogue.*

13. See for example, the published dissertation of Dietrich Bonhoeffer, *The Communion of Saints* (New York: Harper & Row), 1963.

14. Aristotle, *Nicomachean Ethics*, 1169a18–20.

15. *The World Book Encyclopedia Dictionary*, 1963, s.v. "complexity."

16. *The World Book Encyclopedia Dictionary*, 1963, s.v. "difficulty."

17. Neil Postman and Charles Weingartner, *Teaching as Subversive Activity* (New York: Dell, 1969).

18. Mooney, "Professors Are Upbeat About Profession but Uneasy About Students, Standards," A18.

19. Bruce Wilshire, *The Moral Collapse of the University: Professionalism, Purity, and Alienation* (Albany: State University of New York Press, 1990), 13.

20. Cahn, 40, 44.

21. See for example, David Riesman, *The Lonely Crowd* (London: Yale University Press, 1961).

22. Martin, 28.

23. Peterson, "Small Independent Colleges," 9.

24. Michael D. Bayles, *Professional Ethics* (Belmont, CA: Wadsworth Publishing Company, 1981), 42.

25. Bellah, *The Broken Covenant.*

26. Aristotle, *Nicomachean Ethics*, 1113a25–1113b.

27. Bloom, *The Closing of the American Mind*; Hirsch, Jr. *Cultural Literacy: What Every American Needs to Know.*

28. Jeffrey C. Goldfarb, *The Cynical Society: The Culture of Politics and the Politics of Culture in American Life* (Chicago: University of Chicago Press, 1991), 65–81.

29. Bellah, *The Broken Covenant*, 151.

11. Dialogic Teaching: A Vocation

1. Palmer, *To Know as We Are Known*, 8–9.

2. Martin S. Dworkin, ed., *Dewey on Education: Selections* (New York: Teacher's College Press, 1959), 22.

3. Aristotle, *Nicomachean Ethics*, 1172a–15.

4. Bellah, et al, *Habits of the Heart*, 126–27, 129.

5. Christopher Lasch, *The Minimal Self* (New York: W. W. Norton, 1984).

6. Jacoby, 235–36.

7. Booth, 339.

8. Booth, 124.

9. Albert Camus, *The Rebel* (New York: Vintage Books, 1956), 297.

10. Bellah, *Habits of the Heart*, 152–55.

11. Christa McAuliffe, quoted in Robert T. Hohler, *I Touch the Future. . .: The Story of Christa McAuliffe* (New York: Random House, 1986).

12. Paul Watzlawick, et al, *Pragmatics of Human Communication* (New York: W. W. Norton, 1967), 54.

13. Goldie Blumenstyk, "State Officials Deplore Higher Education's Resistance to Change," *The Chronicle of Higher Education* 25 July 1990: A15–16.

14. Gilbert M. Grosvenor, "Superpowers Not So Super in Geography," *National Geographic*, 6 (Dec. 1989), 816–19.

15. Bloom, *The Closing of the American Mind*; Hirsch, *Cultural Literacy: What Every American Needs to Know.*

16. *NCA: A Guide To Self-Study For Commission Evaluation, 1990–1992* (Chicago: North Central Association of Colleges and Schools: Commission on Institutions of Higher Education, 1990), 16.

17. Hirsch, *Cultural Literacy: What Every American Needs to Know.*

18. Watzlawick, et al, 52.

19. See for example, Rudy Henry Weibe, *Peace Shall Destroy Many* (Toronto: McClelland & Stewart Limited, 1962).

20. Bruno Bettelheim, *Love Is Not Enough* (New York: Avon Books, 1971), 30.

21. Slater, 71.

22. Alexander Solzhenitsyn, *One Day in the Life of Ivan Denisovich* (New York: New American Library, 1963), 106.

23. Friedman, *Hidden Human Image*, 276.

24. Bettelheim, *The Uses of Enchantment*, 11.

25. Wilshire, 282.

26. Carl R. Rogers, "The Interpersonal Relationship: The Core of Guidance," in Stewart, *Bridges Not Walls*.

27. Carl R. Rogers and Barry Stevens, *On Becoming a Person* (Boston: Houghlin Mifflin, 1961), 59–69.

28. Buber, *Between Man and Man*, 104–17.

29. Aristotle, *Nicomachean Ethics*, 1155b35.

30. Griffin, 211–12.

31. James A. Jaksa and Michael S. Pritchard, *Communication Ethics: Methods of Analysis* (Belmont, CA: Wadsworth, 1988), 44.

32. Gamson, 112.

33. Wilshire, 31.

34. Clarke E. Cochran, *Character, Community, and Politics* (Tuscaloosa: The University of Alabama Press, 1982), 67–68.

35. Ellul, *Perspectives on Our Age*, 109.

36. Ronald Duncan, ed. *Gandhi: Selected Writings* (New York: Harper & Row, 1972), 42.

37. Maurice Friedman, *Martin Buber and the Eternal* (New York: Human Sciences, 1986), 139–40.

BIBLIOGRAPHY

Adams, James R.C. *John Baldwin: 1922–1987.* North Manchester, IN: Manchester College, 1989.

Adler, Jerry, et al. "Taking Offense." *Newsweek,* 24 Dec. 1990, 48–54.

Anderson, Rob. "Anonymity, Presence, and the Dialogic Self in a Technological Culture." Paper presented at Central States Communication Association Convention, Chicago: 11 Apr. 1991.

Antczak, Frederick J. *Thought and Character: The Rhetoric of Democratic Education.* Ames: Iowa State University Press, 1985.

Aristotle. *Nicomachean Ethics.* Translated by Terence Irwin. Indianapolis: Hackett, 1985.

Arnett, Ronald C. *Communication and Community: Implications of Martin Buber's Dialogue.* Carbondale: Southern Illinois University Press, 1986.

———. "The Hurried Professor: What Is Our Disciplinary Responsibility?" *The Speech Association of Minnesota Journal* 14 (1987): 1–11.

———. "Teacher/Scholar: A Continuing Tradition." *Manchester College Bulletin* 81 (1989): 1, 4.

Asante, Molefi Kete, and Diane Ravitch. "Multiculturalism: An Exchange." *The American Scholar* 60 (1991): 267–76.

Augsburger, David. *When Enough is Enough: Discovering True Hope When All Hope Seems Lost.* Ventura, CA: Regal, 1984.

Babbitt, Katherine Jean. "Instructional Leadership Behaviors of Principals and Teacher's Professional Zone of Acceptance." Ph.D. Diss., Marquette University, Milwaukee, WI, 1990.

Bandman, Bertram, and Robert S. Guttchen, eds. *Philosophical Essays on Teaching.* Philadelphia: J. B. Lippincott, 1969.

Barrett, Harold. *Rhetoric and Civility: Human Development, Narcissism, and the Good Audience.* Albany: State University of New York Press, 1991.

Barrett, William. *The Illusion of Technique.* New York: Anchor Books, 1979.

———. *The Irrational Man.* New York: Doubleday, 1962.

Barzun, Jacques. *Begin Here: The Forgotten Conditions of Teaching and Learning.* Chicago: University of Chicago Press, 1991.

Bayles, Michael D. *Professional Ethics.* Belmont, CA: Wadsworth Publishing Co., 1981.

Belenky, Mary Field, et al. *Women's Ways of Knowing: The Development of Self, Voice, and Mind*. New York: Basic Books, 1986.

Bellah, Robert N. *The Broken Covenant: American Civil Religion in Time of Trial*. New York: Seabury Press, 1975.

———, et al. *Habits of the Heart: Individualism and Commitment in American Life*. Berkeley: University of California Press, 1985.

Bennis, Warren. *Why Leaders Can't Lead: The Unconscious Conspiracy Continues*. San Francisco: Jossey-Bass, 1989.

Berger, Peter, Brigette Berger, and Hansfried Kellner. *The Homeless Mind: Modernization and Consciousness*. New York: Random House, 1974.

Bernstein, Richard J. *Beyond Objectivism and Relativism: Science, Hermeneutics and Praxis*. Philadelphia: University of Pennsylvania Press, 1983.

Bettelheim, Bruno. *Love is Not Enough*. New York: Avon Books, 1971.

———. *The Uses of Enchantment: The Meaning and Importance of Fairy Tales*. New York: Vintage Books, 1977.

Blackman, Ann, et al. "Crybabies: Eternal Victims." *Newsweek*, 12 Aug. 1991, 16–18.

Bloom, Allan. *The Closing of the American Mind*. New York: Simon & Schuster, 1987.

Blumenstyk, Goldie. "State Officials Deplore Higher Education's Resistance to Change." *The Chronicle of Higher Education*, 25 July 1990, A15–16.

Bok, Derek. *Higher Learning*. Cambridge: Harvard University Press, 1988.

Bok, Sissela. *A Strategy for Peace: Human Values and the Threat of War*. New York: Pantheon Books, 1989.

Bonhoeffer, Dietrich. *The Communion of Saints*. New York: Harper & Row, 1963.

———. *The Cost of Discipleship*. New York: MacMillan, 1949.

———. *Life Together*. New York: Harper & Row, 1954.

Booth, Wayne. *Critical Understanding: The Powers and Limits of Pluralism*. Chicago: University of Chicago Press, 1979.

Bormann, Ernest G. *The Force of Fantasy: Restoring the American Dream*. Carbondale: Southern Illinois University Press, 1985.

———. *The Vocation of a Teacher: Rhetorical Occasions*. Chicago: University of Chicago Press, 1988.

Boschmann, Erwin. *Teaching Tools: Ten Secrets to Total Teaching Success*. Dubuque, IA: Kendall/Hunt, 1987.

Boulding, Kenneth. *The Meaning of the Twentieth Century: The Great Transition*. New York: Harper & Row, 1964.

Bowers, C. A. *Elements of a Post-Liberal Theory of Education*. New York: Columbia University Press, 1987.

Boyer, Ernest L. "Buildings Reflect Our Priorities." *Educational Record* 70 (1989): 27.

———. *Campus Life: In Search of Community*. Princeton, NJ: Carnegie Foundation for the Advancement of Teaching, 1990.

———. *College: The Undergraduate Experience in America*. New York: Harper & Row, 1987.

Brown, Charles T., and Paul W. Keller. "A Modest Proposal for Listening Training." *Quarterly Journal of Speech* 48 (1962): 395–99.

———. *Monologue to Dialogue: Exploration of Interpersonal Communication*. Englewood Cliffs, NJ: Prentice Hall, 1973.

Brown, Claude. *Manchild in the Promised Land: A Modern Classic of the Black Experience*. New York: Signet Books, 1965.

Brueggemann, Walter. *The Land: Place as Gift, Promise and Challenge in Biblical Faith*. Philadelphia: Fortress Press, 1977.

Buber, Martin. *A Believing Humanism: Gleanings*. New York: Simon & Schuster, 1969.

———. *Between Man and Man*. New York: Macmillan, 1972.

———. *Good and Evil*. New York: Scribner's, 1952.

———. *The Knowledge of Man: A Philosophy of the Interhuman*. New York: Harper & Row, 1965.

———. *Meetings*. La Salle, IL: Open Court, 1973.

———. *The Way of Response*. New York: Schocken, 1966.

Burns, James MacGregor. *Leadership*. New York: Harper & Row, 1978.

Burroughs, Catherine B. "Teaching and/or Scholarship." *Liberal Education* 76 (1990): 16.

Cage, Mary Crystal. "States Questioning How Much Time Professors Spend Working With Undergraduate Students." *The Chronicle of Higher Education*, 7 Aug. 1991, A1, A20.

Cahn, Steven M. *Saints and Scamps: Ethics in Academia*. Totowa, NJ: Rowan & Littlefield, 1986.

Callahan, Daniel, and Sissela Bok, eds. *Ethics Teaching in Higher Education*. New York: Plenum, 1980.

Campbell, Joseph. *The Hero With a Thousand Faces*. Princeton, NJ: Princeton University Press, 1973.

Camus, Albert. *The Rebel*. New York: Vintage Books, 1956.

Chait, Richard P., et al. *Trustee Responsibility for Academic Affairs*. Washington, D. C.: Association of Governing Boards of Universities and Colleges, 1984.

Cheit, Earl. *The Useful Arts and the Liberal Tradition*. New York: McGraw-Hill, 1975.

Cherwitz, Richard, ed. *Rhetoric and Philosophy*. Hillsdale, NJ: L. Erlbaum Associates, 1990.

Cochran, Clarke E. *Character, Community, and Politics*. Tuscaloosa: University of Alabama Press, 1982.

Cordes, Colleen. "Universities Charging High Overhead Rates Could Be at Disadvantage Under NIH Plan." *The Chronicle of Higher Education*, 14 Aug. 1991, A, A19.

Corson, John J. *Governance of Colleges and Universities*. New York: McGraw-Hill, 1960.

Coser, Lewis. *The Functions of Social Conflict*. New York: Free Press, 1969.

Council for Independent Colleges. *Community, Commitment and Congruence: A Different Kind of Excellence*. Washington, D. C.: Council on Independent Colleges, 1987.

Cousins, Norman. *The Healing Heart*. New York: W. W. Norton, 1983.

Crimmel, Henry H. "The Myth of the Teacher-Scholar," *Liberal Education* 70 (1984): 192.

Darkey, William A., ed. *Three Dialogues on Liberal Education*. Annapolis: St. John's College Press, 1979.

DeLoughry, Thomas J. "Study of Transcripts Finds Little Structure in the Liberal Arts." *Chronicle of Higher Education*, 18 Jan. 1989, A1, A32.

Denney, Joseph Villiers, ed. *Washington, Webster, and Lincoln*. Chicago: Scott Foresman, 1920.

de Tocqueville, Alexis. *Democracy in America*. New York: Modern Library, 1981.

Dewey, John. *Democracy and Education*. New York: Free Press, 1966.

Dobson, James C. *Straight Talk to Men and Their Wives*. Waco, TX: Word Books, 1984.

D'Souza, Dinesh. *Illiberal Education: The Politics of Race and Sex on Campus*. New York: Free Press, 1991.

Duncan, Ronald, ed. *Gandhi: Selected Writings*. New York: Harper & Row, 1972.

Dworkin, Martin S., ed. *Dewey on Education: Selections*. New York: Teacher's College Press, 1959.

Eble, Kenneth. *The Craft of Teaching: A Guide to Mastering the Professor's Art*, 2d ed. San Francisco: Jossey-Bass, 1988.

Eble, Kenneth, and Wilbert J. McKeachie. *Improving Undergraduate Education Through Faculty Development*. San Francisco: Jossey-Bass, 1985.

Ellul, Jacques. *Perspectives on Our Age*. New York: Seabury, 1981.

———. *In Season, Out of Season*. New York: Harper & Row, 1981.

———. *The Technological Society*. New York: Knopf, 1964.

———. *Violence*. New York: Seabury Press, 1969.

Emerson, Thomas I. *The System of Freedom of Expression*. New York: Vintage Books, 1970.

"Faculty at Small Liberal Arts Campuses Report Career Satisfaction, High Morale." *Higher Education and National Affairs* 36 (30 Nov. 1987): 1, 6.

Falender, Andrew J., and John C. Merson, eds. *New Directions for Higher Education: Management Techniques for Small and Specialized Institutions*. San Francisco: Jossey-Bass, 1983.

Fenno, Richard, Jr. *Congressman in Committees*. Boston: Little, Brown & Co., 1973.

Fisher, Walter. *Human Communication as Narration: Toward a Philoso-*

phy of Reason, Value, and Action. Columbia: University of South
Carolina Press, 1987.

———. "Narration as a Human Communication Paradigm: The Case of
Public Moral Argument." *Communication Monographs* 51 (Mar.
1984): 1–22.

Fouts, Jeffrey T., and Loyde W. Hales. "A Controlled Environment: The
Nature of Small, Liberal Arts, Christian Colleges." *Journal of College Student Personnel* 26 (1985): 524–31.

Frankl, Viktor E. *Man's Search for Meaning: An Introduction to Logotherapy*. New York: Pocket Books, 1974.

———. *Psychotherapy and Existentialism: Selected Papers on Logotherapy*. New York: Simon & Schuster, 1967.

Freire, Paulo. *The Pedagogy of the Oppressed*. New York: Seabury, 1974.

Friedman, Maurice. *Hidden Human Image*. New York: Dell, 1974.

———. *Martin Buber and the Eternal*. New York: Human Sciences, 1986.

———. *Martin Buber: The Life of Dialogue*. Chicago: University of Chicago Press, 1976.

———. *Martin Buber's Life and Work: The Early Years 1878–1923*. New
York: E. P. Dutton, 1981.

———. *Martin Buber's Life and Work: The Middle Years 1923–1945*.
New York: E. P. Dutton, 1983.

———. *Touchstones of Reality: Existential Trust and the Community of
Peace*. New York: E. P. Dutton, 1974.

Gadamer, Hans-Georg. *Truth and Method*. New York: Crossroad Publishing, 1986.

Gamson, Zelda F. and Associates. *Liberating Education*. San Francisco:
Jossey-Bass, 1984.

Geertz, Clifford. *The Interpretation of Cultures*. New York: Basic Books,
1973.

Gelman, David. "A Much Riskier Passage." *Newsweek*. Special edition,
Summer/Fall 1990: 16.

Goldfarb, Jeffrey C. *The Cynical Society: The Culture of Politics and the
Politics of Culture in American Life*. Chicago: University of Chicago
Press, 1991.

Gottesman, Ronald, comp. *The Norton Anthology of American Literature*.
New York: Norton, 1979.

Grassmuck, Karen. "Stanford's Kennedy to Step Down in Effort to End
the Controversy on Overhead Costs." *The Chronicle of Higher Education*, 7 Aug. 1991, A1, A10.

Greenberg, Karen Joy, ed. *Conversations on Communication Ethics*. Norwood, NJ: Ablex, 1991.

Greene, Maxine. *Teacher as Stranger: Educational Philosophy for the
Modern Age*. Belmont, CA: Wadsworth, 1973.

Griffin, Em. *Making Friends and Making Them Count*. Downers Grove,
IL: InterVarsity Press, 1987.

Grosvenor, Gilbert M. "Superpowers Not So Super in Geography." *National Geographic* 6 (1989): 816–19.

Gutmann, Amy. *Democratic Education*. Princeton, NJ: Princeton University Press, 1987.

Haiman, T. S. "A Re-examination of the Ethics of Persuasion." *Central States Speech Journal* 3 (1952): 4–9.

Hall, Edward T. *The Silent Language*. New York: Anchor Books, 1990.

Hammarskjold, Dag. *Markings*. New York: Knopf, 1977.

Hardie, W. F. R. *Aristotle's Ethical Theory*. 2d ed. Oxford: Clarendon Press, 1990.

"Hate in the Ivory Tower: A Survey of Intolerance on College Campuses and Academia's Response." People for the American Way. Dec. 1990.

Hauerwas, Stanley. *The Community of Character: Toward a Constructive Christian Social Ethic*. Notre Dame, IN: University of Notre Dame Press, 1981.

Heller, Scott. "Colleges Becoming Havens of 'Political Correctness,' Some Scholars Say." *Chronicle of Higher Education*, 21 Nov. 1990, A1, A14–A15.

Hesse, Herman. *Beneath the Wheel*. New York: Noon Day, 1968.

———. *Siddhartha*. New York: New Directions, 1951.

Hirsch, E. D. Jr. *Cultural Literacy: What Every American Needs to Know*. Boston: Houghton Mifflin, 1987.

Hoffer, Eric. *The True Believer*. New York: New American Library, 1951.

Hohler, Robert T. *I Touch the Future . . . : The Story of Christa McAuliffe*. New York: Random House, 1986.

Hook, Janet. "A Disconcerting Philosopher Challenges the Pretensions of His Discipline." *Chronicle of Higher Education*, 9 Dec. 1981: 25–26.

Hook, Sidney. "The Closing of the American Mind: An Intellectual Best-Seller Re-Visited." *The American Scholar* 58 (1989): 128.

———. *Philosophy and Public Policy*. Carbondale: Southern Illinois University Press, 1980.

Horn, Francis H. "The Dean and the President." *Liberal Education* 50 (1964): 463–75.

Hutchins, Robert M. *The University of Utopia*. Chicago: University of Chicago Press, 1953.

Hyer, Marjorie. "Rev. Curren Crusades for Academic Freedom." *Fort Wayne Journal Gazette*, 24 April 1988: A9–10.

Jacoby, Russell. *The Last Intellectuals: American Culture in the Age of Academe*. New York: Basic Books, 1987.

Jaksa, James A., and Michael S. Pritchard. *Communication Ethics: Methods of Analysis*. Belmont, CA: Wadsworth, 1988.

James, William. *Pragmatism and Other Essays*. New York: Washington Square Press, 1963.

Jaspers, Karl. *The Future of Mankind*. Chicago: University of Chicago Press, 1967.

Johannesen, Richard L. "The Emerging Concept of Communication as Dialogue." *Quarterly Journal of Speech* 57 (1971): 373–82.

————. *Ethics in Human Communication.* 3d ed. Prospect Heights, IL: Waveland Press, 1990.

————. "Virtue Ethics in Political Communication." *Proceedings of the First National Communication Ethics Conference.* (1990): 219–56.

Joughin, Louis, ed. *Academic Freedom and Tenure: A Handbook of the American Association of University Professors.* Madison: University of Wisconsin Press, 1969.

Joy, Charles R., ed. *Albert Schweitzer: An Anthology.* Boston: Beacon, 1967.

Kanter, Donald L., and Philip H. Mirvis, *The Cynical Americans: Living in an Age of Discontent and Disillusionment.* San Francisco: Jossey-Bass, 1989.

Kantrowitz, Barbara, and Pat Wingert. "A Dismal Report Card." *Newsweek,* 17 June 1991, 64–67.

Katchadourian, Herant A., and John Boli. *Careerism and Intellectualism Among College Students.* San Francisco: Jossey-Bass, 1985.

Kazantzakis, Nikos. *Zorba the Greek.* New York: Ballantine, 1952.

Keeton, Morris. *Shared Authority on Campus.* Washington, D. C.: American Association for Higher Education, 1971.

Kennedy, John F. *Profiles in Courage.* New York: Harper & Row, 1964.

Kerr, Clark. *The Uses of the University.* Cambridge, MA: Harvard University Press, 1963.

King, Martin Luther, Jr. Address. Manchester College, North Manchester, IN, 1 Feb. 1968. Audiotape.

Kirschenbaum, Howard, and Valerie Land Henderson, eds. *The Carl Rogers Reader.* Boston: Houghton Mifflin, 1989.

Koestler, Arthur. *Darkness at Noon.* New York: Bantam Books, 1941.

Kreiser, B. Robert, ed. *AAUP: American Association of University Professors—Policy Documents and Reports.* Washington, D. C.: American Association of University Professors, 1990.

Lasch, Christopher. *The Culture of Narcissism: American Life in a Time of Diminishing Expectations.* New York: W. W. Norton, 1979.

————. *Haven in a Heartless World.* New York: Basic Books, 1979.

————. *The Minimal Self.* New York: W. W. Norton, 1984.

————. *The True and Only Heaven: Progress and Its Critics.* New York: W. W. Norton, 1991.

MacIntyre, Alasdair. *After Virtue.* Notre Dame, IN: University of Notre Dame Press, 1984.

Macrorie, Ken. *The Vulnerable Teacher.* Rochelle Park, NJ: Hayden Book Co., 1974.

Marsh, Peter T. *Contesting the Boundaries of Liberal and Professional Education: The Syracuse Experiment.* Syracuse, NY: Syracuse University Press, 1988.

Martin, Warren Bryan. *College of Character.* San Francisco: Jossey-Bass, 1982.

Martines, Lauro. "Large and Little School Teaching." *The American Scholar* 54 (1985): 202.

Maslow, Abraham. *Motivation & Personality*. 2d ed. New York: Harper & Row, 1970.

Matthews, Christopher. *Hardball: How Politics Is Played Told by One Who Knows the Game*. New York: Summit Books, 1988.

McGregor, Douglas. *Leadership and Motivation*. Cambridge: MIT Press, 1966.

Meilaender, Gilbert C. *The Theory and Practice of Virtue*. Notre Dame, IN: University of Notre Dame, 1984.

Merton, Thomas. *No Man Is an Island*. New York: Doubleday, 1955.

Montagu, Ashley. *On Being Human*. New York: Hawthorn Books, 1966.

Montagu, Ashley, and Floyd Matson, *The Human Dialogue*. New York: The Free Press, 1967.

Mooney, Carolyn J. "Academic Group Fighting the 'Politically Correct Left' Gains Momentum." *The Chronicle of Higher Education*, 12 Dec. 1990, A1, A13, A16.

———. "Professors Are Upbeat About Profession but Uneasy About Students, Standards." *The Chronicle of Higher Education*, 8 Nov. 1989, A1, A18.

Morse, Suzanne W. "Leadership for an Uncertain Future." *National Forum: The Phi Kappa Phi Journal* 71 (1991): 2.

NCA: A Guide To Self-Study for Commission Evaluation, 1990–1992. Chicago: North Central Association of Colleges and Schools: Commission on Higher Education, 1990.

Niebuhr, H. Richard. *The Responsible Self*. New York: Harper & Row, 1963.

Niebuhr, Reinhold. *The Irony of American History*. New York: Scribner's, 1952.

Nilsen, Thomas R. *Ethics of Speech Communication*. 2d ed. Indianapolis: Bobbs-Merrill, 1974.

———. "Free Speech, Persuasion, and the Democratic Process." *The Quarterly Journal of Speech* 43 (1958): 235–43.

Nye, Robert D. *Conflict Among Humans*. New York: Springer Publishing Co., 1973.

Olswang, Steven G., and Barbara A. Lee. *Faculty Freedoms and Institutional Accountability for Academic Affairs*. Washington D. C.: Association for the Study of Higher Education, 1984.

Otten, Anna, ed. *Hesse Companion*. Albuquerque: University of New Mexico Press, 1977.

Palmer, Parker J. *The Company of Strangers*. New York: Crossroad, 1989.

———. *To Know as We Are Known: A Spirituality of Education*. San Francisco: Harper & Row, 1983.

Pascarella, Ernest T. "College Environmental Influences on Students' Educational Aspirations." *Journal of Higher Education* 55 (1984): 767.

Pascarella, Ernest T., Corinna A. Ethington, and John C. Smart. "The Influence of College on Humanitarian/Civic Involvement Values." *Journal of Higher Education* 59 (1988): 430.

Peck, M. Scott. *People of the Lie: The Hope for Healing Human Evil*. New York: Simon & Schuster, 1983.

Peterson, Merrill P. *The Humanities and the American Promise: Report of the Colloquium on the Humanities and the American People*. Austin, TX: Texas Committee for Humanities, 1987.

Peterson, Patti McGill. "Small Independent Colleges: A Sector at Risk." *National Forum: Phi Kappa Phi Journal* 65 (1985): 9.

Pirsig, Robert M. *Zen and the Art of Motorcycle Maintenance*. New York: Morrow, 1974.

Polanyi, Michael. *Personal Knowledge: Towards a Post-Critical Philosophy*. New York: Harper & Row, 1964.

Porto, Brian L. "The Small College Experience: Not for Students Only." *Liberal Education* 70 (1984): 229–30.

Postman, Neil. *Amusing Ourselves to Death: Public Discourse in the Age of Show Business*. New York: Viking, 1985.

———. *Conscientious Objections: Stirring Up Trouble About Language, Technology, and Education*. New York: Knopf, 1988.

Postman, Neil, and Charles Weingartner. *Teaching as Subversive Activity*. New York: Dell, 1969.

Pritchard, Ivor. *Moral Education and Character*. Washington, D. C.: U. S. Department of Education, 1988.

Public Papers of the Presidents of the United States—John F. Kennedy, January 20–December 31, 1961. Vol. 1 Washington, D. C.: U. S. Government Printing Office, 1962.

Putnam, Linda, and Michael Pacanowsky, *Communication and Organizations: An Interpretive Approach*. Beverly Hills: Sage, 1983.

Radest, Howard B. *Can We Teach Ethics?* New York: Praeger, 1989.

Reardon, Kathleen K. *Interpersonal Communication: Where Minds Meet*. Belmont, CA: Wadsworth, 1987.

Reich, Robert B., ed. *The Power of Public Ideas*. Cambridge, MA: Ballinger, 1988.

Remley, Audrey W. "Real Versus Ideal—A Response." *Journal of College Student Personnel* 27 (1986): 17.

Rice, R. Eugene. "Report on Institutional Case Studies—'High Morale and Satisfaction Among Faculty: Ten Exemplary Colleges,'" in *Community, Commitment, and Congruence: A Different Kind of Excellence* (Washington, D. C.: Council of Independent Colleges, 1987), 17–22.

Richardson, Alan. *A Theological Word Book of the Bible*. New York: MacMillan, 1952.

Ricoeur, Paul. *Time and Narrative*. Chicago: University of Chicago Press, 1983.

Riesman, David. *The Lonely Crowd*. London: Yale University Press, 1961.

Rogers, Carl R. *On Becoming a Person*. Boston: Houghton Mifflin, 1961.

———. *A Way of Being*. Boston: Houghton Mifflin, 1980.

Rogers, Carl R., and Barry Stevens. *Person to Person: The Problem of*

Being Human—A New Trend in Psychology. New York: Pocket Books, 1972.

Rohde, Marie. "Maguire Must Go, Some Say: But Marquette Resists Pressure to Fire Liberal Theologian for Abortion Stance." *The Milwaukee Journal* 27 Oct. 1985.

Ross, Andrew. *No Respect: Intellectuals and Popular Culture.* London: Routledge, 1989.

Russell, Bertrand. *A History of Western Philosophy.* New York: Simon & Schuster, 1972.

Sakharov, Andrei D. *Progress, Coexistence, and Intellectual Freedom.* New York: W. W. Norton, 1968.

Samovar, Larry, and Richard Porter, eds. *Intercultural Communication: A Reader.* Belmont, CA: Wadsworth, 1991.

Schilpp, Paul Arthur, and Maurice Friedman, eds. *The Philosophy of Martin Buber.* LaSalle, IL: Open Court Press, 1967.

Schrag, Calvin O. *Communicative Praxis and the Space of Subjectivity.* Bloomington: Indiana University Press, 1986.

Schram, Peninnah. *Jewish Stories One Generation Tells Another.* London: Jason Aronson, 1987.

Sherman, Nancy. *The Fabric of Character: Aristotle's Theory of Virtue.* Oxford: Clarendon Press, 1991.

Shils, Edward. "Robert E. Park." *The American Scholar* 60 (1991): 122.

———. "Robert Maynard Hutchins." *The American Scholar* 59 (1990): 220.

Sichel, Betty A. *Moral Education: Character, Community, and Ideals.* Philadelphia: Temple University Press, 1988.

Siegel, Betty L. "Knowledge with Commitment." *Vital Speeches of the Day,* 50 (1984), 394–97.

Skinner, B. F. *Walden Two.* New York: Macmillan, 1948.

Slater, Philip. *The Pursuit of Loneliness.* Boston: Beacon Press, 1976.

Smith, Kenneth L., and Ira G. Zepp, Jr. *Search for the Beloved Community: The Thinking of Martin Luther King, Jr.* Valley Forge, PA: Judsen Press, 1974.

Solzhenitsyn, Alexander. *One Day in the Life of Ivan Denisovich.* New York: New American Library, 1963.

Sommers, Christina Hoff. "Ethics Without Virtue: Moral Education in America." *The American Scholar* 53 (1984): 388.

Stewart, John. "Foundations of Dialogic Communication." *Quarterly Journal of Speech* 64 (1978): 183–201.

Stewart, John, ed. *Bridges Not Walls: A Book About Interpersonal Communication.* 4th ed. New York: Random House, 1986.

Stone, I. F. *The Trial of Socrates.* Boston: Little, Brown & Co., 1988.

Sykes, Charles J. *Prof Scam: Professors and the Demise of Higher Education.* Washington, D. C.: Regnery Gateway, 1988.

Tinder, Glenn. *Community: Reflections on a Tragic Ideal.* Baton Rouge: University of Louisiana Press, 1980.

Toulmin, Stephan. "The Recovery of Practical Philosophy." *The American Scholar* 57 (1988): 337–52.

Wallace, Karl R. "An Ethical Basis of Communication." *The Speech Teacher* 4 (1955): 1–9.

Washington, James Melvin, ed. *A Testament of Hope: The Essential Writings of Martin Luther King Jr.* San Francisco: Harper & Row, 1989.

Watson, Denton L. "Scholars' Focus on Martin Luther King Has Skewed Our Understanding of the Civil Rights Struggle." *Chronicle of Higher Education,* 23 Jan. 1991, A44.

Watzlawick, Paul, et al. *The Pragmatics of Human Communication.* New York: W. W. Norton, 1967.

Weaver, Richard. *Ideas Have Consequences.* Chicago: University of Chicago Press, 1948.

Weibe, Rudy Henry. *Peace Shall Destroy Many.* Toronto: McClelland & Stewart, 1962.

Weiss, Paul. *The Making of Men.* Carbondale: Southern Illinois University Press, 1967.

Whyte, William. *The Organization Man.* Garden City: Doubleday, 1957.

Will, George. "The Fuse that Lit the Fire." *Newsweek,* 13 Apr. 1987, 88.

Wilshire, Bruce. *The Moral Collapse of the University: Professionalism, Purity and Alienation.* Albany: State University of New York Press, 1990.

Wise, W. Max. *The Politics of the Private College: An Inquiry Into the Processes of Collegiate Government.* New Haven, CT: Haven Foundation, 1968.

Young, Robert B. "The Small College Point of View: An Ideology of Student Affairs." *Journal of College Student Personnel* 27 (1986): 4–18.

Young, Robert E. and Kenneth E. Eble, eds. *College Teaching and Learning: Preparing for New Commitments.* San Francisco: Jossey-Bass, 1988.

Zinsser, William. "A Visit to Ed Roush." *The American Scholar* 58 (1989): 113–16.

INDEX

RONALD C. ARNETT is a philosopher of communication interested in practical application and understanding of communication and interpersonal life in organizations. In addition to teaching and research, Arnett has been a communication consultant for businesses and churches. Before returning to teaching, Arnett was the Dean/Vice-President of Academic Affairs at his alma mater, Manchester College in Indiana, and he was previously the chair of the Department of Rhetoric and Communication Studies at Marquette University. He began his teaching career at St. Cloud State University in Minnesota.

Arnett is the author of numerous articles and two books, *Communication and Community: Implications of Martin Buber's Dialogue* and *Dwell in Peace: Applying Nonviolence to Everyday Relationships*. He is the recipient of the 1988 Religious Speech Communication Association Book Award for *Communication and Community*, published by Southern Illinois University Press, and the 1979 Outstanding Article of the Year Award from the Religious Speech Communication Association. He has edited the *Journal of Communication and Religion* and has been on the editorial boards of journals in communication and in applied ethics.